THE POWER OF FRAMEWORI

FOR WINDOWS ™ AND OS/2 ® DEVELOPERS

TALIGENT
PRESS

Addison-Wesley Publishing Company

Reading, Massachusetts   Menlo Park, California   New York
Don Mills, Ontario   Wokingham, England   Amsterdam   Bonn   Sydney
Singapore   Tokyo   Madrid   San Juan   Paris   Seoul   Milan   Mexico City   Taipei

Library of Congress Cataloging-in-Publication Data

The Power of frameworks : for Windows and OS/2 developers.
    p.   cm.
  Includes index.
  ISBN 0-201-48348-3
    1. Object-oriented programming (Computer science) 2. Microsoft
Windows (Computer file) 3. OS/2 (Computer file) 4. Computer
software—Development.   I. Taligent, Inc.
QA76.64.P69 1995
005.26—dc20   95-38031
                                                      CIP

Taligent, the Taligent logo, and People, Places, and Things are registered trademarks and CommonPoint, the CommonPoint logo, *cp*Constructor, *cp*Professional, and Task Centered Computing are trademarks of Taligent, Inc. All other trademarks belong to their respective owners.

Sponsoring Editor: Martha Steffen

Cover and text design: Taligent Technical Communications Group, Gary Ashcavai

ISBN: 0-201-48348-3

Set in 10-point New Baskerville

  1 2 3 4 5 6 7 8 9 -CRS-99 98 97 96 95

First printing, September 1995

Addison-Wesley books are available for bulk purchases by corporations, institutions, and other organizations. For more information please contact the Corporate, Government and Special Sales Department at (800) 238-9682.

CONTENTS

Part 2 Applying frameworks 59

Chapter 9
Designing a number formatting framework for OS/2 183

Chapter 10
Extending the framework for OS/2 213

Chapter 14
The power of frameworks

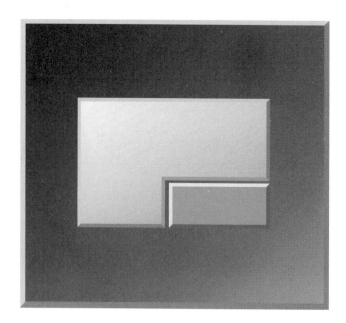

PREFACE

As software systems become more and more complex, software developers have struggled with the task of managing the development process. Many of the advances in the science of software engineering have been motivated by this struggle. Object-oriented programming was a natural progression from the structured design movement and has gained widespread acceptance in industry and academia. Object-oriented technology has taken a long time to mature—its roots go back more than thirty years.

As experience with object-oriented technology has grown, it has become clear that objects alone are not in and of themselves sufficient to manage the complexities of today's software. Frameworks were originally developed to facilitate the creation of user-friendly applications for modern GUI-based systems such as the Mac™OS, OS/2®, and Microsoft Windows. Application frameworks provide developers with a basic application structure and flow of control, reducing complexity and providing for design reuse. Application frameworks also save developers from tasks such as having to create large amounts of infrastructure for event handling, memory management, file input and output: the basic structure of the application framework takes care of these issues for the developer. Freeing developers from these tasks allows them to concentrate on providing features that add value for the end user.

Application frameworks have become increasingly popular over the last few years. Virtually every operating system available today has at least one application framework available for it. Despite their popularity, framework design techniques are poorly understood, with few articles or books published that cover the finer points of framework design.

Further complicating matters, many developers think that frameworks are suitable only for creating GUI-based applications. This is a common misunderstanding because virtually all frameworks available today are application frameworks. In fact, developers can use frameworks to solve virtually any design problem—if they understand exactly what a framework is and how to use it.

This book is intended to address these issues. After reading this book, you should know what a framework is, how to design frameworks, and how to use existing frameworks.

WHAT YOU SHOULD KNOW BEFORE YOU START

Before you read this book, you should be familiar with the basic principles of object-oriented design and programming. You should also be able to read and understand C++ source code, but being able to program in C++ yourself is not absolutely necessary. If you want to learn more about object-oriented technology and/or C++, books and articles are listed in "Recommended materials for further reading" on page 306.

✔ NOTE   Although C++ is used throughout this book in programming examples, the principles are equally applicable to other object-oriented languages, and even, to a lesser extent, to non-object-oriented languages.

HOW TO READ THE BOOK

The book is divided into three major parts:

- Part 1 provides an overview of object-oriented technology and explains the fundamentals of frameworks and the principles of framework design.
- Part 2 shows the step-by-step development of a framework-based application, starting with a simple object-oriented application, then developing a simple framework and extending it to add support for a new end-user feature.
- Part 3 summarizes the framework design process and shows how the CommonPoint application system makes using and developing frameworks easier.

The book concludes with two appendixes: Appendix A describes the class diagram notation used throughout the book; Appendix B describes how to use the companion CD-ROM.

ACKNOWLEDGMENTS

Creating this book/CD required a lot more work than I thought possible, and I gained a new appreciation for the writing profession while working on it. Many people contributed their time and effort to make this book happen, and I'm indebted to them all.

Much credit is due the writers who worked with me on this book. I'm especially grateful to Kate Payne for her effort on Part I, to Jim Showalter for his contributions to the early drafts, and to the folks at IBM who provided OS/2 code and consultation.

I'd also like to thank the editors who took the rough edges off the prose, the reviewers who read and commented on the book's many drafts, and the production folks who transformed our drafts into the book you see before you. Special thanks to Odile Sullivan-Tarazi for her efforts shepherding the project through the development process.

Andrew Shebanow
Taligent Technical Communications
Cupertino, California

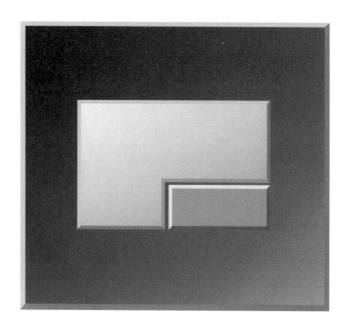

PART 1

INTRODUCING FRAMEWORKS

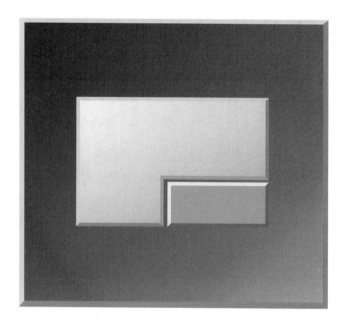

CHAPTER 1

A FIRST LOOK AT FRAMEWORKS

There seems little doubt that object-oriented programming and design are a genuine advance in software development technology.

Every year brings more growth in the use of object-oriented approaches in programming. The industry is adopting object-oriented technology even for mission-critical applications. There are fewer "What is an object?" questions and more queries such as "How can my organization migrate to object-oriented programming?" All over the software landscape class libraries are appearing, even in areas once thought to be the exclusive domain of procedural techniques. Interest in C++ continues to grow.

Tools for object-oriented programming are maturing, and tools for full life-cycle object-oriented development are making their way out of the lab and into the hands of professional software developers. Fortune 500 companies increasingly report success stories about using object-oriented technology. In some cases, reuse metrics have been achieved far exceeding those for procedural programming. The books and articles included in "Recommended materials for further reading" on page 306 can give you more information about advances and successes in object-oriented technologies.

Object-oriented technology is clearly a substantial addition to the developer's arsenal, just as procedural programming, structured analysis, and high-level languages (initially all considered risky, unproven technologies) were major leaps forward in their day.

LIMITS TO OBJECT-ORIENTED PROGRAMMING AND DESIGN

Against the backdrop of expanding industry acceptance of object-oriented programming and design is some well-founded criticism.

The complaint one usually hears goes something like this: "Object-oriented approaches to software development truly do make programs more understandable, better abstracted, robustly encapsulated, and reusable. We've even seen respectable gains in developer productivity. But where are the *major* productivity improvements that were promised?"

This question has some merit. Object-oriented techniques do not, in and of themselves, eliminate the fundamental cause of low developer productivity, which is that developers have to design and implement too much code. Using the techniques of object-oriented technology alone—objects, classes, and class libraries—does not guarantee reuse of design and code. You need specific strategies for using these design and programming techniques to reduce the workload and improve productivity.

Issues for the developer

Merely changing from procedural to object-oriented techniques does not significantly reduce the amount of design or the volume of code that you must write. These techniques do not automatically capture design solutions for future applications. Class libraries provide fine-grained functionality in the form of classes and objects, but you still have to put the pieces together to provide the overall infrastructure of a program. You have to understand how large class libraries, the origin of your classes, interrelate so that you can create the code that controls their interaction.

With or without objects, as the developer you are responsible for providing the behavior and flow of control of your program. A system library is basically passive: it doesn't do anything unless you specify how to make it happen. You control the interactions among all the objects in the program, including defining which functions to call, when, and for which objects.

At times, it seems that the software industry has traded the traditional procedural programming model for the object-oriented programming model.

In programming, concerns go beyond simply the volume of code to design and write for each application. How much time and effort should you spend on program maintenance and evolution? Can you build groups of applications that work together and are consistent? How many times have you solved the same problem without capturing the solution in a reusable design? All these factors add to the issues inherent in software development.

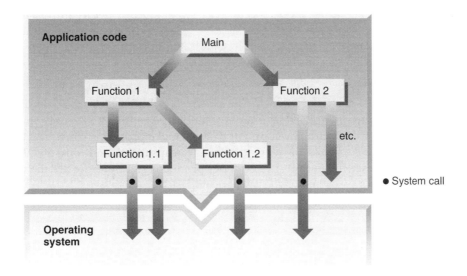

PROCEDURAL PROGRAM STRUCTURE FOR A TRADITIONAL OPERATING SYSTEM

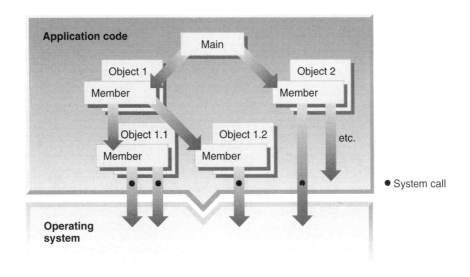

OBJECT-ORIENTED–BASED PROGRAM STRUCTURE FOR A TRADITIONAL OPERATING SYSTEM

Limits to productivity   When each developer is responsible for program infrastructure using a class library—the repository of classes and objects—some negative effects influence overall productivity. As suggested by Cotter and Potel (Cotter with Potel 1995), working with large class libraries:

- **Steepens the learning curve.** You must learn the relationships among classes to use them—nothing inherent in a class library expresses or enforces proper use of its classes. Large class libraries require you to learn about hundreds of classes and their relationships before you can use them effectively to modify their default behavior or create new functionality. Documentation and design guidance help you determine what was intended by the class library developers—such as how and when functions call other functions or from which classes you can derive new classes. With a large class library, this creates a steep learning curve.

- **Imposes considerable overhead on the developer.** If you create your own class library, you or your team of developers typically must assume responsibility for a large infrastructure that you must design, implement, test, document, support, maintain, and extend.

- **Misallocates expertise.** You might be forced to write and maintain large amounts of code that have little or nothing to do with the actual problem the application is intended to address. You cannot focus your efforts on your particular area of expertise. Instead, because you are forced to design and implement code for problem domains in which you are not an expert, you are more likely to make mistakes.

  What if you want to write a spell checker and, in the process, need to provide code for error handling, help, data storage, and other utilities? This overhead slows down the development process, reduces productivity, and creates a barrier for the independent developer.

- **Limits reuse and interoperability.** Class libraries promote code reuse; each developer can use the same classes to create an application. But, because the class library leaves infrastructure to the clients, developers can use the same pieces in different combinations. Two different developers can use the same set of class libraries to write two programs that do exactly the same thing, but whose structures vary. Because they don't share similar designs, two applications that perform a similar task (such as word processing) have little or no high-level code in common, cannot exchange data without converting it to some lowest-common-denominator format (for instance, ASCII), and are likely to have different commands, menus, and so on. This limits the reuse and interoperability of programs created for related tasks, makes the transfer of domain expertise from application to application difficult, and adds to maintenance problems.

Enter frameworks

What you really want is a way to reduce the amount of design you need to create and code you need to write in the first place, and to increase the reusability of the design and the interoperability of the code that you've written. Only this approach fundamentally addresses the problem of low developer productivity.

One solution to this problem is called a *framework*. Frameworks carry the object-oriented paradigm further than do class libraries and, in so doing, deliver on the promise of greatly improved developer productivity.

Delivering developer productivity

Whether you are developing commercial applications as an independent software vendor or custom applications in a corporate setting, building and using frameworks increases productivity. Frameworks and systems that are based on frameworks, such as the Taligent® CommonPoint™ application system (also called "CommonPoint"), help developers achieve improved design and code reuse, including reduced development requirements, reduced maintenance, and higher reliability.

Improving developer productivity is a major challenge for the entire software industry. While current approaches have advanced to provide the productivity and development leverage needed to solve today's complex computing problems, the next generation of software should fully exploit object-oriented technology.

The issue is one of properly implementing object-oriented technology, rather than just switching to objects. The success of object-oriented approaches hinges on an infrastructure (such as frameworks) that enables developers:

- To change their programming mindset to design general solutions
- To design software that is more reusable and maintainable
- To create innovative software that addresses business problems

WHAT ARE FRAMEWORKS?

A framework embodies a generic design, comprised of a set of cooperating classes, which can be adapted to a variety of specific problems within a given domain (Cotter with Potel 1995).

Frameworks are aggregates of classes in the same way that classes are aggregates of functions and data—but frameworks are more than just collections of classes. They are architectural; that is, they provide structure. This reduces the amount of design you must create and code you must write, which, in turn, improves productivity.

The growth of framework technology

The first object-oriented frameworks were designed to solve mathematical problems in Simula and Smalltalk. The spread of computing hardware in the 1980s, and the emerging interactive paradigm of Graphical User Interface (GUI) systems, made windows and events (not mathematical simulations) the real domains where programmers needed help writing their software.

The most popular GUIs included those for the Macintosh®, the X Window System, and Microsoft Windows. Each of these systems presented application developers with complex procedural APIs, and a multitude of data structures for dealing with low-level issues such as file input/output, memory management, and printing.

The difficulty of building GUI applications on these systems demanded a solution, and a different kind of framework started to gain popularity with frustrated programmers. MacApp® and InterViews were two of these new *GUI frameworks*, and they shared the following characteristics: they organized application initialization chores; they provided useful, generic abstractions for drawing views and windows; and they offered an event-handling mechanism based on the Model/View/Controller (MVC) concepts from Smalltalk. Most importantly,

writing an application with any of these frameworks was much easier, and resulted in a more stable code base, than writing directly in the basic GUI APIs.

The developers of the first application frameworks saw that typical applications shared common patterns, and modified their frameworks to address more areas of the clients program. MacApp, for example, provided a powerful facility that made it much easier to represent application documents and their commands. This started the trend toward comprehensive *application frameworks*.

Today, application frameworks vary in their scope, type of problem solved, method of implementation, and level of sophistication. Some frameworks are academic research projects; some are commercial-quality packages that provide solutions in the software industry. Frameworks are available for most computers and operating systems. The Macintosh has MacApp, the Think Class Library (TCL), PowerPlant, and the OpenDoc™ Developer Framework. UNIX systems have ET++. Microsoft Windows has the Borland Object Windows Library (OWL) and the Microsoft Foundation Classes (MFC). Third-party vendors sell application frameworks that run on one or more of these platforms.

Because of this broad functionality, you can use frameworks to address programming problems as well as to develop GUI applications. In fact, frameworks are an appropriate solution wherever a problem needs to be solved in a generalized, extensible way. For example, a database access framework such as Rogue Wave db++.h or the Taligent Data Access Framework can make working with an SQL database much easier.

By applying framework design principles throughout the entire application system, Taligent has taken framework technology beyond what others have done. Because the same design principles are applied throughout, the frameworks in the Taligent system all "speak with one voice": they work together as a single system smoothly and efficiently. Fully utilizing object-oriented architecture, individual frameworks in the Taligent system employ many sophisticated new features that don't exist in other application frameworks. And the coverage is broader—in addition to frameworks for text and user interface applications, the Taligent application system includes frameworks for system software functions such as networking, multimedia, and database access.

Frameworks represent partial-to-complete solutions to a particular problem. You can use a framework exactly as it was created. However, in many cases, you want to extend or customize the framework for your specific problem.

Capturing domain expertise

A framework represents a generic design solution. It is a meta-solution encompassing a set of possible solutions, rather than any one solution, within a particular problem domain. A framework reflects many solutions in the domain at once, without necessarily solving any one particular problem.

"A framework abstracts the essential entities, state, and behavior in the problem domain. It provides key mechanisms, provides the interaction protocols for key scenarios, and encapsulates and enforces fundamental invariants." (Andert 1994) It has strong "wired-in" connections among its objects. These connections capture design decisions common to its problem domain.

The following figure illustrates the elements that you combine to create a framework. The framework encompasses possible problems in the domain to provide a generic solution. Based on the common parts of those problems, you provide the specific domain expertise in the form of processes, rules, and policies for that particular area. Object-oriented techniques are especially useful for defining frameworks, and you can use your object-oriented design and language expertise to implement the solution. Adding framework design expertise ties the solution together in a flexible, usable form.

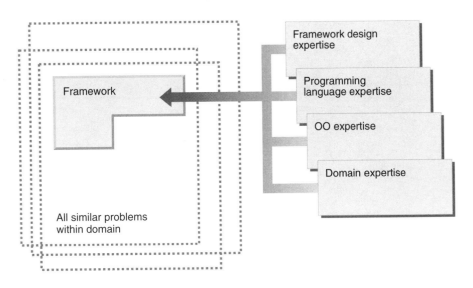

A FRAMEWORK ENCOMPASSES EXPERTISE TO PROVIDE A GENERIC SOLUTION

In this manner, a framework embodies the domain expertise of the designer of the framework—it encompasses the programming expertise necessary to solve a particular kind of problem.

For example, a financial domain expert can encompass domain expertise dealing with currency conversion, exchange rates, and securities purchasing for international markets to create a framework as the basis for multiple specialized arbitrage applications.

Creating applications with frameworks

A framework also defines and enforces the responsibilities of a developer who wants to use the framework, as well as the degrees of freedom available to a developer who wants to customize the framework. "The framework dictates the architecture of your application. It will define the overall structure, its partitioning into classes and objects, the key responsibilities thereof, how the classes and objects collaborate, and the thread of control." (Gamma et al. 1995)

Working within the constraints imposed by the framework, you tailor the framework to solve your particular problem. You do this by adding expertise specific to your problem, in design and in implementation language, to solve the requirements of the specific framework client. The framework contributes the domain expertise. This way, you turn the generic solution represented by the framework into a concrete instance of an application, as shown in the following figure.

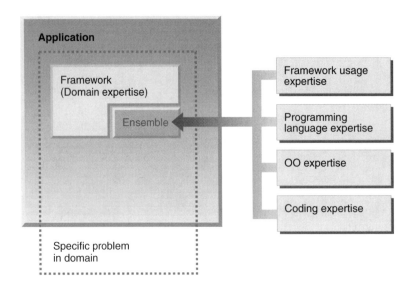

AN APPLICATION COMBINES A FRAMEWORK WITH CLIENT EXPERTISE

Although you need to know how to use the framework to solve the problem, you need not be a domain expert. By using the framework, you reuse the design captured by the framework. In effect, you inherit the domain expertise and problem-solving ability of the designer of the framework.

In contrast, as the following figure illustrates, to solve a problem without a framework, you must be a domain expert (or have access to a domain expert) and, in addition, you must design and implement a complete solution.

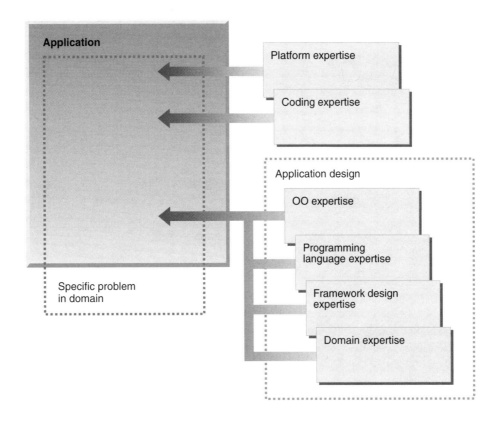

CREATING AN APPLICATION WITHOUT FRAMEWORKS

Ensembles

Developing an application using a framework consists of writing the additional code that captures the specifics of a particular solution within the framework's domain, but which is not already addressed in the general solution of the framework itself. This code is called an *ensemble*.

An ensemble incorporates the domain knowledge, expertise, rules, and policies of a particular solution. It is the part of the solution that varies from one problem to another within the domain, as opposed to the framework, which captures the invariant parts of a solution for that domain. The ensemble code conforms to the protocols established by the framework and extends or completes it for the specific solution (Andert 1994), as shown in the following figure.

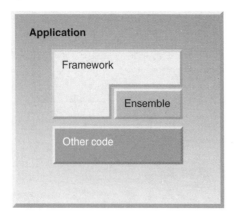

ENSEMBLE CODE WORKING WITH A FRAMEWORK MAKES AN APPLICATION

In the simplest form, a framework and an ensemble make up an application as shown in the preceding figure. The blocks provide the abstract overview; you implement the ensemble by providing code that communicates with and extends the various classes in the framework.

Together with its corresponding framework, an ensemble is a complete concrete implementation of the service provided by the framework—in other words, an application of that framework. The coding, language, object-oriented, and framework client expertise form the ensemble; the ensemble and the framework together form the application (or part of a larger application) that solves the specific domain problem. The following figure illustrates this relationship.

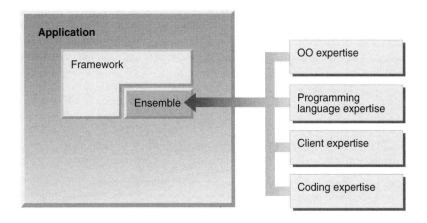

THE ENSEMBLE ISOLATES PROBLEM-SPECIFIC EXPERTISE

For example, a user interface framework can embody the way user interfaces work in a general sense, while at the same time make no statement about how windows look, how menus are activated, or how the details for a specific interface are handled. An ensemble for that framework would specify precisely how windows look, how menus are activated, and so forth.

Multiple frameworks   So far, applications and frameworks have been described in terms of a one-to-one relationship: one application per framework, one framework per application. In practice, you can implement an application using multiple frameworks. The following figure demonstrates a situation that calls for multiple frameworks.

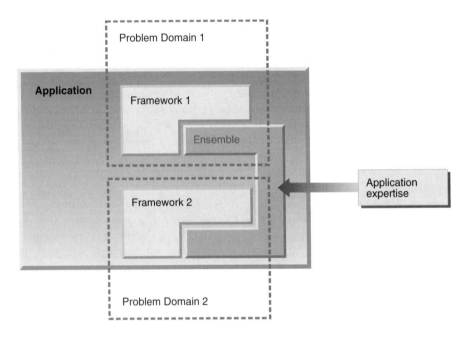

AN APPLICATION BASED ON MULTIPLE FRAMEWORKS

The application uses Framework 1 to solve the problem in Domain 1 and Framework 2 to solve the problem in Domain 2. The added expertise forms the ensemble, which contains specific solution information for both Frameworks 1 and 2 and expertise to allow them to interact to provide the specific domain solution. An application might need a user-interface framework together with an accounting framework to create an end-user home-loan calculator.

In more complex framework structures, frameworks can use other frameworks, thus layering solutions on different levels to solve different aspects of the problem.

When you require multiple frameworks for an application, the ensemble for the application consists of code for each of the frameworks.

How to use frameworks

More so than procedural or class libraries, frameworks are very flexible programming constructs. You can use frameworks in three different and complementary ways. These are listed below and appear in *Inside Taligent Technology* (Cotter with Potel 1995):

- **Use as is.** Use the framework without modifying it, like a specialized class library. Some frameworks provide sufficient default behavior that you can use them as they are, without making changes. This use doesn't preclude more sophisticated use of the framework—it just means that the more sophisticated uses are optional, rather than required.

- **Complete.** Add code to the framework to implement specific capabilities. A framework represents a generic design solution, not any one solution. A framework doesn't have to exhibit complete default behavior—it can be partially filled in. A framework might not even be able to execute as delivered—it might be abstract, requiring developer-supplied code to make it concrete.

- **Customize.** Replace parts of the framework implementation. This is the most sophisticated, and radical, way to use a framework. Through customization, you replace some of the code in the framework to change the behavior of the framework. You can replace some code or the entire implementation. You can even implement some or all of the code in hardware (for example, a graphics accelerator).

In all three of these implementations, the framework maintains the same interface. Changes that you make to the framework's underlying implementation don't affect the programs that use the framework for services.

You can compare these methods across the spectrum of the white-box (customize) and black-box (use-as-is) frameworks (Johnson and Foote 1988) and the "open-closed principle" (Meyer 1988).

Client and customization APIs

Frameworks are represented by two basic application programming interfaces (APIs): client and customization.

- **Client API.** Use the client API when you want to use a framework as is or by completing it. You work with the framework without changing its fundamental internal operations. The client API manifests the default behavior of the framework.

- **Customization API.** Use the customization API to change some fundamental behavior of the framework.

The difference between how you use the client and customization APIs is not exact. Some of the same classes and member functions from one framework might belong to both APIs. The distinction is in the degree to which they are used and how that impacts the behavior of the framework. Interestingly, for low-level frameworks often the only client of the framework is a framework in the next layer up, rather than a developer writing an application. Despite this "fuzziness," the idea that a framework has these two kinds of APIs is useful for thinking about and describing the design of a framework.

Finding frameworks in the real world

Ironically, while frameworks are a new and somewhat unfamiliar concept in the field of software development, they are actually ubiquitous in everyday life. In fact, they are so commonplace that it is arguable that frameworks are the way in which we accomplish almost anything—software is the exception!

Frameworks aren't a radical concept at all—quite the opposite. It is unlikely that we could manage our lives without frameworks. But software developers have not yet widely embraced this concept. They often build a single solution to a specific problem, rather than use a general framework to implement a specific solution from a group of solutions.

Fortunately, although frameworks have been tardy in making their appearance in the software industry, they have now begun to do so.

Frameworks in the everyday world

The concept of frameworks in the everyday world carries over into software design. In a sense, you can describe much of life as a framework, and we all work with frameworks every day without thinking about it. Each process works a bit differently each time, allowing flexibility within clearly defined limits.

Consider these simple examples:

- Build-to-suit real estate, where a company can rent a building shell and have the interior finished to the company's specifications.
- Pre-cut tailored suits, where the pieces have been cut out and basted together so that the tailor can fit the suit to a client, and then complete the final stitching.

- A board game such as Trivial Pursuit, where players use the same board, tokens, dice, and rules, but with different sets of cards (for example, sports trivia, '60s trivia).

These frameworks are static and fairly inflexible. It is difficult to alter their fundamental structure, and the relationships among the various entities are fixed. Much closer to the idea of a software framework are the more complex and dynamic conceptual frameworks that we use to perform a complex yet familiar task.

A wedding represents a complex framework that you find in the everyday world. A large set of protocols ("traditions") exists for how to choreograph a wedding. These protocols vary with different religions and cultures. Formal traditional American weddings share certain customs: brides wear white; the Best Man manages the rings; flowers are thrown. Guidelines dictate what ushers wear, where family members sit, and so forth. The rules are so complex that you can hire a consultant to help you design your wedding and various experts to orchestrate parts or all of the procedure.

And yet, within this structure, no two weddings are exactly alike. Some differences are obvious—the bride and groom pair is unique. Other differences range from the music they select to the color of the cummerbunds the male members of the entourage wear to which church or location serves as the venue.

And some very wild customizations are possible: marriages while skydiving, at Star Trek conventions, and so on.

WHAT ADVANTAGES DO FRAMEWORKS PROVIDE?

Frameworks return a number of benefits to developers. Some of these benefits are directly attributable to frameworks supporting considerable reuse of code (also present, to a lesser extent, when using well-designed class libraries). Other benefits are unique to frameworks and are advantages that frameworks have over both procedural and class libraries. *Inside Taligent Technology* (Cotter with Potel 1995) and several sources in "Recommended materials for further reading" on page 306 describe the many benefits of frameworks. The following list describes some of those benefits:

- **Less code to design and implement.** By providing the infrastructure—design, structure, and code for an application—the framework dramatically decreases the amount of standard software that you must design, code, test, and debug. Because the infrastructure of the framework is already in place, you write code only as required by the framework or to override some default behavior of the framework that is inappropriate for the application (this is sometimes called "programming by differences"). Typically, the amount of code required for an ensemble is a fraction of the code required to create the same application. This provides a corresponding decrease in the effort, time, and cost required to implement the functionality, as well as an increase in quality and a possible decrease in footprint (depending on the framework's implementation).

  Consider, for example, a user interface framework that handles routine tasks: drawing windows, scroll bars, and menus; tracking the mouse; highlighting menu items; detecting menu selections. Using the framework, you might need to specify only the items in the menus. The framework enforces and encapsulates the user interface policies and processes and promotes reuse when you customize or extend the interface.

- **Leverage domain experts' experience.** When using a framework, you can focus on the area where you can add the most value to your code. All you need to understand is how to use other frameworks to support your domain-specific application. Just as standard programming interfaces insulate software routines from system dependencies and standard utilities facilitate development, frameworks provide standard solutions. This frees developers who are not experts in a certain area from the complexity of the underlying details. Frameworks create an environment in which solving domain problems—not programming problems—is possible.

- **Proliferation of expertise.** Good software design in a particular area requires domain knowledge that you typically acquire only by experience. Corporate and commercial development organizations as well as systems integrators have acquired this experience in particular areas, such as manufacturing, accounting, insurance, or financial instruments. Frameworks allow organizations to package the common characteristics of their expertise. This opens business opportunities for organizations to resell specialized knowledge.

  For example, frameworks give systems integration companies with expertise in vertical markets a distribution mechanism for packaging, reselling, and deploying their expertise.

- **Enculturation.** The more developers use frameworks, the more likely they are to design and implement generic rather than special solutions. This shift in the development culture means more frameworks become available so that you and other developers can reuse them.

- **Improved consistency.** Because frameworks embody expertise, you solve the problems once—when first creating, buying, or leasing the framework—and you can use the business rules and designs captured in the framework consistently across all problems in the framework's domain.

  Additionally, frameworks enforce the relationships among the objects and classes in the framework, providing a higher degree of consistency than is obtained with either procedural or class libraries.

- **Improved integration and interoperability.** Frameworks support a high degree of integration among multiple customizations. Much as individual objects hide their internal complexity and present a simplified interface for use by other objects, many different programs can use frameworks at the same time in a way that allows the programs to share common behavior without interfering with each other's specialized implementations. This is possible because the client API of the framework remains unchanged.

  When applications use the same frameworks, they can work together (for example, cut-copy-paste or drag-and-drop) in more substantial ways. The result is that applications are better integrated from a user's point of view, while requiring less work by developers to create compatible applications.

- **Reduced maintenance overhead.** Because your applications are based on a framework, generally any change you make to the framework—fixing a bug or adding a new feature—automatically updates in the applications. And because you make the changes in only one place, you minimize the chance of introducing errors in the code.

  Maintenance is far easier, because you amortize maintenance of a framework over many ensembles. A properly implemented ensemble adds or changes only the pieces that are unique to the particular ensemble, so you have to create less new code. More common code means more common maintenance; less unique code means fewer unique bugs.

As you and your clients constantly reuse the framework, you refine the features and bugs in the code. From this process evolves a very robust framework. Code you reuse by using a framework has already been tested and integrated with the rest of the framework (and with other frameworks in the system). This allows an organization to build from a base that has been proven to work in the past and minimizes the amount of testing required. Thus, a new product contains significant amounts of mature code from the framework, plus a smaller amount of new code in the ensemble, resulting in higher overall quality.

■ **Orderly program evolution.** Frameworks provide a mechanism for reliably extending functionality. While objects and class libraries provide interfaces for extending functionality at a fine-grained level, frameworks provide this flexibility at a higher level. In this manner, you can develop applications by using the framework as a starting point and writing smaller amounts of code to modify or extend the framework's behavior. You can add these extensions without sacrificing compatibility or interoperability because the interfaces are well defined.

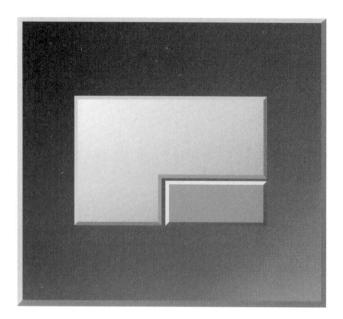

CHAPTER 2

HOW FRAMEWORKS WORK

In most situations, frameworks work by shifting the direction of the flow of control between an application and the software on which it is based—frameworks call applications, rather than applications calling frameworks. To use frameworks effectively, you have to change the way you think about the interaction between the code that you design and write and the code other developers design and write.

When you use a class or procedural library, you write the main body of the application and call the code that you want to reuse. When you use a framework, however, you reuse the main body of the application and write the code that *it* calls. Writing an application using frameworks involves dividing responsibilities among the various pieces of software that the framework calls, rather than specifying how the different pieces should work together.

By owning the flow of control, a framework defines the infrastructure for the solution. It establishes which objects call which other objects, and when, and why. Your objects participate in this flow of control at the points determined by the framework. A framework has been compared to a puppeteer, pulling the strings; your code is the puppet. This relationship contrasts directly to what exists with procedural or class libraries, where your program must provide all the structure and flow of execution and make calls to system libraries whenever necessary.

SHIFTING TO DYNAMIC BEHAVIOR

Developing applications using frameworks requires a shift in location and behavior of the flow of control. This shift, from sequential to dynamic flow, is necessary as more applications depend on customers to determine the flow of tasks. Frameworks provide solutions that allow you to reuse the common control code and extend user activities for your particular domain.

Evolution of the concept

The idea of turning over the flow of the control to the system has evolved over years of application development. The following figure shows these stages.

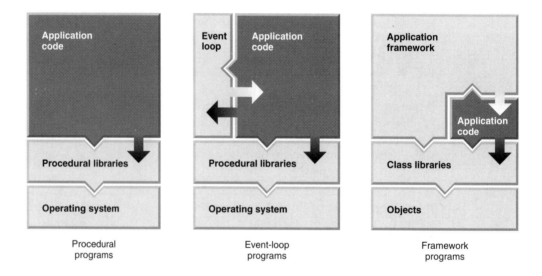

EVOLUTION OF APPLICATION PROGRAMMING STRUCTURES

- **Procedural programming.** In this earliest approach, you provide all code for flow of control. The operating system has libraries with procedures to perform certain tasks that you can call. You control the flow in a program that executes sequentially, instruction by instruction, down the page from start to finish. The system takes action only when your program calls it.

■ **Event loops.** With the introduction of graphical user interfaces (GUI), end users started to interact with applications in fundamentally different ways. This called for a different solution to the control problem, because end users could now decide which actions to perform and select the order of those actions. A sequential control flow could no longer accommodate the user's choices.

One solution devised to handle this problem involves the concept of the *event loop*. Interacting with a GUI, the user indicates choices and actions through input devices—mouse, keyboard, trackball, and so on—which the event loop senses. The user chooses the order in which events happen. When the user makes a choice, the event loop calls sections of your application program that handle the action the user requests.

However, you are still responsible for flow of control within the sections of your program that the event loop calls to respond to user actions. These sections of code call operating system libraries to carry out user requests. In addition, parts of the application are not appropriate for an event-loop approach, and so do not benefit.

■ **Application frameworks.** In an application framework environment, the framework code takes care of almost all flow of control and calls your code only when necessary. You need not design and write the control code required by the event-loop programs or code common to many applications that you want to write once and reuse.

When you write a framework-based application, you turn over control to the user (as with event-loop programs) and to the original framework developers. From the combined effort with the framework developers, you can create more feature-rich, interoperating applications systems, rather than individually re-create repetitive solutions for similar problems.

**Examining flow
of control**

Consider the following sample programs as examples of the shift of flow of
control. These samples contrast the procedural and framework approach to flow
of control by showing a debugger stack trace that follows the calls that each
sample makes. The illustrations show the logical arrangement of the modules
with the corresponding series of calls from the stack trace.

The following figure illustrates a traditional procedural-based application, in
which application modules make calls to other application modules and
occasionally to the operating system libraries for services.

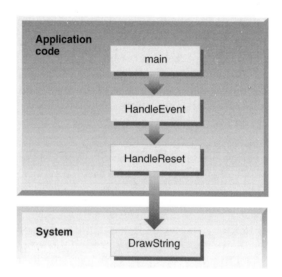

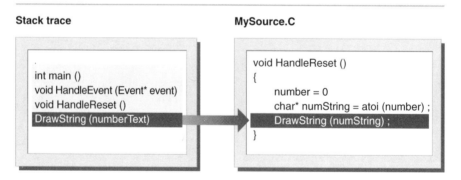

TRADITIONAL PROCEDURAL CODE TRACE

The following figure illustrates a simple framework-based application, in which framework member functions call each other and occasionally call your ensemble code when the framework uses your functions. This is the opposite of the procedural approach to flow of control.

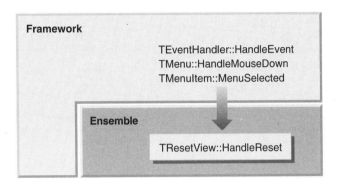

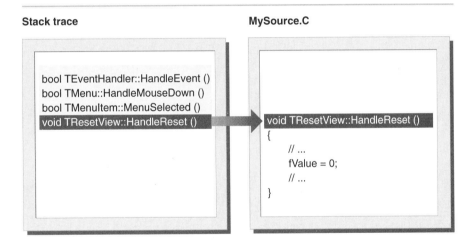

SIMPLE FRAMEWORK CODE STRUCTURE

The following figure illustrates a more complex framework structure, in which both frameworks use the ensemble code.

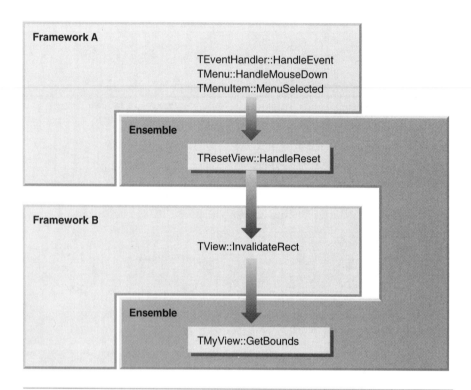

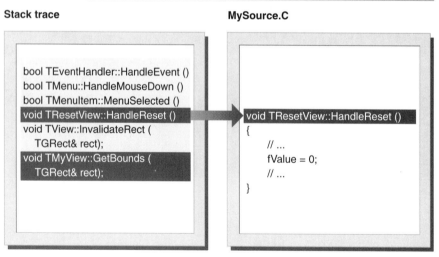

MULTIPLE FRAMEWORK CODE STRUCTURE

Shifting control flow: not an absolute

The shift in direction of control flow when using a framework is not absolute. Calls are not made universally in one direction: ensemble code often calls framework code.

The shifting of control flow is a question of degree, with the goal being to shift as much of the flow-of-control code into the framework as possible. Ideally, you design and write only a small fraction of the total flow-of-control code required to implement the application. A well-designed framework can handle all flow of control for the generic solution.

All programs exist on a scale somewhere between 0% and 100% framework-owned control flow. Application frameworks move the average location of a program on this scale as far as possible in the direction of 100% framework-owned.

ANALYZING A SIMPLE APPLICATION

To see these concepts illustrated, let's analyze a very simple example of an application. This example illustrates the complexity of handling simple tasks with direct code. It provides a concrete example to show how applications have progressed from a procedural to a more object-oriented approach, and where you might find frameworks useful. You are unlikely to build a framework for this particular application, but it gives you some idea of scope of the problem and the level of effort involved.

Functional description

This simple application generates and displays a single number. The application's window is a fixed size, big enough to display all numbers in the range covered by the application; it has no scroll bars, does not zoom, and has no other window controls except for a close box in the upper left corner. The application has a single menu, the title of which appears at the top of the window.

A user can work through the features of the application using the following steps:

1 To start the application, double-click its icon on the desktop.

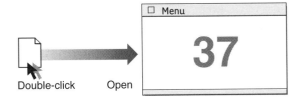

2 To close the application, click in the application window's close box.

3 To reopen the application, double-click its icon on the desktop.

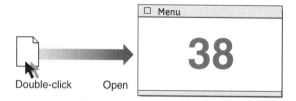

Each time the user starts the application, the number it displays is incremented from the value that it displayed the last time it was started and closed. Because the application keeps a running count, each time it is executed it provides a new value that is suitable to use, for example, as a unique serial number.

4 To reset the application counter to 0, select Reset from the menu.

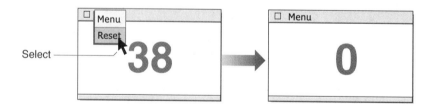

The application's menu contains a single entry, Reset, which resets the counter to 0 if selected.

This is a very simple example, but it serves as a basis for explaining framework concepts, as shown in the following sections.

Writing pseudocode   Suppose you are asked to design and implement this application, and you have no frameworks available. As a first step, you might write out pseudocode for the overall flow of control of the system, particularly as it relates to your application. A portion of the result would look something like this:

- Track the mouse as it moves over the desktop, watching for mouse-down events.
- When you detect a mouse-down event, check the location of the cursor. Depending on the location of the cursor and the current state of the system, take actions such as:
  - Bringing a window to the foreground (which involves clipping other windows that are now fully or partially obscured by the window that you brought to the foreground, and so on).
  - Highlighting an icon on the desktop.
  - Activating a menu.
  - Closing, zooming, or minimizing a window.
- If you detect a second mouse-down event very close to the previous mouse-down, handle this as a double-click.

  Check the location of the cursor. Then, depending on the location of the cursor, take actions, such as launching a document.
- Watch for mouse-up events. If you detect a mouse-up event, check the location of the cursor. Depending on the location of the cursor and the current state of the system, take actions, such as selecting a particular menu item.

From this very high-level (and complex) analysis, you then isolate each individual activity that pertains to your application and write out its pseudocode.

For example, a portion of the result of this more detailed analysis for the activity "launch a document" would look something like this:

1 Display an application window appropriate for the document on the screen. (This includes displaying any menus associated with the window.)

2 Find the file or files representing the document on disk.

3 Read in the part of the file(s) needed for display.

4 Display the information in the window.

You then write pseudocode for each subactivity you have identified, and each sub-subactivity, and so on. What you are implementing includes many features of an operating system, so eventually you can produce hundreds to thousands of pages of fairly detailed pseudocode. Because this functionality requires so much support code, you have to describe other services, which can lead to as much as hundreds of thousands of lines of finished code. Then all you have to do is turn the pseudocode into real code, compile, and you're done. Within possibly hundreds of developer years, you get your simple application (with its operating system support) up and running.

Factoring

Admittedly, the process just described is artificial. Nobody using today's systems would actually design and implement a simple application this way, because the system handles at least some of the routine activities. For example, all modern systems provide at least some degree of mouse tracking for the developer. Toolkits and class libraries can handle additional actions. But the issue of reusing the overall design of the problem solution still remains.

However, before dismissing this example as completely artificial, look at the activities. On a typical system, are all these activities handled automatically for developers? Another way to formulate this question is to ask, out of all the code it would take to implement the functionality required by your simple application, what is the *absolute minimum* amount of code that you should have to design and implement versus the amount of code the system can provide?

The answer, of course, is that you should have to write code only for elements that are unique to your application (that is, that the system would not know how to do). Using this criterion to factor the pseudocode into system responsibilities and your responsibilities, you find that the only things unique to your application in the pages of pseudocode are:

- Details to direct the system to handle the appearance of the user interface
  - Size of the window
  - Title of the menu
  - Number of items in the menu
  - Title of the item in the menu
  - How the document icon appears on the desktop
- What to do when the user selects the item in your menu (and how to do it)
- Which data your application manages and manipulates
- How to read your data from and save your data to disk (including incrementing the count when saving)
- How to display your data in your window

Your ensemble should contain nothing but these elements. Everything else, from your standpoint, is system-level detail. The system handles the following activities (along with many others):

- Making state transitions when mouse events come into the system
- Allocating screen real estate, opening and closing windows, and preserving foreground/background relationships among the various windows on the screen (and refreshing newly unhidden areas as they occur)
- Associating the document icon with the correct file(s) representing the document
- Accessing the physical disk
- Activating menus

If the system provides everything that is not unique to your application, you have to write only the most minimal amount of code.

EXPANDING ON THE SIMPLE APPLICATION

Programmers familiar with a GUI API (such as MacApp, the X Window System, or Microsoft Windows) won't find the previous application example particularly compelling, because these GUI systems handle most, if not all, of the functionality described in the pseudocode. Taligent wants to make much more complex, distributed examples equally as simple.

Implementing more complex functionality

For example, suppose that you want to implement a more complex feature, a robust multilevel undo/redo capability in a text editor that you're developing. With this capability, your end users can undo their most recent change, and the one before that, and the one before that, and so forth, all the way back to when they first opened the file for this editing session. Similarly, users can then redo forward in time, to return to the most recent change to the document.

Think about this problem for a moment. What is required to make this undo/redo feature work well enough that users would trust it with their data? Without going to the same level of detail as in the previous example, can you write a one-sentence pseudocode description for each of the more complex aspects of this problem?

Creating pseudocode   Using one possible solution, your program should have the following minimum capabilities:

- Encapsulating each discrete change users make to the file—defining a way to represent user operations, such as "Cut" and "SetToBold."
- Applying an encapsulated change to the appropriate part of the file—defining a way to represent the item to "Cut" or "SetToBold."
- Reverting the file to the previous state (undo) or advancing to the next state (redo) using the encapsulated changes and their targets.
- Encapsulating each change as a single transaction so that if an error occurs in the middle of a change, users can recover by reverting to the previously completed transaction.
- Documenting each change to a log to support the roll-back and roll-forward capability
- Keeping the change log together with the edited file, but independent of the file (otherwise, an error writing the file also destroys the log).

These capabilities are more difficult to support than those of the previous example, and such support is certainly beyond the scope of what today's application frameworks directly support.

Factoring   Now factor this sample application into actions the system can perform (and which the system should, therefore, be able to perform in a framework) and actions that only you can perform for your application.

In this solution, the only actions the system should not perform are the following:

- Encapsulating the changes specific to your application
- Targeting the encapsulated changes in ways specific to your application

Everything else is generic: transactions, logging, roll back, roll forward, and so forth. The system should take care of all of this automatically, and then, when the specific target and specific encapsulated change needs to be applied, the system calls your code.

In the Taligent CommonPoint application system, the encapsulated change is a *command*, and the target is a *selection*. You write those two objects and the system provides the rest. For a simple application, you typically need to write fewer than 200 lines of code, and you can use your solution over the network collaboratively as well. This is the power of frameworks.

HOW FRAMEWORKS CALL ENSEMBLE CODE

Thus far, you know that frameworks call developer code, but you don't know anything about how frameworks do this. Everything discussed up to this point applies to all frameworks, but the actual mechanism whereby developer code is inserted into a framework's flow of control is design- and implementation-dependent and can vary widely from one framework to another.

Despite the variety, all mechanisms for calling your code from framework code belong to one of two major categories:

- The framework must be delivered to developers as source code.
- The framework can be delivered to developers in binary form (that is, with only the interface to the framework provided as source code and the corresponding implementation compiled into a binary).

Delivering source code frameworks

Frameworks delivered as source code are based on the simple idea that you lexically intermingle your developer source code with the framework's source code, then compile the combination to produce an executable.

Two basic types of source code delivery are available:

- As source files
- Through code generation

Delivery as source files

With source code delivery as source files, you receive the actual headers and source files for the framework.

Because the framework code is available for modification, the framework can call your code without using any special mechanisms to incorporate code. In fact, in its simplest form, all you need is a text editor—you then edit the framework's source code to make it call your ensemble routines. You can also more easily debug flow-of-control problems from the source code.

However, do not confuse a framework delivered as source files with a simple application skeleton (or, for that matter, with reuse that uses a copy-and-paste procedure). The distinction is in the quality of support that the framework provides for orderly extension and modification and in the degree to which the framework properly factors the invariant portions of the problem domain into its flow of control.

MacApp is an example of an extremely well thought-out source code framework.

Delivery as code generation

Source code delivery as code generation uses one or more mechanisms to semi-automate the intermingling of your code with the framework's code. This can reduce the amount of code you need to write and limit the chance for error.

Macro expansion

A rudimentary form of code generation is achieved through *macro expansion*, where you fill in various macros with arguments as appropriate for your problem. A preprocessor then expands these macros into the necessary boilerplate, which is then compiled. This technique is limited by the expressive power of the macro language used and by how well the designers of the macro set anticipated the needs of the developer.

Parameterized types

In some languages, you can achieve code generation through use of *parameterized types*, called "templates" in C++ and "generics" in Ada and Eiffel. A parameterized type is a class to which other types are supplied as arguments during instantiation, thereby completing the specification and implementation of the class. In the same way that instantiating a normal class creates an object, specializing a parameterized type creates a class (which is then instantiated to create an object). Parameterized types are not as common as the other language mechanisms discussed in this book.

The parameterized type represents the invariant portions of the class. The parameters represent the parts of the class that vary depending on the specific problem addressed by the instantiation. In a sense, a parameterized type is itself a mini-framework.

The textbook example of a parameterized type is a ListOf class. This class abstracts the list-supporting properties, while at the same time leaving it to the instantiator to specify the type of object to be stored in the list.

To some extent, parameterized types are a glorified macro expansion technique (in fact, compilers often implement parameterized types using macro expansion). However, parameterized types have the advantage of being more type-safe and more object-oriented than macros, as well as offering the possibility of code sharing to reduce footprint, which is generally not feasible with macros. Parameterized types assume more importance in languages such as C++, where objects do not all descend from a common ancestor; in this case, without parameterized types there is no type-safe way to define a general ListOf class.

Tool support

Providing a point-and-click interface can simplify code generation; through this mechanism you can select bits of functionality, toggle modes using menu entries, respond to dialog boxes with the names of types, and so forth. When you've established all the settings, the tool generates source code in accordance with the settings, which is then compiled. These sorts of tools are commonly referred to as "application generators" or "application builders."

It might seem odd to categorize an application builder as a way to deliver a framework as source, but in a sufficiently sophisticated application builder, the builder *itself* embodies domain knowledge about how to solve a particular kind of problem. The builder uses this knowledge to generate an instance of an application within its area of expertise, tailored by the developer's responses to the builder's prompts.

Binary frameworks

While source code delivery is simple, it also has several drawbacks:

- Source code delivery exposes developers to software piracy. The implementation is entirely exposed for anyone to use.

- The framework developer might not provide the necessary documentation to learn and use the framework. (This is especially true for large frameworks.) The source code alone is not sufficient to use effectively.

- Source code delivery thwarts the goals of consistency and interoperability, because different developers can make arbitrary changes not only to the implementation of the framework but also to its public interface.

- The source code is recompiled for each instance of the framework. This can create footprint issues and increase turnaround time.

Although most vendors ship frameworks as source code today, for the reasons discussed, most would generally prefer binary delivery of frameworks. But delivering a framework in binary is much more difficult than delivering a framework in source code, for the following reasons:

- You cannot insert developer code into the flow of control with an editor. You must now insert it through a language or runtime mechanism.

- The framework can be more difficult to understand and the learning curve steeper, because developers cannot look at the source code to determine what is going on. Accordingly, better documentation and training are required.

    In addition, debugging requires more sophisticated tools. It must be possible for you, as the developer, to visualize the flow of control of the application when it steps into framework code, despite the fact that the framework code is just a binary image, and you have limited information from the stack trace.

- The vendor of the framework must be very responsive to bugs, because developers cannot fix—and often cannot even work around—a bug in the framework's code.

- The design of the framework must be better, because developers cannot modify the interface. The framework must be more general, more flexible, more modular, and more complete than if it were delivered as source code.

Despite these drawbacks, framework suppliers gain consistency, interoperability, and prevention of piracy. With binary delivery, clients share the same binary for the framework itself—only the code in their ensemble contributes to footprint on shared library systems. These advantages are worth the extra effort. This is particularly true for high-quality production-level frameworks that are a major strategic asset for a company and a source of considerable competitive advantage revenue.

Using language mechanisms

The language mechanisms used to call developer code from framework code are quite varied. However, they fall into two broad categories that reflect two fundamentally different approaches to designing a framework:

- Composition-focused
- Inheritance-focused

These terms reflect how a framework is used by a developer—whether the developer instantiates and combines existing classes to change the framework's behavior (composition-focused) or derives new classes to accomplish this goal (inheritance-focused).

	Composition-focused	Inheritance-focused
Advantages	■ Easy to use, use-as-is, "plug and play" ■ No subclassing, which requires less programming sophistication	■ More flexible ■ Can create more new, unanticipated solutions, allowing more general solutions
Disadvantages	■ Inflexible, only applies to a portion of the problem solution ■ Limited to only the anticipated problem solutions	■ Requires creating subclasses; more complex to create and maintain

Ideally, composition-focused solutions should be broad-based, as flexible as possible, and parameterized; inheritance-focused solutions should be just a few things that you need to override the change in your application's behavior. A framework can use a combination of methods and fall somewhere along a spectrum between pure composition ("plug-and-play") and pure inheritance focus.

Composition-focused frameworks

Composition-focused frameworks rely primarily on assembling or "composing" collections of objects to create the structure that calls developer code. Clients customize the behavior of the framework by passing to it different combinations of programming constructs in components or code. The constructs that clients pass into a framework affect what the framework does. However, the framework specifies in its interface which constructs it accepts, and it defines in its implementation how the passed-in constructs interact, thus preserving the invariants in the problem domain.

Callbacks

One type of programming construct that can pass to a framework is a *callback*. A callback is a function or procedure that the framework executes at some point in the flow of control. When the framework executes the callback, control passes to the developer's code in the callback. By supplying various callbacks to the framework, you can produce a range of different behaviors. This is a widely used technique for some frameworks, such as the X Window System.

For example, a menu can consist of a list of callbacks, each having an associated title that the menu displays. When the user selects a particular item in the menu, the framework invokes the callback associated with that item.

The following application example implements the Reset menu item as a callback.

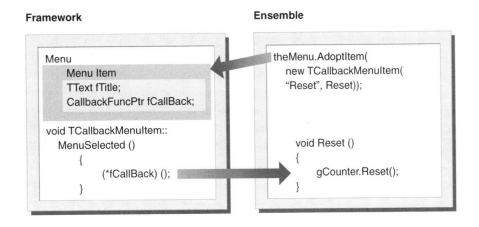

IMPLEMENTING A CALLBACK

Functors

Another simple programming construct that can pass to a framework is a *functor* (Coplien 1992). Functors are objects that serve the same purpose as a callback. A functor has only one significant function. The framework calls this function in the same way (expecting the same return value) that a framework executes a callback.

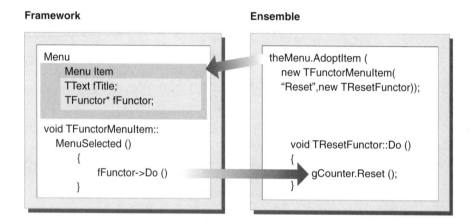

Framework

```
Menu
      Menu Item
      TText fTitle;
      TFunctor* fFunctor;

void TFunctorMenuItem::
   MenuSelected ()
      {
         fFunctor->Do ()
      }
```

Ensemble

```
theMenu.AdoptItem (
   new TFunctorMenuItem(
   "Reset",new TResetFunctor));



void TResetFunctor::Do ()
   {
      gCounter.Reset ();
   }
```

IMPLEMENTING A FUNCTOR

Functors are more flexible than callbacks, for the same reasons that objects are more flexible than functions and procedures. For example, you can write a functor to, or read it from, storage; however, you cannot do this with a callback in most languages. A functor can also contain local state, and, if you clone it, you can reset the state in the copy.

In contrast, a callback can contain (in some languages) local state, but there is only one instance of that callback in the entire system, and so its local state is shared by necessity among all invocations of the callback. In other languages, a callback can reference only global state, which is even more limiting.

Ordinary objects

A further generalization is achieved by having frameworks accept ordinary objects, rather than the more constrained (to a single function) functors. The framework can call several functions on the object at various points in the flow of control, can copy the object, can hand the object to some other object (which might also have been supplied by the developer), and so on. This allows more flexibility in design.

For example, in your simple application you might have a data model object that contains your persistent state. At various points during the execution of your application, the framework might call functions on your data model both to read it from the file and to write it to the file. It might also call a cloning function on your model when performing a copy-and-paste operation from your application's window to a new document.

Other constructs

Other mechanisms are available to support composition-focused coding. For example:

- In some languages, such as Smalltalk and the Common Lisp Object System (CLOS), classes are first-class objects. In such languages, you can pass classes to a framework as just another form of data.
- Dataflow languages support composition of processes, filters, and pipes.
- Parameterized types can be used for composition.

Inheritance-focused frameworks

Inheritance-focused frameworks rely primarily on subclasses and overrides to call developer code.

An inheritance-focused framework defines a set of interacting classes (some of which may have no actual implementation associated with them) that capture the invariants in the problem domain. Clients derive application-specific classes from the base classes provided by the framework, and override, as necessary, their member functions. It is these subclasses and overrides that contain the developer's code. The following figure illustrates this relationship.

Your code is executed when the framework calls the functions that have been overridden in its base classes. Your code lives "underneath" the system, rather than on top as in a conventional system. The exact details depend on the specific implementation language.

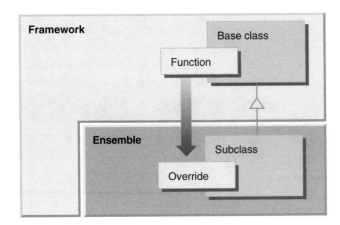

FRAMEWORK EXECUTING ENSEMBLE CODE

For example, suppose a user interface framework defines a base class, View, to be used for displaying information on the screen. Suppose further that every application window has a View object associated with it. Finally, suppose that View defines a member function, DrawSelf, that does the actual drawing. (View might define a number of other functions, but for this discussion focus solely on DrawSelf.) The following figure graphically describes the flow of the application.

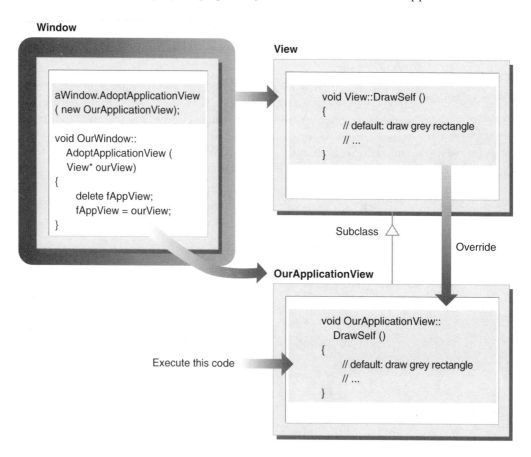

Window

```
aWindow.AdoptApplicationView
( new OurApplicationView);

void OurWindow::
   AdoptApplicationView (
   View* ourView)
{
    delete fAppView;
    fAppView = ourView;
}
```

View

```
void View::DrawSelf ()
{
    // default: draw grey rectangle
    // ...
}
```

Subclass

Override

OurApplicationView

Execute this code

```
void OurApplicationView::
   DrawSelf ()
{
    // default: draw grey rectangle
    // ...
}
```

FLOW OF THE SAMPLE APPLICATION

The user interface framework calls the DrawSelf function whenever it determines that a particular application window's view needs to be refreshed (as might happen, for example, when a window that has been obscured is brought to the foreground). The implementation of DrawSelf in the base class View provides the default drawing behavior of the user interface framework, which is to draw a grey rectangle inside the application's window.

To implement your simple application, display the current value of the counter. To do this, create a subclass of View called OurApplicationView, and override DrawSelf with your own implementation, which displays the counter value. You then tell the window to use your OurApplicationView subclass instead of the default View.

Whenever the framework determines that your view needs to be redrawn, it calls the DrawSelf function for the view associated with your application window. However, because your view is an OurApplicationView, not just a View, the framework calls your DrawSelf function instead of the default implementation provided by the user interface framework.

Composition- and inheritance-focused APIs

Frameworks that are heavily inheritance-driven can be difficult to use because they require clients to write a substantial amount of code to produce new and useful behavior. Purely composition-focused frameworks are generally easy to use, but they can be inflexible. They depend on the availability of sufficient plug-and-play, off-the-shelf components to create the behavior you need in your application. If you don't have these components and you can't use inheritance to create new subclasses, you can't extend the behavior of the framework.

Frameworks fall on a spectrum from being completely plug-and-play to needing to create a large number of subclasses. The composition-focused API consists of mechanisms that you use to pass your code into the framework. The inheritance-focused API consists of the base classes from which you derive new classes and functions that you override to make the framework call your code through inheritance.

One approach for building frameworks that is both easy to use and extensible is to provide an inheritance-focused base with a composition-focused layer; that is, provide a set of ready-to-use, off-the-shelf components that you can plug together (composition-focused) and an API that allows you to customize (inheritance-focused). It is helpful to think of such frameworks as having two different APIs: composition-focused and inheritance-focused.

For example, in the sample application described in "Inheritance-focused frameworks" on page 39, we use the composition-focused API of the user interface framework to substitute your OurApplicationView for the application window's default View.

API matrix

		Usage	
		Client API	Customization API
Mechanism	Composition-focused API		
	Inheritance-focused API		

A framework's composition-focused and inheritance-focused APIs are related to its client and customization APIs. In fact, the two pairs of APIs form a matrix of possibilities, in which the mechanisms in the composition-focused and inheritance-focused APIs can be used both by clients and for customization. You can use this matrix to describe how a particular ensemble works.

An ensemble can contain code that uses all four or some combination of a framework's APIs.

For example, the ensemble for the simple application would contain code to add the Reset functor to the menu (which involves the client and composition-focused APIs), and code to subclass View and override DrawSelf (which involves the client and

inheritance-focused APIs). Because the application is so simple, the ensemble probably would not contain code that involves the customization API.

As a rule, the customization API for a framework tends to involve the inheritance-focused API more than the composition-focused API, because subclassing usually provides more flexibility than composition.

Where ensemble code resides

The ensemble contains the code that you use to modify the behavior of the basic framework. This code is not isolated in a single block of physical code. You design and write code that physically resides throughout the framework code in the form of added components and subclasses containing overrides.

The following figure shows the structure and interaction of the framework and ensemble code at the class level. In inheritance-focused frameworks, shown in this example, the frameworks call functions in subclasses to override functions in a base class. Using composition-focused frameworks, the frameworks call the components you provide. You modify the behavior of the framework in many different code sections of the framework, rather than in a monolithic block of ensemble code. Your code is intermixed with the actual framework code at the level of classes, subclasses and overrides, and calls to components.

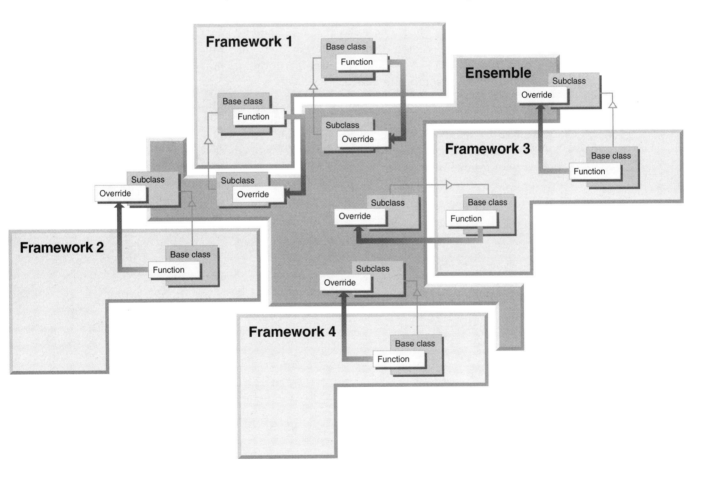

ENSEMBLE CODE INTERACTS WITH FRAMEWORK CODE

WORKING WITH FRAMEWORK CODE

Frameworks are the result of advancing strategies for developing applications. The shift to dynamic behavior, demanded by user-driven applications, has required shifting the flow of control from the developer's application code to event-driven systems controlled by user input. Frameworks represent the next step in this evolutionary process.

As you design your framework, you need to consider and balance the trade-offs involved:

- How to deliver frameworks—source code or binary code delivery (along with the mechanisms needed to incorporate ensemble code into your application).
- Whether to use inheritance- versus composition-focused framework implementation. These methods are complementary and compatible; you can use them together to create a more flexible framework.
- Which type of API best supports your application implementation— inheritance- or composition-focused APIs.

Using a framework to build an application, you "plug in" components or create subclasses and use overrides to create your ensemble code. The framework calls the ensemble code to produce the behavior that you want in your application. This code, logically contained as ensemble code, is physically spread out throughout your framework.

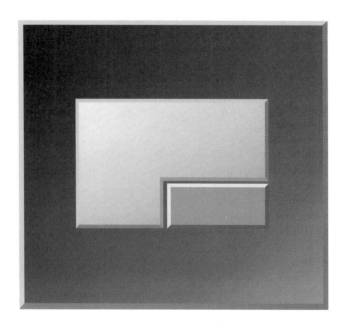

CHAPTER 3

DEVELOPING FRAMEWORKS

Chapter 1, "A first look at frameworks," explains that the cost, in time and money, of producing a framework is substantially higher than that of the more narrowly focused, single application or library of similar functionality. Generally, you would create a framework only when the cost of producing the framework is amortized over many application projects.

While the easiest solution is using an existing framework, the frameworks you need might not be available. If you have a situation in which you can reuse a design over many applications, you might want to design the framework yourself. However, as useful as they are, frameworks can be difficult to develop: they require deliberate, concerted effort.

The most obvious consideration is whether designing a general, extensible framework is more work than repeatedly doing a design for a single application. To create a new framework, you must be willing to put in the time up front, but in the long run, designing for extensibility up front saves you and your organization time and money.

This chapter introduces you to some general goals and guidelines to consider when you design your own frameworks. It describes a top-down approach to developing frameworks. You can see these applied to the frameworks explained in Parts 2 and 3.

WHAT MAKES A SUCCESSFUL FRAMEWORK DESIGNER?

Developing a framework differs from developing a standalone application. A successful framework solves problems that, on the surface, are quite different from the problem that justified its creation. You must capture the problem-solving expertise so that it is an abstraction of both the original problem and the future solutions in which you use it; however, each program that uses the framework should appear to be the one for which you designed it.

You have to identify clearly the class of problem a framework addresses. For your clients to adapt the framework to new problems, they must understand both the solution the framework provides and how to incorporate it into their programs. Because other developers have to understand how to use your frameworks, it is critical that you follow good software design practices.

Framework design demands considerable skill from designers. They need excellent analytic, modeling, and general problem-solving skills in addition to substantial experience with objects. Experience writing applications in the problem domain helps to identify common design elements for framework solutions. Most organizations find that their need for designers with these skills outstrips their ability to hire or internally develop them, which makes buying expertise already packaged in commercially-available frameworks attractive.

To achieve the high reuse demands of a framework, designers must look beyond current needs and anticipate the needs of future ensembles. They must understand both present and likely future behaviors. The framework must correctly abstract the full range of essential entities in the problem domain. This abstraction is crucial for a new ensemble to be able to reuse the framework's existing designs. Looking beyond current needs to anticipate those of future ensembles helps you to avoid the creeping requirements and continual design changes that makes it difficult to distinguish between necessary framework evolution and a design out of control.

ANALYZING YOUR PROBLEM DOMAIN

Think of frameworks as abstractions of possible solutions to problems. To determine which frameworks you need, examine families of applications rather than individual programs:

- Look for software solutions that you build repeatedly, particularly in key business areas.
- Identify what the solutions have in common and what is unique to each program.

If you are familiar with the problem domain, you can draw from your past experience and former designs to abstract common elements and begin designing your framework. If you're not familiar with the problem domain, examine similar applications that you've written or those written by others and consider writing an application in the domain. The problem that you are trying to solve is likely to be very specific: abstract out the parts that are common to the entire problem domain, and use these as the foundation of a framework to suit the entire domain. Factor these pieces into small, focused frameworks.

Factor the aggregate of these behaviors so that fundamental behaviors are allocated to the framework. Andert (1994) discusses factoring as follows:

"Proper factoring is difficult and requires a great deal of domain knowledge. The framework must provide default behavior yet still allow future ensembles considerable latitude to vary that behavior. Thus, the designer of a framework must have broad and deep domain expertise—much more than that required for the more narrowly focused single application or library."

"This encapsulation keeps the rules out of the client code, which makes writing client code easier. But more important, it greatly simplifies the evolution of that knowledge. Proper partitioning of domain knowledge between the framework and the ensembles depends on the domain and the business problem to be solved by the framework. The best designs encapsulate each piece of knowledge in just one place. Thus, the fundamental invariants are encapsulated in the framework, while variable rules and policies are encapsulated in the ensambles."

Wherever you have a suite of applications that solve similar problems, you have an opportunity for developing a framework. Look for potential frameworks in:

- Real-world models
- Processes performed by end users
- Source code for current software solutions

After you've identified the frameworks from the problem domain, you can go on to create the individual frameworks.

DESIGNING YOUR FRAMEWORK

The first step in developing a framework is to analyze your problem domain and identify the individual frameworks you need. Once you've decided which framework or frameworks to build, you create each framework using the following steps:

1 Identify the primary abstractions.

2 Design how clients interact with the framework.

3 Implement, test, and refine the design.

Identifying primary abstractions

Identify the abstractions that your clients need to describe their problems and then provide the logic for producing a valid solution with those abstractions. If the problem maps to a process, describe the process from the user's perspective or from the perspective of the external events affecting the process. For each framework, identify the process it models. Once you've outlined the process, you should be able to identify the necessary abstractions.

The easiest way to identify the abstractions is with a bottom-up approach—start by examining existing solutions. First analyze the data structures and algorithms, then organize the abstractions. Always identify the objects before you map out the class hierarchy and dependencies.

When identifying abstractions, as suggested by Birrer and Eggenschwiler (1993), you should:

- Consolidate similar functionality across the system and implement it through common abstraction.
- Try to break down large abstractions, dividing them into several smaller abstractions. Each of the smaller abstractions should have a small, focused set of responsibilities.
- Implement each variation of an abstraction as an object. This increases the flexibility of the design.
- Use composition instead of inheritance where possible. This reduces the number of classes and the complexity for the framework client.

If the framework models a process, you can determine a pattern in the process—which steps the framework performs and which steps the client performs. By describing the design of a framework in terms of patterns, you describe both the design and the rationale behind the design. As you begin to design how the framework works, you might also discover that you can break down the framework into a collection of recurring *design patterns*, much the way you decompose the initial problem into a set of frameworks (Gamma et al. 1995).

"Good designers know many design patterns and techniques that they know lead to good designs. Applying recurring patterns to the design of a framework is one form of reuse. Using formalized 'design patterns' also helps to document the framework, making it easier for clients to understand, use, and extend the framework." (Johnson 1993)

When you design a framework, look for recurring patterns that can be applied to other problems. Reusing common patterns opens up an additional level of design reuse, where the implementations vary, but the micro-architectures represented by the patterns still apply.

Design patterns point to better frameworks

Design patterns identify, name, and abstract common themes in object-oriented design. They capture the intent behind a design by identifying objects, how objects interact, and how responsibilities are distributed among the objects. They constitute a base of experience for building reusable software, and they act as building blocks from which more complex designs can be built.

Each design pattern is a micro-architecture for a recurring element. Patterns can represent generic software elements or elements particular to a problem domain. Some patterns are generic and some are specific to a problem domain. Each pattern can be characterized by its elements:

- Preconditions—The patterns that must be satisfied for this pattern to be valid.

- Problem—The problem addressed by the pattern.

- Constraints—The conflicting forces acting on any solution to the problem and the priorities of those constraints.

- Solution—The solution to the problem.

Architect Christopher Alexander first introduced the concept of patterns as a tool to encode the knowledge of the design and construction of communities and buildings. Alexander's patterns describe recurring elements and rules for how and when to create the patterns. Designers of object-oriented software have begun to embrace this concept of patterns and use it as a language for planning, discussing, and documenting designs.

(Gamma et al. 1993)

Designing your client-framework interactions

You need to define your constraints and assumptions clearly. This helps clients determine whether a framework is applicable to their problem. In your framework design, focus on how the client interacts with the framework—which classes and member functions does the client use?

To be successful, design your framework to be:

- **Complete**—Frameworks support features needed by clients and provide default implementations and default functionality where possible. Provide concrete derivations for the abstract classes in your frameworks and default member function implementations to make it easier for your clients to understand the framework and allow them to focus on the areas they need to customize.
- **Flexible**—Abstractions can be used in different contexts.
- **Extensible**—Clients can easily add and modify functionality. Provide hooks so that your clients can customize the behavior of the framework by deriving new classes or through other mechanisms.
- **Understandable**—Client interactions with the frameworks are clear.

Designing for flexibility and extensibility

"If applications are hard to design, and toolkits are harder, then frameworks are hardest of all. A framework designer gambles that one architecture will work for all applications in the domain. Any substantive change to the framework's design would reduce its benefits considerably, since the framework's main contribution to the application is the architecture it defines. Therefore it's imperative to design the framework to be as flexible and extensible as possible." (Gamma et al. 1995)

Consider the following elements in this process:

- Look for ways to reduce the amount of code that your clients must write:
  - Provide concrete implementations clients can use directly.
  - Minimize the number of classes clients must derive.
  - Minimize the number of member functions clients must override.
- Simplify clients' interactions with the framework to help prevent client error. Make it as clear as possible in both your interfaces and documentation what is required of your clients.
- Isolate platform-dependent code to make it easier to port your framework. Designing for portability reduces the impact porting has on your clients.
- Determine how the framework classes and member functions interact with client code:
  - Which objects are created when the client calls framework functions?
  - When does the framework call client overrides?
  - What can you do to protect against errors in developer's code, for example, by catching exceptions?

When you design your framework, consider the following guidelines illustrated by examples from the CommonPoint application system:

- Do as much in the framework as possible so that your developer's code is as simple as possible. For example, if you need locking for thread safety, acquire the lock, call the developer's code, then release the lock, so that your developer's code can be single-threaded. Consider that you need to balance flexibility and extensibility—the more your framework does, the more constrained and difficult to change it is. If your framework does more than necessary for the domain, it can needlessly degrade performance.

- High-level functionality tends to make limiting assumptions. Factor your code so that clients can remove or easily override the code encapsulating the assumption.

- Provide notification hooks that developers can use to react to important state changes within the framework. For example, a cursor tool tracking movement in a GUI needs to know when it has crossed a view boundary, and a view needs to know when it has been added to the view hierarchy.

- Avoid lexical cycles to prevent deadlock. Otherwise, the framework calls an extension that calls the framework and the system freezes in the cycle. When you cannot avoid cycles, the framework must handle locking so that it can detect and overcome callbacks into the framework from outcalls to developer's code.

Supporting customization   "A framework helps developers provide solutions for problem domains and better maintain those solutions. It provides a well-designed and thought-out infrastructure so that when better pieces are created, they can be substituted with minimal impact on the other pieces in the framework." (Nelson 1994)

One of the things to consider is how to support customization—adding new pieces to the code while maintaining the same interfaces. With customization, you want to provide as flexible a framework as possible, but you also want to maintain the focus of the framework and minimize the complexity for the client. If you provide an overly flexible framework, it is difficult for your clients to learn and difficult for you to support.

One approach is to build a very flexible, general framework from which you derive additional frameworks for narrower problem domains. These additional frameworks provide specialized default behavior and built-in functionality, while the general framework provides the flexibility.

As you design the framework, also consider how the design can help communicate how to use the framework. Class names, function names, and pure virtual functions (in C++) can all provide clues for using the framework.

Refining your framework	As your framework takes shape, continually look for ways to refine it by adding more default behavior and additional ways for users to view and interact with the data.

Building a framework is an iterative process. Beginning with your initial design, work with your clients to determine how the framework can be improved—implement features, test them, and verify them with your clients. During this process, go back and reanalyze the problem domain and refine your design based on testing, client feedback, and your own insights. Wirfs-Brock (1990) states that it takes three real applications to get a framework right. Thus, you need to use your framework to solve real problems in more than one application before you can have confidence in its design.

Because the framework controls design, changes in framework interfaces, both syntactic and semantic, have an impact on your existing applications. As a framework expands and changes, applications must change to accommodate it. You must keep your frameworks loosely coupled to control the impact of changes.

As your framework matures, you'll probably find more features to add and identify opportunities for additional frameworks. These might be entirely new frameworks or frameworks that support a particular subset of the problem domain.

The concept of prototyping is not unique to framework development, but it is very useful. A common approach is to implement a framework that applies to a specific subset of a larger problem domain and then rework it to support more general cases.

Simplifying your frameworks	"The most profoundly elegant framework will never be reused unless the cost of understanding it and then using its abstractions is lower than the programmer's perceived cost of writing them from scratch." (Booch 1994)

As you refine your framework, keep the following goals in mind:

- **Design for ease of use—the most important consideration.** From the client's perspective, an easy-to-use framework performs useful functions with little or no added effort. The framework works with little or no client code, even if the default implementations are simply placeholders, and it supports small, incremental steps to get from the default behavior to sophisticated solutions. When in doubt, err on the side of making it simpler for your clients to use the framework, even if doing so makes implementing the framework more difficult. A good framework designer strives to make the ensemble developer's job as easy as possible. The ideal framework enables nonframework domain experts to produce ensembles.

- **Keep your frameworks small.** Look for ways to break down frameworks into small, focused frameworks. If they're designed to interoperate, small frameworks are more flexible and can be reused more often. By breaking down the original workflow framework into a set of small frameworks, you can use the resulting frameworks in other contexts.

- **Look for additional ways to make your clients' tasks easier.** In some cases, it makes sense to provide special tools with your frameworks. Code generators, CASE tools, and GUI builders can make programming with frameworks easier, just as they do for traditional software development.

Iterate to simplify, but choose a point when your framework is finished. Until you release your framework to a wider user group, you won't gain any of the benefits or learn about other needed enhancements. A simple framework requires fewer iterations than more complex frameworks—another advantage of developing smaller, focused frameworks.

Quick guidelines for developing frameworks

To design a framework, you first analyze the problem domain. As you look at the problem, break it into smaller, workable elements.

- **Analyze your problem domain**—Look for the set of solutions to your problem.

- **Identify potential frameworks**—Find common solutions to a family of processes or actions.

When you've decided on a particular framework, you can design client-framework interactions for that specific framework.

- **Identify common elements**
  - Abstractions—Objects that encapsulate the data structures and algorithms that solve the problem.
  - Design patterns—Collections of recurring elements that solve domain problems.

- **Design for flexibility, extensibility, and ease of use**
  - Reduce the amount of client code.
  - Identify and simplify client interaction with the framework to minimize client errors.

- Isolate platform-dependent code for portability.
- Determine how framework classes and members interact with client code.

- **Decide how to support customization**

As you use your new framework, you have the opportunity to iterate and refine it.

- **Simplify**—Keep your frameworks small, simple, and easy to understand.

- **Derive from existing frameworks**—Build new solutions from working frameworks.

Deriving from frameworks   Once you've developed a general framework that provides a strong architectural base, you can derive additional frameworks that apply to particular problem sets. The overall framework provides generalized components and constraints to which the derived frameworks conform. Derived frameworks introduce additional components and constraints that support more specific solutions. They support a narrower set of applications than their more general base, and they give you a safe way to provide more domain-specific default behavior. You can contain potentially restrictive design decisions in derived frameworks without "corrupting" the basic framework.

Derived frameworks are another method of providing default behavior for your clients. You can provide the default behavior in the derived framework, rather than in the core framework. If your framework consists of a number of abstract classes, you might want to create one or more derived frameworks that provide concrete implementations and additional built-in functionality.

PART 2

APPLYING FRAMEWORKS

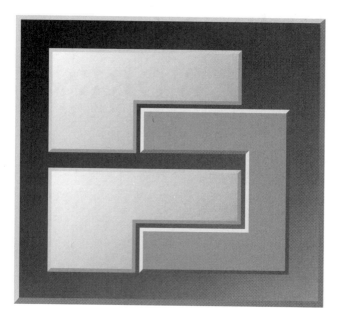

Chapter 4

Applying frameworks to a real-world programming problem

Now that you have a basic understanding of what a framework is and what the benefits of framework-based programming are, it's time to apply frameworks to a problem that a programmer developing a "real" application would face.

The problem we've selected is one that many applications must handle: formatting numbers for display to the user. Spreadsheet programs are the most common type of program to address this problem, so our sample application takes the form of a very simple spreadsheet.

Over the course of the next six chapters, we'll walk through the creation and extension of the application. We've implemented the application for both Microsoft Windows and for IBM® OS/2, the two most popular operating systems for PC-compatibles.

A BRIEF USER INTERFACE SPECIFICATION

A 2-by-10 grid of editable cells is presented to the user. Each cell within the grid contains a number. The user can select a cell using the mouse and enter a number using the keyboard. The user can then set the display format for each cell using a dialog box, as shown in the following figure.

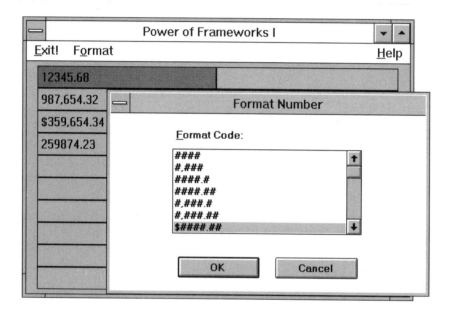

FORMATTING A CELL

Unlike in a true spreadsheet, the cells in the sample application cannot be "tied together" by functions. The application resembles a spreadsheet in form only, not in function.

APPLICATION DESIGN ISSUES

This is an overly simplified sample application: an "industrial-strength" application would need to add many additional features to be usable. On the other hand, this sample does illustrate the kinds of design and implementation issues a real application would need to address.

Converting numbers to text

The first of these issues is formatting numbers as text according to what the user wants.

At the most basic level, converting a floating-point or integer number to text for display is easy. We can use the C++ stream package or any one of a number of other standard C/C++ functions to do the conversion. All of these functions are simple to learn and use, and they get the job done.

For example, let's say the user can control the number of digits that appear after the decimal point. We can do this in C++ using the standard streams package:

```
void ConvertNumToString(double num, int numDigits, ostrstream& str)
{
    str << setprecision(numDigits) << num;
}
```

What if we want the user to be able to control whether or not numbers show up in scientific notation? We can do it, but the code becomes more complicated:

```
void ConvertNumToString(double num, int numDigits,
                    int useScientific, ostrstream& str)
{
    if (useScientific)
        str.setf(ios::scientific);
    else str.setf(0);
    str << setprecision(numDigits) << num;
}
```

What if we need to support having commas separating the thousands? How do we handle currency formatting for different countries? None of the C/C++ standard library routines supports this kind of formatting directly; however, we could use a number of calls to streaming operators, each with its own hardcoded format string, to achieve the same effect. Neither the Windows 3.1 nor the Windows 95 APIs provide a direct solution, although they do provide a way to determine the thousands separator and currency symbol characters on the currently running version of the system. The only solution is to write our own routines to convert numbers to text.

> **✅ NOTE**   Some operating systems, such as Windows NT 3.5 and MacOS, provide routines that will properly format numbers for you and handle other localization issues as well. Developing the sample applications shown in this book on such an operating system would be correspondingly easier, but any developer who wants to develop an application that runs on other operating systems would still have to address these issues.

Localizing numbers

We also need to address the issue of software localization.

Designing an application to support localization is an important part of application design, because it allows a program developed in one country to be used in other parts of the world. Even though we aren't going to export our sample application, we should consider the implications of localization for the domestic market. If we were working on a currency trading program for an investment bank, for example, that application would have to support the simultaneous display of currencies from many different countries.

Fortunately, there are some simple things we can do that will make development easier in the future (and easier too for any company that wants to sell our software in another country). The most important thing we need, though, is a basic understanding of the issues involved in localizing applications.

Let's look at the issues of currency formatting. Many countries, including the U.S., use a leading symbol ($, £, and so on), while others, such as Japan, use a trailing symbol (¥). Similarly, we have to know how many significant digits should be printed after the decimal point; how to print negative values; what the monetary symbol, decimal point, and thousands separator characters are; whether to use thousands separators; and whether to use spaces between the monetary symbol and the numeric value. All of these monetary system characteristics can change from country to country.

As mentioned, Windows, along with most other GUI-based operating systems, provides a set of API routines that we can call to get information about the current locale's currency formatting conventions. Converting this information into a correctly formatted currency string is the responsibility of the application. Similarly, the application must handle formatting noncurrency numbers, dates, and so forth, although the Windows API provides the information we need to set it up.

Formatting numbers within a spreadsheet

Another issue we need to look at is the manner in which we allow the user to specify the number format.

Our spreadsheet-like example lets the user choose between various number formats using the Format Cell dialog box. This dialog box lets the user set the number of significant digits after the decimal place, control whether a thousands separator character is shown, and decide whether to show a currency symbol. It does so using a Microsoft Excel-style format string, with special characters representing the various components of a formatted number.

Character Digit	Represents
#	Single digit
,	Thousands separator character
.	Decimal point character
e	Scientific notation exponent separator character
$	Currency symbol character

To illustrate the use of format strings and show a few of the possible combinations that the application needs to represent, some examples follow.

The format string

```
$#,###.##
```

shows currency, with a thousands separator and with two digits following the decimal place. If you format the floating-point number

```
3555.98765
```

using this format, it would display in the U.S. as

```
$3,555.99
```

In Switzerland, the same number would display as

```
Fr. 3'555.99
```

On the other hand, the format string

```
#.#########e##
```

would display the same number (in the U.S.) as

```
3.55598765e03
```

The actual characters used to format the numbers vary from country to country, based on the locale information returned by Windows.

DEVELOPMENT PLATFORM ISSUES

Depending on which operating system you develop applications for, you must make some decisions about your development platform. We used C++ to develop both the OS/2 and Windows versions of the application, but avoided using any of the existing application frameworks such as the Borland ObjectWindows Library (OWL) or the Microsoft Foundation Classes (MFC). Using either of these frameworks would have made the spreadsheet application a lot simpler, but it also would have limited the audience of the book to those who use a particular application framework. If you haven't used one of these frameworks before, you should investigate one or more of them, or, better still, use the CommonPoint application system for your next application programming project.

Windows development platform

In Chapters 5, 6, and 7, the Windows application development was done using the Borland C++ 4.5 development system running on Microsoft Windows 3.1. The sample application should also run on any operating system that supports 16-bit Windows applications, such as Windows NT and OS/2.

OS/2 development platform

In Chapters 8, 9, and 10, the OS/2 application development was done using the IBM C Set ++® 2.1 development system running on OS/2 Warp™ Version 3, using the OS/2 2.1 toolkit.

WHERE TO GO FROM HERE

If you prefer to follow the development of the application on Microsoft Windows, continue with Chapter 5.

If you would rather follow the development of the application on OS/2, you should skip Chapters 5 through 7 and continue with Chapter 8.

The accompanying CD-ROM includes the source code for both versions of the sample application. The CD-ROM also contains an interactive version of the Windows development material, which you can use instead of reading it in book form.

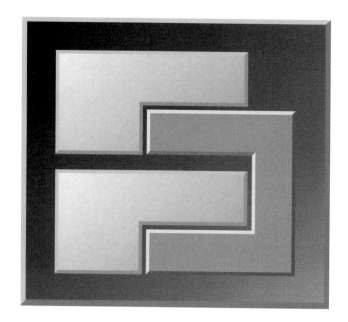

Applying frameworks on Microsoft Windows

CHAPTER 5

CREATING THE APPLICATION FOR WINDOWS

In Chapter 4, we created a specification for the initial version of the application. In this chapter, we convert that specification into a functioning piece of code.

The application, like most Windows applications, begins with a main function and a window message handler. Because the Windows API calls these functions, and Windows does not support the use of C++ member functions as handlers, these routines are written as standard C functions. To take advantage of object-oriented features of C++, we'll use these global functions as a liaison between the Windows API and the application's classes. Thus, the application can be roughly divided into two parts: a Windows application layer, and a set of classes that allows the user to see and edit the spreadsheet data.

DESIGNING THE WINDOWS APPLICATION LAYER

We'll begin by designing the Windows application layer, which provides two key pieces of functionality: a main function and a window message handler.

Initializing the application

The main function of the application, WinMain, is responsible for initializing the application. This is a standard part of any Windows application that corresponds to the main function in a standard C program. WinMain needs to create the application window and initiate the Windows message-dispatching loop.

Window message dispatcher

WndProc is called when a message is sent to the application's window. WndProc dispatches these messages to the appropriate piece of code in the application. As the primary dispatch function, WndProc acts as the interface between the application layer and the spreadsheet classes that manipulate the application's data.

Other functions

The application layer also includes several functions needed by other parts of the program, such as a message handler routine for the Format Cell dialog box. We'll discuss the design and implementation of these functions as they're needed by other parts of the application.

DESIGNING THE SPREADSHEET CLASSES

The spreadsheet classes are divided into two distinct sets. The first set provides the user interface for our application and handles the messages that WndProc delegates to them. The second set is responsible for converting numbers into text.

User interface objects

Because the spreadsheet's user interface models a grid of cells, the first class to create is a NumberGrid. NumberGrid maintains a list of cells and keeps track of the currently selected cell for the user.

We also need to create a class, NumberCell, that represents a single cell. NumberCell manages the editing and display of the cell's contents.

Number formatting objects

Next, we need to create a class to handle the formatting process. Because our design goal is to separate data representation from the user interface as much as possible, we'll make a class, FormattableNumber, that represents a number that knows how to format itself as text, but doesn't perform any display or editing operations.

Many variables affect the formatting process. To allow these variables to be manipulated as a set, we create a NumberFormat class that keeps track of the number format. FormattableNumber uses a NumberFormat object to perform the formatting operation.

The class hierarchy of the spreadsheet classes is shown in the following figure.

✅ NOTE   The notation used for the class hierarchy diagrams shown in this book
is described in "Appendix A: Reading notation diagrams."

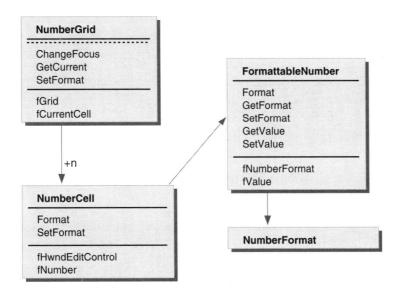

SPREADSHEET CLASS HIERARCHY

Now that we've determined the basic set of classes, we'll continue by filling out
the class design.

NumberGrid class design

NumberGrid provides three different sets of member functions:

- Standard C++ member functions, including the constructor and destructor
- Cell editing member functions, which handle basic user interface operations
- Data accessor member functions, which allow you to manipulate the state of the NumberGrid

Let's look at the declarations of each of these sets of functions.

Standard C++ member functions

The class declaration begins with the constructor and destructor. The NumberGrid constructor takes the arguments needed to create the spreadsheet grid, including the number of rows, number of columns, and the column width (in characters) of each cell.

```
class NumberGrid {
public:
    //----------------------------------------------------------------------------
    // Standard C++ member functions

    // constructor and destructor
        NumberGrid(HINSTANCE hInst, HWND hwnd , int xPos = 0, int yPos = 0,
                int rows = 0, int cols = 0, int nCharsPerCell = 0);
    virtual ~NumberGrid();
```

Editing member functions

The most important functions in NumberGrid handle our user interface functions. These functions are typically called by the application's user interface code.

```
    // Format current cell according to a format code set by the user
    // from the main menu
    virtual void        FormatCurrentCell(int nFormatCode);

    // Reformat a cell in the grid according to its current user-specified format.
    virtual int         UpdateCell(int nCellNo);

    // Change the focus to cell number nCellNo.
    virtual int         ChangeFocus(int nCellNo);

    // Does nCellNo contain a valid numeric string?
    virtual BOOL        IsValidEntry(int nCellNo);

    // Move the upper-left corner of the grid to a new x,y position
    virtual void        Move(int x = 0, int y = 0);

    // Center the grid in the client area.
    virtual void        Center(HWND hwnd);
```

Accessor member functions

The remaining member functions provide access to the state of the cell grid. Convenience member functions are provided to make it easier to perform common operations on the current cell. These member functions are usually called by the framework itself, rather than by clients.

```
// access the currently selected cell's id
virtual int        GetCurrentCell();
virtual int        SetCurrentCell(int nCurrent);

// set the format of the specified cell
virtual int        SetFormat(int nCellNo, const NumberFormat& nf);

// Get the Windows edit handle to nCellNo.
virtual HWND       GetHandle(int nCellNo);

// Get the edit control's enclosing NumberCell.
virtual NumberCell* GetCell(int nCellNo);
```

Data members

The class declaration concludes with the class's private data member declarations. Of these data members, the two worth noting are fGrid, which is a pointer to our array of cells, and fCurrentCell, which keeps track of the current cell.

```
private:
    NumberCell***   fGrid;          // Pointer to the 2D grid of NumberCells.
    int             fNRows, fNCols; // Number of rows, cols in grid.
    int             fTop, fLeft;    // Position of top, left corner of grid
    int             fCellWidth, fCellHeight;
    int             fCurrentCell;   // The cell index of the current cell
};
```

NumberCell class design

The NumberCell class is more complicated than NumberGrid. A NumberCell serves as a kind of pivot-point: it associates a C++ object (a cell) with a critical Windows user interface element, and it shuttles the raw and formatted user input data between this Windows user interface element and the C++ class responsible for formatting.

What is this "critical Windows user interface element"? For the application to actually display a NumberCell, the cell must encapsulate some user interface element that Windows understands. Windows knows nothing about the NumberCell object. Because we expect the user to select a cell (using the mouse) and enter a number into it (using the keyboard), it seems logical to have the NumberCell class be a wrapper for a Windows EditControl element. (An EditControl is a text-entry user interface element with some built-in, primitive editing functions such as select, append, insert, and delete.)

For reasons that will become apparent, we also need to design a two-way communication path between NumberCell and its encapsulated EditControl. It's easy to see how a NumberCell can access its EditControl: we just make the EditControl a data member of the NumberCell. But how does a Windows EditControl access its NumberCell? That's a little more complex. We'll discuss that when we implement the NumberCell class in "Implementing NumberCell" on page 92.

NumberCell is also pivotal in its role of shuttling raw and formatted user input values between the EditControl and the class that's actually responsible for formatting, but we have not yet described that formatting class. In Chapter 4, you saw how the user of the application specifies a display format for a particular spreadsheet cell by first selecting the cell (actually, the cell's EditControl), then choosing a format from the Format Cell dialog box. Although, from the user's perspective, it appears that the chosen format is applied directly to the cell, we opted to less closely couple the NumberCell and its display format, which is stored in a FormattableNumber.

Designing some distance between the cell and its format creates a buffer of independence, which improves the potential for reuse. This makes each of the two classes, NumberCell and FormattableNumber, more reusable because it separates the cell's member functions for handling actions such as keyboard input and display updating from the member functions responsible for formatting the cell input value.

Standard member functions

As usual, the class declaration begins with the constructor and destructor. The hInst and hwndParent parameters are passed to the constructor by the NumberGrid object when it creates the grid of cells.

```
class NumberCell
{
public:
                    NumberCell(HINSTANCE hInst, HWND hwndParent,
                               int xPos = 0, int yPos = 0,
                               int width = 0, int height = 0);
        virtual     ~NumberCell();
```

Editing member functions

To support editing operations, NumberCell provides member functions to move the cell, update the cell's value based on the EditControl text, and redraw the cell's text.

```
// Move the cell to x,y with width w and height h
void            Move(int x = 0, int y = 0, int w = 0, int h = 0);
// Set the cell format to the edit format.
void            Edit();
// Reformat the cell based on its new format.
int             Update();
```

Accessor member functions

NumberCell also provides a number of accessor member functions to access the state of the cell.

```
void            SetFormat(const NumberFormat &nf);

HWND            GetEditHandle();
WORD            GetID();

BOOL            GetFormatErrorStatus();
void            SetFormatErrorStatus(BOOL errorStatus);

BOOL            HasBeenAltered();
BOOL            SetAlteredStatus(BOOL newStatus);
```

Data members

Lastly, NumberCell declares its data members, including a handle to its EditControl, the FormattableNumber, and a dirty flag.

NumberCell also declares several static data members. It keeps track of the last cell ID number used in the static data member fCellNumber, ensuring that each Windows EditControl object has a unique ID. NumberCell also tracks the EditControl's overridden and original message handler to help implement the application's customized EditControl.

```
    static int          fCellNumber;        // last cell id used
    static FARPROC      fLpfnNewEditProc;
    static FARPROC      fLpfnOldEditProc;

private:
    HWND                fHwndEditControl;   // Handle to the enclosed edit control.
    FormattableNumber   fNumber;            // Formattable number enclosed in the cell.
    BOOL                fErrorInFormat;     // Error status flag.
    BOOL                fAltered;           // Altered status flag.
};
```

FormattableNumber class design

FormattableNumber translates a number into formatted text. Its key member function is Format, which does the actual work of converting the FormattableNumber object's current value and format options into a text string. FormattableNumber also provides member functions to access the format options and the value.

```cpp
class FormattableNumber {
public:
    // Standard member functions
                    FormattableNumber(double d = 0.0);
                    FormattableNumber(double d, const NumberFormat& nf);
    virtual         ~FormattableNumber() {};

    virtual FormattableNumber&
                    operator=(const FormattableNumber &fn);
    virtual FormattableNumber&
                    operator=(double v);

    // Formatting member function
    virtual void    Format(char* fresult);

    // Accessor member functions
    virtual double  GetValue();
    virtual void    SetValue(double d) const;

    virtual const NumberFormat&
                    GetFormat();
    virtual void    SetFormat(const NumberFormat& nf) const;

private:
    double          fValue;     // Value part.
    NumberFormat    fFormat;     // Current format.
};
```

NumberFormat class design

The design of NumberFormat is straightforward. It provides accessors to allow the caller to get and set the values of its various formatting data members. It also provides a static member function GetGeneralNumberFormat that you can use to set a NumberFormat to the defaults for the current locale.

```
class NumberFormat {
public:
    static const char kCommaChar;
    static const char kDollarSignChar;
    static const char kPeriodChar;
    static const int kDefaultPrecision;
    static const int kZeroPrecision;

    // Standard C++ member functions
            NumberFormat(int prec = kDefaultPrecision,
                        BOOL delimtd = TRUE, BOOL curncy = FALSE,
                        char intSep = kCommaChar, char decSep = kPeriodChar,
                        char curncySym = kDollarSignChar);
            NumberFormat(const NumberFormat &nf);
            NumberFormat& operator=(const NumberFormat& nf);
            ~NumberFormat()  { };

    // Accessor member functions
    void    Set(int prec = kZeroPrecision,
                BOOL delimtd = FALSE, BOOL curncy = FALSE,
                char intSep = kCommaChar, char decSep = kPeriodChar,
                char curncySym = kDollarSignChar);

    int         GetPrecision() const;

    BOOL        IsThousandsDelimitted() const;
    BOOL        IsCurrency() const;

    char        GetIntSeparator() const;
    char        GetDecSeparator() const;
    char        GetCurrencySymbol() const;

    // utility member function: creates a basic number format
    static NumberFormat
                GetGeneralNumberFormat();

private:
    int         fPrecision;
    BOOL        fThousandsDelimitted;
    BOOL        fCurrency;
    char        fIntSeparator;
    char        fDecSeparator;
    char        fCurrencySymbol;
};
```

✅ NOTE   This version of the application is not fully usable in countries other than the U.S., because the GetGeneralNumberFormat member function hard-codes the values of the currency and separator characters to correspond to those used in the U.S. As we'll discuss in Chapter 6, correcting this deficiency is a major framework design task for the next version of this application.

IMPLEMENTING THE WINDOWS INTERFACE

Now that the basic application design is in place, we can implement the application. We'll begin with the Windows interface code.

Implementing WinMain

As with most Windows programs written in C or C++, WinMain is the initial entry point for our program. C programmers who are not familiar with Windows programming conventions can think of this function as equivalent to the main function in a standard C program.

When WinMain is invoked by the Windows application runtime, it initializes its WNDCLASS and creates a window. WinMain then drops into the message loop, which is responsible for receiving keyboard and mouse events and dispatching them to the appropriate application function where these events are processed.

```
int PASCAL WinMain(HANDLE hInstance, HANDLE hPrevInstance,
            LPSTR lpszCmdParam, int nCmdShow)
{
    HWND        hwnd;
    MSG         msg;
    WNDCLASS    wndclass;

    hInst = hInstance;

    // set up our window class structure if this is our first instance
    if (!hPrevInstance)
    {
        wndclass.style          = CS_HREDRAW | CS_VREDRAW;
        wndclass.lpfnWndProc    = (WNDPROC) WndProc;
        wndclass.cbClsExtra     = 0;
        wndclass.cbWndExtra     = 0;
        wndclass.hInstance      = hInstance;
        wndclass.hIcon          = LoadIcon(NULL, IDI_APPLICATION);
        wndclass.hCursor        = LoadCursor(NULL, IDC_ARROW);
        wndclass.hbrBackground  = GetStockObject(LTGRAY_BRUSH);
        wndclass.lpszMenuName   = MAKEINTRESOURCE(MENU_1);
        wndclass.lpszClassName  = szAppName;
        RegisterClass(&wndclass);
    }
```

```
// create our window
hwnd = CreateWindow(szAppName,                // window class name
                    "Power of Frameworks I",  // window caption
                    WS_OVERLAPPEDWINDOW,      //style
                    CW_USEDEFAULT,            // initial x position
                    CW_USEDEFAULT,            // initial y position
                    CW_USEDEFAULT,            // initial x size
                    CW_USEDEFAULT,            // initial y size
                    NULL,                     // parent window handle
                    NULL,                     // window handle menu
                    hInstance,                // program instance handle
                    NULL);                    // creation parameters

ShowWindow(hwnd, nCmdShow);
UpdateWindow(hwnd);

// handle incoming messages til we're told to quit
while (GetMessage(&msg, NULL, 0, 0))
{
    TranslateMessage(&msg);
    DispatchMessage(&msg);
}

return msg.wParam;
}
```

Implementing WndProc

When a message is sent to the application window, the Windows routine DispatchMessage passes that message to the WndProc function. WndProc's primary job is to take this message and redispatch it within the application.

WndProc handles several different types of messages, including window manipulation messages, menu commands, and some special number formatting messages generated by the application.

Window manipulation messages

Generally speaking, WndProc handles its window-related messages, WM_CREATE, WM_SIZE, WM_CTLCOLOR, and WM_DESTROY, by calling the appropriate routines from the Windows API.

Menu command messages

WM_COMMAND messages are sent when the user chooses a menu command, using the mouse or a keyboard accelerator. WndProc passes WM_COMMAND messages to another global subroutine, WndCommand, for further processing.

**Application-defined
formatting messages**

At certain points in the execution of the application, it can be difficult to update the user interface directly by calling application routines. Windows programs allow applications to create and send their own custom message types to tell the user interface to perform special actions. We use this technique in our program in two ways:

- WM_FORMATCELL messages are generated by the Format Cell dialog box when the user clicks the OK button or double-clicks a format in the dialog box's scrolling list. The dialog box message handler sends this message back to the application to tell WndProc to update the cell's format.

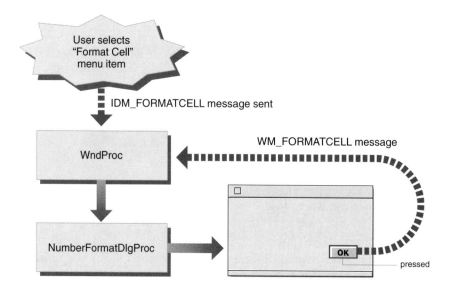

FORMAT CELL COMMAND PROCESSING

- WM_FORMATERROR messages are generated during focus-change operations when the user enters an illegal number. When this message is processed, it forces the focus to return to the cell containing the error and beeps, giving the user the opportunity to correct the problem.

The code for WndProc is show here in its entirety.

```
long _export FAR PASCAL WndProc(HWND hwnd, WORD message,
                                WORD wParam, LONG lParam)
{
    HDC hdc;
    POINT point;

    // create the grid if it hasn't been initialized previously
    if (!theGrid)
        theGrid = new NumberGrid((hInst, hwnd, 0, 0,
                                 KNROWS, KNCOLS, KNCHARSPERCELL);

    // default background color
    const COLORREF KRGBLTGRAY = RGB(0xC0, 0xC0, 0xC0);
    // cell with focus background color
    const COLORREF KRGBDKGRAY = RGB(0x80, 0x80, 0x80);

    static HBRUSH hBrushLtGray, hBrushDkGray;

    switch (message)
    {
        case WM_CREATE :
            // Use a fixed-spaced font
            hdc = GetDC(hwnd);
            SelectObject(hdc, GetStockObject(SYSTEM_FIXED_FONT));
            ReleaseDC(hwnd, hdc);

            // set focus to first cell in grid
            theGrid->ChangeFocus();

            // create our gray brushes
            hBrushLtGray = CreateSolidBrush(KRGBLTGRAY);
            hBrushDkGray = CreateSolidBrush(KRGBDKGRAY);
            return 0;

        case WM_SIZE:
            // Center the grid:
            theGrid->Center(hwnd);
            return 0;
```

```
            case WM_CTLCOLOR:
                // repaint edit controls in grid
                if ((int) HIWORD(lParam) == CTLCOLOR_EDIT)
                {
                    point.x = point.y = 0;
                    ClientToScreen(hwnd, &point);

                    // if we're handling the current cell
                    if (GetWindowWord((HWND)LOWORD(lParam), GWW_ID) ==
                        theGrid->GetCurrentCell())
                    {
                        // draw hilited
                        SetBkColor((HDC) wParam, KRGBDKGRAY);
                        UnrealizeObject(hBrushDkGray);
                        SetBrushOrg((HDC) wParam, point.x, point.y);
                        return ((DWORD) hBrushDkGray);
                    }
                    else
                    {
                        // draw unhilited
                        SetBkColor((HDC) wParam, KRGBLTGRAY);
                        UnrealizeObject(hBrushLtGray);
                        SetBrushOrg((HDC) wParam, point.x, point.y);
                        return ((DWORD) hBrushLtGray);
                    }
                }
                break;

        case WM_COMMAND:
            // handle user command (from menus, etc.)
            return WndCommand(hwnd, message, wParam, lParam);

        case WM_FORMATCELL:
            // reformat and display the cell text using the new format
            theGrid->FormatCurrentCell((int) lParam);
            return 0;

        case WM_FORMATERROR:
            // Format error, reset focus to cell with error
            SetFocus(LOWORD(lParam));
            SendMessage(LOWORD(lParam), EM_SETSEL, 0, MAKELONG(0, 0x7fff));
            return 0;

        case WM_DESTROY:
            DeleteObject(hBrushLtGray);
            DeleteObject(hBrushDkGray);
            PostQuitMessage(0);
            return 0;
    }

    return DefWindowProc(hwnd, message, wParam, lParam);
}
```

Implementing WndCommand

WndCommand is called by WndProc to handle any command messages that are sent to the application. These command messages are typically sent by menus.

WndCommand performs the following actions:

1 Checks whether the command message changes the focus from one cell to another.

If so, WndCommand calls ProcessFocusChange and returns.

2 Caches the current cell number and its corresponding EditControl for future use.

This saves many calls to retrieve the current cell number and edit handle later in the function.

3 Executes the correct command handler for the command number using a switch statement.

Three distinct commands are handled: the IDM_EXIT command message tells the application to quit by converting the command into a WM_CLOSE message; the IDM_ABOUT command displays a simple about box; the IDM_FORMATCELL command displays the Format Cell dialog box, after verifying that the cell contains valid numeric data.

WndCommand's implementation is shown here.

```
long WndCommand(HWND hwnd, WORD message, WORD wParam, LONG lParam)
{
    NumberCell* ncp;

    // if user has clicked on a new cell.
    if (HIWORD(lParam)  == EN_KILLFOCUS || HIWORD(lParam)  == EN_SETFOCUS)
    {
        // Reset the format on the cell losing the focus, if necessary.
        ProcessFocusChange(hwnd, lParam, theGrid);
        return 0;
    }

    // get current cell and its handle
    int current = theGrid->GetCurrentCell();
    HWND handle = theGrid->GetHandle(current);
```

```
switch (wParam)
{
    case IDM_EXIT:
        SendMessage(hwnd, WM_CLOSE, 0, 0l);
        return 0;

    case IDM_FORMATCELL:
        ncp = (NumberCell*) GetProp(handle, (LPSTR) KNUMBERCELLPROP);
        if (! ncp->HasBeenAltered())
            ncp->Edit();

        // if the cell does not contain a valid numeric string
        if (!theGrid->IsValidEntry(current))
        {
            (theGrid->GetCell(current))->SetFormatErrorStatus(TRUE);
            MessageBeep(0);
            MessageBox(hwnd, "Invalid Numeric Format",
                    "Number Cell Error", MB_ICONEXCLAMATION);
            SetFocus(handle);
            SendMessage(handle, EM_SETSEL, 0, MAKELONG(0, 0x7fff));
            // return -- don't open the dialog
            return 0;
        }

        // valid numeric format, display the format number cell dialog
        lpfnNumberFormatDlgProc = (DLGPROC) MakeProcInstance(
                                (FARPROC) NumberFormatDlgProc, hInst);
        DialogBox(hInst, MAKEINTRESOURCE(DIALOG_1), hwnd,
                                lpfnNumberFormatDlgProc);
        FreeProcInstance(lpfnNumberFormatDlgProc);
        return 0;

    case IDM_ABOUT:
        MessageBox(hwnd, "Power of Frameworks Sample Application\n"
                    "               Copyright 1995 Taligent, Inc.",
                "Power of Frameworks I", MB_ICONINFORMATION | MB_OK);
        return 0;

    default:
        return DefWindowProc(hwnd, message, wParam, lParam);
    }
}
```

**Implementing
ProcessFocusChange**

ProcessFocusChange is called by WndCommand if the command message passed in has the EN_KILLFOCUS or EN_SETFOCUS parameter set.

ProcessFocusChange reformats and displays the cells that are losing and receiving focus. The cell losing focus is displayed in the format the user selected when that cell was current. The cell receiving focus is redisplayed in a generic format suitable for editing.

Because ProcessFocusChange is a fairly complicated function, we'll walk through its implementation step-by-step.

**Getting the new
NumberCell object**

To begin with, ProcessFocusChange gets a pointer to the cell that is receiving focus (that is, the cell that was just mouse-clicked by the user).

```
void ProcessFocusChange(HWND hwnd, LONG lParam, NumberGrid* grid)
{
    // NumberCell id of cell losing the focus
    int nOldCurrent;
    // Windows handle of edit control losing the focus
    HWND hwndOldCurrent;

    // Get a pointer to the enclosing NumberCell
    NumberCell* newCell = (NumberCell*) GetProp(LOWORD(lParam),
                                       (LPSTR) KNUMBERCELLPROP);
```

As described earlier, the NumberCell constructor stores a pointer to the NumberCell in its EditControl member's property list. The ProcessFocusChange function is passed a handle to the EditControl that is receiving focus in its lParam parameter.

**Getting the old
NumberCell object**

Next, ProcessFocusChange retrieves the NumberCell associated with the EditControl that is losing focus. The following code does this.

```
    // if we need to process a focus change
    if (HIWORD(lParam) == EN_SETFOCUS)
    {
        // the edit control has received input focus...
        // save the cell number of the cell losing the focus
        nOldCurrent = grid->GetCurrentCell();

        // get a handle to the edit control losing the focus
        hwndOldCurrent = grid->GetHandle(nOldCurrent);

        // get a handle to the NumberCell enclosing the edit control
        NumberCell* ncpOldCurrent = (NumberCell*)
                    GetProp(hwndOldCurrent, (LPSTR) KNUMBERCELLPROP);
```

The first statement asks the NumberGrid for its index to the current cell. At this point in the focus-change process, NumberGrid still considers the current cell to be the one that is losing, not receiving, the focus. (We'll update NumberGrid's current cell information later in this function.) Next, ProcessFocusChange retrieves the handle of the EditControl that corresponds to the cell's index. Finally, ProcessFocusChange gets a pointer to the NumberCell that encapsulates this EditControl; it uses the property list just as it did for the cell receiving focus.

Updating the old NumberCell's value

Now that ProcessFocusChange knows about the old and new NumberCell objects, it can take the text the user entered in the old cell and convert it back to a number. A number of error conditions can arise when doing this conversion. To handle these errors, ProcessFocusChange verifies whether the cell has a format error both before and after it attempts the conversion, and, if an error condition exists, ProcessFocusChange passes a WM_FORMATERROR message to the application's event queue and returns.

```
// if there's already a numeric format error
if (ncpOldCurrent->GetFormatErrorStatus())
{
    // return to the cell to edit it
    PostMessage(hwnd, WM_FORMATERROR, 0, hwndOldCurrent);
    // and try again
    ncpOldCurrent->SetFormatErrorStatus(FALSE);
    return;
}

// update appropriately sets the format error status
ncpOldCurrent->Update();

// if we have a format error produced by update
if (ncpOldCurrent->GetFormatErrorStatus())
{
    // return to the cell and edit it
    PostMessage(hwnd, WM_FORMATERROR, 0, hwndOldCurrent);
    return;
}
```

Finishing the focus change

Now that the text of the EditControl has been converted into a number, ProcessFocusChange can complete the focus-change operation. It tells the grid to change its currently selected cell and forces the window to redraw both the old and new cells so that their background color reflects the new selection. Finally, ProcessFocusChange tells the newly activated cell's EditControl to start its text editing loop.

```
        // OK update, highlight the new current cell
        // set the current cell number to the cell receiving the focus
        grid->SetCurrentCell(GetWindowWord(ncp->GetEditHandle(), GWW_ID));

        // invalidate (the rectangle) of the edit control losing the input focus
        InvalidateRect(grid->GetHandle(nOldCurrent), NULL, TRUE);

        // force the old EditControl to paint, thus turning off the
        // highlighting for this cell
        SendMessage(grid->GetHandle(nOldCurrent), WM_PAINT, 0, 0L);

        // force it to paint, thus turning off the highlighting for this cell
        InvalidateRect(grid->GetHandle(grid->GetCurrentCell()), NULL, TRUE);
        SendMessage(grid->GetHandle(grid->GetCurrentCell()), WM_PAINT, 0, 0L);

        // activate editing for the new current cell
        ncp->Edit();
    }
}
```

IMPLEMENTING THE SPREADSHEET CLASSES

With the Windows application layer in place, we can implement our spreadsheet classes.

Implementing NumberGrid

We'll start by implementing the NumberGrid class.

NumberGrid constructor

The NumberGrid constructor sets up the application's default font, creates a grid of cells, and initializes the selection to point to the first cell.

```
NumberGrid::NumberGrid(HINSTANCE hInst, HWND hwnd , int xPos, int yPos,
                       int rows, int cols, int nCharsPerCell)
{
    int i, j;
    int xChar, yChar;

    HDC hdc;
    TEXTMETRIC tm;

    // Get fixed font width and height:
    hdc = GetDC(hwnd);
    SelectObject(hdc, GetStockObject(SYSTEM_FIXED_FONT));
    GetTextMetrics(hdc, &tm);
    xChar = tm.tmAveCharWidth;
    yChar = tm.tmHeight + tm.tmExternalLeading + tm.tmHeight / 2;
    ReleaseDC(hwnd, hdc);

    // create the grid cells:
    fCellHeight = yChar;
    fCellWidth = nCharsPerCell * xChar;
    fNRows = rows;
    fNCols = cols;
    fGrid = new NumberCell ** [rows];
    for (i = 0; i < rows; ++i)
        fGrid[i] = new NumberCell * [cols];

    for (i = 0; i < rows; ++i)
        for (j = 0; j < cols; ++j)
          fGrid[i][j] = new NumberCell(hInst, hwnd,
                                  xPos + j * fCellWidth,
                                  yPos + i * fCellHeight,
                                  fCellWidth, fCellHeight);

    // first cell in the grid is the current cell
    fCurrentCell = 0;
}
```

Maintaining the currently selected cell

NumberGrid has a number of member functions which maintain the current selection. When the focus changes, NumberGrid changes the ID of the currently selected cell and tells Windows to set the editing focus to the EditControl of that cell.

```
int NumberGrid::ChangeFocus(int nCellNo)
{
    // return 0 if new cell invalid
    if (nCellNo < 0 || nCellNo > fNRows * fNCols)
        return 0;

    // set focus
    SetFocus(fGrid[nCellNo/fNCols][nCellNo % fNCols]->GetEditHandle());

    // make it the current cell
    SetCurrentCell(nCellNo);

    return 1;
}
```

NumberGrid also has member functions to get and set the currently selected·cell ID and convenience member functions such as GetCell to provide easy access to cell information. For the implementations of these member functions, refer to the source code on the CD-ROM that accompanies this book.

Handling cell formatting

When the user clicks the OK button or double-clicks a format item in the scrolling list, the dialog box posts a WM_FORMATCELL message with its lParam set to the index of the format. The message is eventually handled by WndProc, which then calls NumberGrid's FormatCurrentCell member function to change the format of the currently selected cell.

FormatCurrentCell then creates and initializes a NumberFormat that corresponds to the format the user wants, changes the cell's format to match, and then forces an update of that cell.

```
void NumberGrid::FormatCurrentCell(int nFormatCode)
{
    NumberFormat theFormat;

    // change the format according to the user Format menu choice
    switch (nFormatCode)
    {
        case 0:
            theFormat.Set(0, FALSE, FALSE);
            break;
        case 1:
            theFormat.Set(0, TRUE, FALSE);
            break;
        case 2:
            theFormat.Set(1, FALSE, FALSE);
            break;
        case 3:
            theFormat.Set(2, FALSE, FALSE);
            break;
```

```
                    case 4:
                        theFormat.Set(1, TRUE, FALSE);
                        break;
                    case 5:
                        theFormat.Set(2, TRUE, FALSE);
                        break;
                    case 6:
                        theFormat.Set(2, FALSE, TRUE);
                        break;
                    case 7:
                        theFormat.Set(2, TRUE, TRUE);
                        break;
            }

            // set the current cell to the appropriate format
            fGrid[fCurrentCell/fNCols][fCurrentCell % fNCols]->SetFormat(theFormat);

            // update it
            fGrid[fCurrentCell/fNCols][fCurrentCell % fNCols]->Edit();
            fGrid[fCurrentCell/fNCols][fCurrentCell % fNCols]->Update();
        }
```

The implementation of the NumberGrid class is now complete.

Implementing NumberCell

NumberCell's implementation is more complicated than that of NumberGrid, due mostly to its interactions with the Windows EditControl it owns.

NumberCell constructor

The NumberCell constructor creates the EditControl object and replaces its standard EditProc with its own custom version, EditWndProc, which notifies the NumberCell when the text of the EditControl has been altered. NumberCell stores the old EditProc handle so that it can call it from the EditWndProc routine to do the actual text editing. In this respect, Windows' handler system allows us to achieve a simplified form of polymorphism, which is a lot less work than creating a complete text editing control from scratch.

The constructor then stores a pointer to this NumberCell object in a named property of the EditControl. NumberCell uses this pointer to convert an EditControl handle, passed to it by Windows, into a NumberCell object pointer.

Finally, NumberCell initializes its data members as usual.

```
NumberCell::NumberCell(HINSTANCE hInst, HWND hwndParent , int xPos, int yPos,
                        int width, int height) : fNumber()
{
    fHwndEditControl = CreateWindow("edit", NULL,
                    WS_CHILD | WS_VISIBLE | WS_BORDER | ES_LEFT | ES_AUTOHSCROLL,
                    xPos, yPos, width, height,
                    hwndParent, fCellNumber++,
                    hInst, NULL);

    // create a single thunk for the new edit proc
    if (!fLpfnNewEditProc)
        fLpfnNewEditProc = MakeProcInstance((FARPROC) EditWndProc, hInst);

    // subclass the old edit proc
    fLpfnOldEditProc = (FARPROC) GetWindowLong(fHwndEditControl, GWL_WNDPROC);
    SetWindowLong(fHwndEditControl, GWL_WNDPROC, (LONG) fLpfnNewEditProc);

    // store the handle to the NumberCell in the edit control property list
    SetProp(fHwndEditControl, (LPSTR) KNUMBERCELLPROP, (HANDLE) this);

    // new cell, has never been altered, format is OK
    fAltered = FALSE;
    fErrorInFormat = FALSE;
}
```

Text editing support

For NumberCell to know when to update the number in its
FormattableNumber object when the user types a new value, NumberCell keeps
track of when the user makes a change to the EditControl. As mentioned
previously, this is done in a custom EditWndProc. The implementation of
EditWndProc is simple. When the user types a character, EditWndProc sets the
dirty bit of the EditControl's cell object.

```
long _export FAR PASCAL EditWndProc(HWND hwnd, WORD message,
                                WORD wParam, LONG lParam)
{
    // This procedure is used to subclass the edit control.
    // The new edit proc intercepts keystrokes and "marks"
    // the NumberCell as "altered."
    switch (message)
    {
        case WM_KEYDOWN:
            // user has typed character into edit control, set to altered
            NumberCell* cell = (NumberCell*) GetProp(hwnd, (LPSTR) KNUMBERCELLPROP);
            cell->SetAlteredStatus(TRUE);
            break;
    }

    // Call the old Windows edit proc
    return CallWindowProc(NumberCell::fLpfnOldEditProc, hwnd, message, wParam,
    lParam);
}
```

Next, NumberCell handles the preparations for editing. When the user clicks in a cell, the NumberCell reformats the number without any excess punctuation such as dollar signs and commas. This makes it easier to validate the input, and lets users see exactly what they're entering. To prepare, the Edit member function creates a temporary FormattableNumber and uses it to get the simplified text version of the number. It then sets the EditControl to that text.

```
void NumberCell::Edit()
{
    char szBuffer[32], szEditStr[32];

    // if the cell has been altered, done editing
    if (fAltered)
        return;

    // is the cell text empty? if so, return
    if (!GetWindowText(fHwndEditControl, szEditStr, sizeof(szEditStr)))
        return;

    // Not empty, edit the cell in-place:
    // create a temporary FormattableNumber
    FormattableNumber aTempFNumber(fNumber.GetValue(), fNumber.GetFormat());

    // set it to the "general format"
    NumberFormat editFormat(2, FALSE, FALSE, NULL, '.');
    aTempFNumber.SetFormat(editFormat);

    // Format its edit text
    aTempFNumber.Format(szBuffer);

    // Replace the edit control text with the newly formatted string
    SetWindowText(fHwndEditControl, szBuffer);
    fAltered = TRUE;
}
```

Updating the cell's display

When an event occurs that causes editing to complete, such as a focus-change message, NumberCell updates the FormattableNumber's value from the EditControl's text. This is done in the Update member function.

Update verifies whether the text in the EditControl was altered. If not, it returns immediately. If the text did change, Update extracts it and uses the standard library function strtod to do the conversion. If no error occurs, Update changes the text of the EditControl to match the newly formatted number, because the user doesn't need to see the stripped-down editing format once editing is complete.

If an error does occur, Update displays an error dialog box and aborts the update process.

```c
int NumberCell::Update()
{
    char szBuffer[32], *endPtr;
    double dTemp;

    if (!fAltered)
        return 1;

    // is the cell empty?
    if (!GetWindowText(fHwndEditControl, szBuffer, sizeof(szBuffer)))
    {
        // if so, format is OK
        fErrorInFormat = FALSE;
        fAltered = FALSE;
        return 1;
    }

    // if we have a bad numeric format, abandon update.
    if (fErrorInFormat)
        return 0;

    // attempt numeric conversion
    dTemp = strtod(szBuffer, &endPtr);

    // if endPtr is NULL, conversion was successful
    if (!*endPtr)
    {
        // update FormattableNumber value member
        fNumber = dTemp;

        // compute the new format
        fNumber.Format(szBuffer);

        // set the edit cell to that format
        SetWindowText(fHwndEditControl, (LPSTR) szBuffer);

        fErrorInFormat = FALSE;
        fAltered = FALSE;
        return 1;
    }

    // Record that the user has typed-in a bad numeric format
    fErrorInFormat = TRUE;

    // Signal an error
    MessageBeep(0);
    MessageBox(fHwndEditControl, "Invalid Numeric Format",
               "Number Cell Error", MB_ICONEXCLAMATION);

    return 0;  // unsuccessful update
}
```

Implementing NumberFormat

NumberFormat is a convenience class, and, as such, its implementation is very simple. It consists almost entirely of getters for its component data members. It also has a single member function, Set, which can be used to update the entire format with a single call. The implementations of Set and GetIntSeparator, a typical getter member function, are shown here.

```
void NumberFormat::Set(int prec, BOOL delimtd, BOOL curncy,
                       char intSep, char decSep, char curncySym)
{
    fPrecision = prec;
    fThousandsDelimitted = delimtd;
    fCurrency = curncy;
    fIntSeparator = intSep;
    fDecSeparator = decSep;
    fCurrencySymbol = curncySym;
}

char NumberFormat::GetIntSeparator() const
{
    return fIntSeparator;
}
```

Implementing FormattableNumber

FormattableNumber is responsible for the conversion of numbers to text. The bulk of the class's implementation consists of accessor members.

As with the other classes in the application, FormattableNumber provides accessor member functions that allow its format and numeric value to be manipulated. The code for the format state accessors is shown here.

```
const NumberFormat& FormattableNumber::GetFormat() const
{
    return fMyFormat;
}

void FormattableNumber::SetFormat(const NumberFormat &nf)
{
    fMyFormat = nf;
}
```

Format member function

The most important member function in FormattableNumber is Format, which is responsible for converting the value and format into a string. To perform this conversion, Format first divides the numeric value into its component parts by calling the standard library function fcvt.

It then creates a formatted string by applying the sign, currency character, and thousands separators to the number as needed. Notice that the positioning of these characters in the number is fixed in this version of the application, which is not very international-friendly.

```
void FormattableNumber::Format(char *fresult)
{
    int  decimal, sign;
    char *buffer;
    const int BUFFLEN = 81;
    char outbuf[BUFFLEN];
    ostrstream ostrstr(outbuf, BUFFLEN);

    buffer = fcvt(fValue, fMyFormat.GetPrecision(), &decimal, &sign);

    // negative sign?
    if (sign)
        ostrstr << "-";

    // Currency?
    if (fMyFormat.IsCurrency())
        ostrstr << fMyFormat.GetCurrencySymbol();

    // print the decimal part:
    for (char* digits = buffer; digits < (buffer + decimal); ++digits)
      {
        ostrstr << *digits;
        // delimitted integer format?
        if (fMyFormat.IsThousandsDelimitted())
          {
           if ((digits < (buffer + decimal - 1)) &&
               ((buffer + decimal - digits - 1) / sizeof(char)) % 3 == 0)
             ostrstr << fMyFormat.GetIntSeparator();
          }
      }
    if (fMyFormat.GetPrecision() > 0) // there's a decimal point
        ostrstr << fMyFormat.GetDecimalSeparator();

    while (*p)  // print the decimal part
        ostrstr << *p++;

    ostrstr << NULL;

    strcpy(fresult, outbuf);
}
```

PUTTING THE APPLICATION TOGETHER

This version of the application is now complete. We have a simple but serviceable spreadsheet, one that a user can use to edit and format numbers. Even though the application has some problems with international formatting, its design lays the foundation for a version that handles these issues correctly.

Chapter 6

Designing a number formatting framework for Windows

At this point, we have a workable, if somewhat simplistic, Windows application, which we will run through the usual process of testing and then shipping to customers.

As customers use the product, they report bugs and submit feature requests. Some of the feature requests are minor (use a different font, and so on), while others are more complex. Of the feature requests we receive, two of the most common are the ability to format numbers as fractions (to display stock prices) and the ability to use the program in other countries. Time is short, so we decide to concentrate on adding support for other countries first, but we also want to make sure that it's possible to add support for fractions later without having to redesign or rewrite a lot of code.

Our current implementation of the program has room for improvement. Even though we've divided the problem into a set of objects, adding support for international number formatting to the existing application forces us to make significant changes to the design and implementation of our NumberCell and NumberFormat classes.

However, because the application wasn't designed to be extensible, we can see that these types of problems will probably reappear the next time we have to add features.

Rather than just do a patch on the existing design, we decide to develop a general solution to the number formatting problem: creating a number formatting framework. We'll still be able to reuse, with some editing, much of the code created for the first version of the sample, including virtually all the existing code for the user interface.

DESIGNING THE FRAMEWORK

In the current implementation of the application, the FormattableNumber class is responsible for building the formatted number string. While having a single object that can format itself seemed reasonable at the time, it poses a few problems now. For example, to add support for displaying fractions to the FormattableNumber, we'll need to add case and if statements to many different formatting routines.

We also want to be able to add new number formatting capabilities to the application later, without adding lots of new classes or revisiting existing ones. Thus, the core of the framework should be a class that formats numbers generically, TNumberFormatter. We'll create subclasses of TNumberFormatter to format numbers in more specific ways. For example, to format floating-point numbers, we'll add a TFloatingPointFormatter class to the framework.

Because the current application design allows only the double value kept by FormattableNumber to be used, we also want to provide a more general way of passing numbers to TNumberFormatter. In its place, the framework provides a more general TFormattableNumber class that can be passed to any TNumberFormatter object. Like the old NumberFormatter class, TNumberFormatter uses a double to represent the number being formatted.

Unlike NumberFormatter, this design lets us create a subclass of TFormattableNumber to represent new data types, which in turn lets us format numeric data types about which the framework itself knows nothing. A future version of the application could use a Binary-Coded Decimal (BCD) class for its calculations, and by using a TFormattableBCDNumber class, the application would be able to format these values without modifying the underlying framework.

This kind of flexibility is one of the keys to good framework design. The framework provides reasonable default behavior that lets us format floating-point numbers, but it also allows for future extensibility without affecting the underlying framework design and implementation.

We also need a way to communicate formatting errors to framework clients. Correctly designed classes usually respond to error conditions by throwing exceptions or returning error codes, either of which is perfectly appropriate when there are no shades of grey in the success or failure of a particular operation.

However, when formatting a number, error conditions are not always so clear. Number formatting operations rarely fail outright, but it is possible that the result won't serve the needs of the client. For example, the space available to display the number can be fixed in width, and you might want to display the number in a different format (such as scientific notation) to allow it to fit into the allocated space. To address this issue, we need to create a class that allows us to return more detailed results to the client. This class, TFormatResult, includes error information and more general information about the formatting results.

Finally, we need a TNumberFormatLocale class, which stores the common formatter types used for a given area of the world. This class is used to isolate the international dependencies from the rest of the framework.

The class hierarchy of the framework is shown in the following figure.

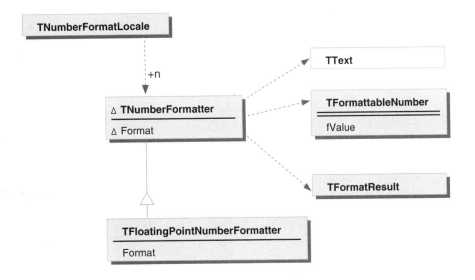

CLASS HIERARCHY OF THE NUMBER FORMATTING FRAMEWORK

This method of formatting offers advantages over the previous technique we used. For one, the TFormattableNumber object does not have to carry specialized functions to format itself. It's "just" data. Formatting knowledge is kept in the TNumberFormatter class hierarchy. This separation makes it easier to use, maintain, and extend these classes.

Using these classes in the application requires minor revisions to the NumberCell class, described in "Updating NumberCell" on page 122.

✅ NOTE   The framework also uses a TText class, which represents a standard ASCII string. Because its implementation is straightforward, the design and implementation of this class is not shown in the book. The source code for this class is included on the accompanying CD-ROM.

Now that our basic design is in place, we'll begin filling out the design of the framework's classes.

**Designing
TNumberFormatter**

The first class we need to design is TNumberFormatter. TNumberFormatter's primary function is to "remember" a formatting style and to convert a numeric value into a textual representation using that style.

Format member functions

The Format member functions are the core of the TNumberFormatter class, and are the primary member functions called by clients of the framework. They take a TFormattableNumber, convert it to text according to the format set in the TNumberFormatter, and return the text to the caller, along with an optional TFormatResult object that provides additional information about the conversion process.

```
virtual bool    Format(constTFormattableNumber& num, TText& resultText);
virtual bool    Format(constTFormattableNumber& num, TText& resultText,
                    TFormatResult& result);
```

**Formatting support
member functions**

The Format member function relies on two protected member functions, SetUpFormattableNumber and FormattableNumberToText, to handle the bulk of its formatting efforts. SetupFormattableNumber tells TFormattableNumber how it should process the numeric properties of its value.

FormattableNumberToText does the actual work of converting the numeric properties of the TFormattableNumber into text. Subclasses of TNumberFormatter need to override these member functions to provide more specialized behavior. The default versions of these functions implemented by TNumberFormatter can handle only simple floating-point numbers without exponents.

```
virtual void    SetUpFormattableNumber(TFormattableNumber& num);
virtual void    FormattableNumberToText(const TFormattableNumber& num,
                    TText& text, TNumberFormatResult& result);
```

**Accessor member
functions**

TNumberFormatter also provides a set of accessor member functions that allows the formatting of the number to be controlled. TNumberFormatter doesn't know whether the number should be formatted as a floating-point number or as an integral number, so it can control only the formatting of the sign of the number. Note that TNumberFormatter also provides accessors that control the setting of prefix and suffix strings for both positive and negative numbers, allowing TNumberFormatter to show negative numbers with parentheses.

```
virtual void    GetPlus(TText& prefix, TText& suffix) const;
virtual void    SetPlus(const TText& prefix, const TText& suffix);
virtual void    GetMinus TText& prefix, TText& suffix) const;
virtual void    SetMinus(const TText& prefix, const TText& suffix);
virtual bool    GetShowPlusSign() const;
virtual void    SetShowPlusSign(bool);
```

Miscellaneous member functions and data members

The remainder of the member functions for the class consists of standard C++ constructors and an assignment operator. The data members store the suffix and prefix strings, along with a flag that keeps track of whether we want to display the positive sign prefix and suffix to the user.

```
TNumberFormatter&   operator=(const TNumberFormatter&);

                    TNumberFormatter(const TNumberFormatter& format);
                    TNumberFormatter();
virtual             ~TNumberFormatter();

private:
    TText           fPlusPrefix;
    TText           fPlusSuffix;
    TText           fMinusPrefix;
    TText           fMinusSuffix;
    bool            fShowPlusSign;
};
```

Designing TFormattableNumber

TFormattableNumber's primary role is to provide the input number to the TNumberFormatter, along with information about the number's properties. Its class declaration is as follows:

```
class TFormattableNumber {
public:
                    TFormattableNumber();
                    TFormattableNumber(const double number);
                    TFormattableNumber(const TFormattableNumber& copy);
virtual             ~TFormattableNumber();

virtual TFormattableNumber& operator=(const TFormattableNumber& toCopy);

typedef unsigned char Digit;
enum  { kNoSignificandDigit = 253 };

//----------------------------------------------------------------------
// Accessors for number's properties
//----------------------------------------------------------------------

// access the value of the number
virtual double  GetNumber() const;
virtual void    SetNumber(double);

// Is the number negative
virtual bool    IsNegative() const;
```

In addition to storing the number as a double, TFormattableNumber provides access to the individual digits of the number for use by the text converter. It does so using a string of byte-encoded digits (with "0" having a numeric value of zero), called the *significand*. The implicit decimal point is placed after the first digit in the string, as in scientific notation. Special values exist for infinity, illegal numeric values (NaNs), and zero.

Before retrieving the significand, the user must allocate storage for the significand buffer that is at least as large as GetSignificandLength multiplied by the size of a Digit.

```
virtual void    GetSignificand(Digit* theSignificand) const;
virtual size_t  GetSignificandLength() const;

// Exponent represents powers of 10.
virtual long    GetExponent() const;

// bool tests for Infinity, NaN and Zero (sign irrelevant)
virtual bool    IsZero();
virtual bool    IsInfinity();
virtual bool    IsNan();
```

Setting conversion parameters

The accessor functions described above provide information about the properties of the number. Determining these properties requires an analysis of the value, and TFormattableNumber provides routines to control the number of significant digits to preserve when doing this analysis.

```
// Get/SetDigitsFromDecimalPoint controls rounding to a fixed number of
// digits from the decimal point in the significand string when converting.
virtual short   GetDigitsFromDecimalPoint() const ;
virtual void    SetDigitsFromDecimalPoint(short digitsFromDecimalPoint);
```

Numeric analysis member functions

As part of TFormattableNumber's protected interface, we provide routines to analyze the numeric properties of the number and set its internal fields. The setters are protected virtual functions; therefore they can be overridden if necessary by a subclass to fine-tune the analysis process.

```
protected:
    // analyze the numeric value to determine its properties, using the
    // rounding and precision settings of the number. Called automatically whenever
    // the number value or any of the rounding/precision values is changed.
    virtual void    AnalyzeValue();

    // set the properties of the number (used by analyzer routine)
    virtual void    SetAnalysisDirtyFlag(bool flag = TRUE);
    virtual void    SetSignBit(bool signIsMinus);
    virtual void    SetSignificand(Digit significand[], size_t length);
    virtual void    SetExponent(long theExponent);
    virtual void    SetInfinity();
    virtual void    SetNan(unsigned short nanCode);
```

The class declaration concludes with the definition of TFormattableNumber's private data members, which keep track of the number and its properties.

```
private:
    enum      {kBufferLength = 122};
    enum      {kInfinityDigit = 254};
    enum      {kNaNDigit = 255};

    double          fNumber;
    bool            fIsSignMinus;
    long            fExponent;
    size_t          fSignificandLength;
    Digit           fSignificand[kBufferLength+2];
    unsigned short  fTotalDigitCount;
    unsigned short  fDigitsFromDecimalPoint;
    double          fRoundToMultiple;
    bool            fAnalysisDirtyFlag;
};
```

Designing TFloatingPointNumber Formatter

The TFloatingPointNumberFormatter class adds the ability to format floating-point numbers to the basic formatting capabilities provided by TNumberFormatter.

The class declaration begins with the definitions of types and enumerations that define some of the allowable formatting parameters that the user can set.

```
class TFloatingPointNumberFormatter : public TNumberFormatter {
public:
    typedef unsigned short DigitCount;
    enum ESign { kMinusSign = -1, kNoSign = 0, kPlusSign = 1 };
```

The following are the standard constructors, destructor, and assignment operator for this class.

```
TFloatingPointNumberFormatter();
TFloatingPointNumberFormatter(const TFloatingPointNumberFormatter& format);
virtual ~TFloatingPointNumberFormatter();
TFloatingPointNumberFormatter&
        operator=(const TFloatingPointNumberFormatter&);
```

TNumberFormatter formatting overrides

The numeric conversion routines SetupFormattableNumber and FormattableNumberToText, originally defined by TNumberFormatter, are overridden by TFloatingPointNumberFormatter. These routines do the actual work of formatting the text string, using the current format state. The overridden FormattableNumberToText function calls two new protected functions, FormattableNumberToExponentText and FormattableNumberToDecimalText, to handle the formatting of the exponent and decimal portions of the number.

```
virtual void    SetUpFormattableNumber(TFormattableNumber& num);

virtual void    FormattableNumberToText(const TFormattableNumber&, TText&,
                         TNumberFormatResult&);
virtual void    FormattableNumberToExponentText(const TFormattableNumber&,
                         TText&, TNumberFormatResult&);
virtual void    FormattableNumberToDecimalText(const TFormattableNumber&,
                         TText&, TNumberFormatResult&);
```

Formatting control accessor functions

The remainder of the class is made up of accessors that control the formatting of floating-point numbers.

```
public:
    //========================================================================
    // Getters and setters.

    // in text 1,234,567, the digit group separator text is ",",
    // the separator spacing is 3.
    // Call SetIntegerSeparator(TRUE) if the digit group separator
    // is to be shown for the integer part.
    virtual void      GetDigitGroupSeparator(TText&) const;
    virtual void      SetDigitGroupSeparator(const TText&);
    virtual DigitCount GetSeparatorSpacing() const;
    virtual void      SetSeparatorSpacing(DigitCount);
    virtual bool      GetIntegerSeparator() const;
    virtual void      SetIntegerSeparator(bool);

    // minDigitCount is the minimum number of digits to display when formatting
    // a number as text. Also known as zero-padding.
    virtual DigitCount GetMinIntegerDigits() const;
    virtual void      SetMinIntegerDigits(DigitCount);

    virtual void      GetNanSign(TText&) const;
    virtual void      GetInfinitySign(TText&) const;
    virtual void      SetNanSign(const TText&);
    virtual void      SetInfinitySign(const TText&);

    // SetDecimalSeparator sets the text to be used to separate the integer
    // and the fraction parts of numbers. It defaults to a space
    virtual void      GetDecimalSeparator(TText&) const;
    virtual void      SetDecimalSeparator(const TText&);
```

```
// SetDecimalWithInteger indicates if the decimal point should be
// displayed for integer numbers.
virtual bool    GetDecimalWithInteger() const;
virtual void    SetDecimalWithInteger(bool);

// SetFractionSeparator indicates if the digit group separator text,
// which is set through TNumberFormatter::SetDigitGroupSeparator,
// should be displayed for the fraction part. It defaults to FALSE.
virtual bool    GetFractionSeparator() const;
virtual void    SetFractionSeparator(bool);

// SetExponentSeparatorText indicates the text to be used for
// the exponent separator. The default is 'E'.
virtual void    GetExponentSeparatorText(TText&) const;
virtual void    SetExponentSeparatorText(const TText&);

virtual DigitCount  GetMinFractionDigits() const;
virtual void        SetMinFractionDigits(DigitCount);
virtual DigitCount  GetMaxFractionDigits() const;
virtual void        SetMaxFractionDigits(DigitCount);

 // == 1 for scientific, 3 for engineering formats
virtual DigitCount  GetExponentPhase() const;
virtual void        SetExponentPhase(DigitCount);

virtual double  GetUpperExponentThreshold() const;
virtual void    SetUpperExponentThreshold(double);
virtual double  GetLowerExponentThreshold() const;
virtual void    SetLowerExponentThreshold(double);
```

Despite their simplicity, these functions are important to the design of the
framework because they provide a great deal of control over how numbers are
formatted. In fact, they provide more control than is strictly necessary for this
sample program. This is a common by-product of the framework design process:
we have to do more design and implementation work up front to make the
framework truly general. The alternative, of course, is to develop a framework
that is not truly general, and we end up having to redesign and reimplement
everything whenever we want to add new functionality.

Is the cost of adding all this generality worth it? It is if we would have to do most
of the work involved in designing the framework anyway. The previous version of
the program wouldn't work in countries other than the U.S., and it only
supported a limited number of number formats. Adding support for these
features to the previous version of the framework would require us to add a
similar amount of code to achieve the same level of functionality.

The remainder of the class consists of the data members needed to store all of this state.

```
private:
    TText           fNanSign;
    TText           fInfinitySign;
    TText           fDigitGroupSeparator;  // e.g. thousands separator ","
    DigitCount      fMinIntegerDigits;     // 0-pad at least this many digits
    DigitCount      fSeparatorSpacing;     // digit group length for separator
    bool            fHasIntegerSeparator;
    TText           fDecimalSeparator;     // '.' in 1.23
    TText           fExponentSeparator;    // 'E' in 1E-3
    double          fExponentUpperThreshold;// when to switch to E notation
    double          fExponentLowerThreshold;
    DigitCount      fExponentPhase;        // multiples of exponent to show
    DigitCount      fMinFractionDigits;    // 0-pad to fill
    DigitCount      fMaxFractionDigits;
    bool            fDecimalWithInteger;
    bool            fHasFractionSeparator; // use digit group separator?
    bool            fHasExponentSeparator; // use digit group separator?
    bool            fSignedExponent;
    EMantissaType   fMantissaType;
    EShowBaseType   fShowBaseType;
};
```

Designing TNumberFormatLocale

The TNumberFormatLocale class provides a number of member functions to create default formatters for both currency and floating-point formats. There is always a default locale which corresponds to the user's location, and it can be accessed by calling TNumberFormatLocale::GetUserLocale.

```
class TNumberFormatLocale {
public:
                        TNumberFormatLocale();
                        TNumberFormatLocale(const TNumberFormatLocale&);
    virtual             ~TNumberFormatLocale();

    // member functions to create standard formatters for the current locale.
    virtual TNumberFormatter*   CreateCurrencyFormatter() const;
    virtual TNumberFormatter*   CreateFloatingPointFormatter() const;

    static const TNumberFormatLocale& GetUserLocale();

private:
    static TNumberFormatLocale* gUserLocale;
};
```

We use this class to isolate the locale dependencies from the rest of the framework. The current design supports accessing the current locale only. Future enhancements might include the addition of support for setting the locale under program control and the use of the locale object to support access to other localized classes. For this example, the current design is sufficient.

**Implementing
TNumberFormatter**

Now that the design of the framework's classes is in place, it's time to implement the framework. Since it is assumed that you are familiar with constructors and destructors, and because the getter and setter functions are so simple, not every step of the implementation process is described here. The complete source code is available on the CD-ROM that accompanies this book. This discussion concentrates on the key member functions of the framework.

The key function of TNumberFormatter is the Format member function. Format takes a TFormattableNumber and converts it to text using the current settings of the TNumberFormatter.

```
void TNumberFormatter::Format(const TFormattableNumber& value, TText& theText,
                        TNumberFormatResult& result)
{
    theText.del(0,theText.length());
    SetUpFormattableNumber(value);

    FormattableNumberToText(value, theText, result);

    TText prefix;
    TText suffix;

    bool isNegative;
    isNegative = value.GetSignBit();
    if (isNegative)
        GetMinus(prefix, suffix);
    else if (GetShowPlusSign())
        GetPlus(prefix, suffix);

    theText += suffix;
    theText.prepend(prefix);

    result.SetIntegerBoundary(result.GetIntegerBoundary() + prefix.GetLength());
    result.SetDigitSequenceEnd(result.GetDigitSequenceEnd() + prefix.GetLength());
}
```

FormattableNumber setup and conversion functions

The Format member function calls two member functions to handle most of the number formatting operation. The first of these, SetUpFormattableNumber, sets up the analysis parameters of the TFormattableNumber object. Subclasses of TNumberFormatter can override this member function to customize the behavior of the TFormattableNumber, as we do later when we describe the implementation of TFloatingPointNumberFormatter.

```
void TNumberFormatter::SetUpFormattableNumber(TFormattableNumber& num)
{
    num.SetDigitsFromDecimalPoint(TFormattableNumber::kNoSignificandDigit);
}
```

The second of these member functions is FormattableNumberToText. FormattableNumberToText does most of the work of formatting for the Format member function, and it is usually overridden by subclasses. The default version supplied by TNumberFormatter handles thousands separators, but prints numbers without exponents, filling with zeroes as needed.

```
void TNumberFormatter::FormattableNumberToText(const TFormattableNumber& num,
                                       TText& text, TNumberFormatResult& result)
{
    char uc;

    // delete any existing text
    text.Delete(TTextRange(TTextOffset(0), text.GetLength()));

    if (!num.IsInfinity() && !num.IsNan())
    {
        int numDigits = num.GetSignificandLength();
        if (numDigits <= 0)
        {
            ConvertToNumeral(TFormattableNumber::Digit(0),uc);
            text.prepend(uc);
            return;
        }

        // first, determine and allocate the correct size digit buffer
        // must be at least as big as FormattableNumber returns, but
        // may need extra space for leading zeros.
        int n = num.GetExponent() + 1;
        int exponent = n;
        long places = ( exponent > numDigits ? exponent : numDigits );
        TFormattableNumber::Digit* digits = new
                          TFormattableNumber::Digit[places];
        num.GetSignificand(digits);
```

```
// fill with zeros at end
if (exponent > numDigits)
    for (int i = numDigits; i < exponent; i++)
        digits[ i ] = TFormattableNumber::Digit(0);

// work back through number, filling in digits
int consecutiveDigits = 0;
int digit = 0;
for (int theDigit = exponent - 1; theDigit >= 0; theDigit--)
{
    ConvertToNumeral(digits[theDigit], uc);
    text.prepend(uc);
    if (GetIntegerSeparator()
            && ++consecutiveDigits == GetSeparatorSpacing()
            && (theDigit < exponent - 1)
            && (theDigit > 0))
    {
        TText separatorText;
        GetDigitGroupSeparator(separatorText);
        text.prepend(separatorText);
        consecutiveDigits = 0;
    }
}

// zero pad integral portion as needed
TFloatingPointNumberFormatter::DigitCount minIntegerDigits =
                GetMinIntegerDigits();
if ((minIntegerDigits > 0) && (minIntegerDigits > n))
{
    ConvertToNumeral(0, uc);
    for (int i = n; i < minIntegerDigits; i++)
    {
        text.prepend(uc);
    }
}

result.SetIntegerBoundary(text.length());
result.SetDigitSequenceEnd(text.length());

delete [] digits;

// it currently just sets the confidence to be kPerfect.
result.SetConfidence(TNumberFormatResult::kPerfect);
    }
}
```

Implementing TFormattableNumber

TFormattableNumber contains a large number of accessor functions used to retrieve information about the number, including its exponent, its sign, and so on. Whenever a member function that returns analysis results is called, TFormattableNumber checks a dirty flag to see whether it should reanalyze the number's properties, as shown in the IsNegative member function:

```
bool TFormattableNumber::IsNegative() const
{
    if (fAnalysisDirtyFlag)
        AnalyzeValue();
    return fIsSignMinus;
}
```

Similarly, when a member function is called that might change the analysis results, TFormattableNumber sets the dirty flag in that member function, as shown in the SetNumber member function:

```
void TFormattableNumber::SetNumber(double number)
{
    fNumber = number;
    SetAnalysisDirtyFlag(TRUE);
}
```

The AnalyzeValue member function analyzes the number and extracts its numeric properties, using the conversion settings provided. It uses the ANSI C standard function fcvt to convert the number into its components.

```
void TFormattableNumber::AnalyzeValue()
{
    int  decimal, sign;
    Digit* buffer;
    int siglen = 0;
    long digits = fDigitsFromDecimalPoint;
    if (digits > 12)
      digits = 12;

    // fcvt determines the exponent, mantissa, and sign for us,
    // but it uses ascii characters, which isn't very general, so we
    // convert them to our internal Digit format.
    buffer = (Digit*) fcvt(fNumber, digits, &decimal, &sign);
    siglen = strlen(buffer);
    for (int i = 0; i < siglen; i++)
      buffer[i] = buffer[i] - '0';

    SetSignBit(( sign != 0 ? TRUE: FALSE));
    SetSignificand((Digit*) buffer, siglen);
    SetExponent((long) decimal - 1);

    SetAnalysisDirtyFlag(FALSE);
}
```

Implementing TFloatingPointNumberFormatter

The key member functions of TFloatingPointNumberFormatter are the two overridden member functions of TNumberFormatter, SetUpFormattableNumber and FormattableNumberToText.

Implementing SetUpFormattableNumber

The SetUpFormattableNumber member function sets up the conversion parameters of the formattable number that the class has been asked to format. The overridden implementation first calls the SetUpFormattable member function it inherited from TNumberFormatter and then overrides the setting that controls the number of decimal points to match the maximum permitted digits parameter of TFloatingPointNumberFormatter.

```
void TFloatingPointNumberFormatter::SetUpFormattableNumber(TFormattableNumber& num)
{
    TNumberFormatter::SetUpFormattableNumber(num);

    num.SetDigitsFromDecimalPoint(GetMaxFractionDigits());
}
```

FormattableNumberToText

TFloatingPointNumberFormatter overrides the FormattableNumberToText member function to handle both scientific and engineering notation for floating-point numbers. It delegates the work to two new member functions, FormattableNumberToExponentText and FormattableNumberToDecimalText.

```
void TFloatingPointNumberFormatter::FormattableNumberToText(
                    const TFormattableNumber& num,
                    TText& text, TNumberFormatResult& result)
{
    if (!num.IsInfinity() && !num.IsNan())
    {
        // get absolute value of number
        double number = num.GetNumber();
        if (number < 0)
            number = -number;

        // determine whether to print as scientific notation or not, using
        // the exponent threshold parameters.
        if (number != 0.0 && (number < GetLowerExponentThreshold() ||
                        number > GetUpperExponentThreshold()))
            FormattableNumberToExponentText(num, text, result);
        else FormattableNumberToDecimalText(num, text, result);

        // we currently just set the confidence to be kPerfect.
        result.SetConfidence(TNumberFormatResult::kPerfect);
    }
    else
    {
        // let the TNumberFormatter take care of the edge cases
        TNumberFormatter::FormattableNumberToText(num,text,result);
    }
}
```

FormattableNumberToExponentText

FormattableNumberToExponentText generates a text string in scientific
notation. Rather than duplicate all the code to print a basic number, it uses a
TNumberFormatter to format the exponent as though it were a whole number
and then calls FormattableNumberToDecimalText to format the mantissa. Using
the appropriate separator text, it subsequently puts the two numbers together.

```
void TFloatingPointNumberFormatter::FormattableNumberToExponentText(
        const TFormattableNumber& num, TText& text,
        TNumberFormatResult& result)
{
    long exponent = num.GetExponent();
    long exponentAdjuster = 0;// used later to process mantissa
    long phase = (long) GetExponentPhase();
    if (phase > 1)
        {
            // we round the exponent down using the phase value
            // for engineering notation, phase is 3, so we get an
            // exponent value rounded down to the nearest multiple
            // of 3
            long idealExponent;
            if (exponent < 0)
                idealExponent = (((-1 - exponent) / phase) * -phase) - phase;
            else idealExponent = (exponent / phase) * phase;

            exponentAdjuster = exponent - idealExponent;
            exponent = idealExponent;
        }

    // first we format the exponent, using a basic TNumberFormatter which
    // we handily initialize with this object's settings
    TNumberFormatter exponentFormat(*this);
    TText exponentText;
    TNumberFormatResult exponentResult;
    TFormattableNumber formattableExponent((double) exponent);
    exponentFormat.Format(formattableExponent, exponentText, exponentResult);

    // now we format the integral part of our number
    // we make a new number which reflects only the mantissa, with the correct
    // number of digits to match the exponent we've already printed
    TFormattableNumber formattableMantissa(num.GetNumber() /
                            pow(10.0, exponentAdjuster));
    FormattableNumberToDecimalText(num, text, result);

    TText exponentSeparator;
    GetExponentSeparatorText(exponentSeparator);
    text += exponentSeparator;
    text += exponentText;

    result.SetDigitSequenceEnd(text.GetLength());
}
```

FormattableNumberToDecimalText

FormattableNumberToDecimalText is responsible for formatting a floating-point number in the standard (nonscientific) format. Its implementation is similar to that of TNumberFormatter::FormattableNumberToText, but it provides more control over the formatting.

```
void TFloatingPointNumberFormatter::FormattableNumberToDecimalText(
                              const TFormattableNumber& num,
                              TText& text, TNumberFormatResult& result)
{
    double number = 0.0;
    TFormattableNumber::Digit theDigit;
    char uc;

    if (!num.IsInfinity() && !num.IsNan())
        number = num.GetNumber();

    long numDigits = num.GetSignificandLength();
    TFormattableNumber::Digit* digits = new TFormattableNumber::Digit[numDigits];
    num.GetSignificand(digits);
    long exponent = num.GetExponent() + 1;
    long minPlaces = exponent + GetMinFractionDigits();
    long maxPlaces = exponent + GetMaxFractionDigits();

    long places = numDigits;

    if (places < minPlaces)    places = minPlaces;
    if (places > maxPlaces)    places = maxPlaces;

    //  First the stuff to the left of the decimal place
    long consecutiveDigits = 0;
    for (long i = exponent - 1; i >= 0; i--)
    {
        theDigit = (i >= numDigits ? 0 : digits[i]);
        ConvertToNumeral(theDigit, uc);

        text.prepend(uc);
        if (GetIntegerSeparator()//  i.e., insert ","
            && ++consecutiveDigits == GetSeparatorSpacing() //  insert it here
            && i < exponent - 1
            && i > 0)
        {
            //  more digits coming
            TText separatorText;
            GetDigitGroupSeparator(separatorText);
            text.prepend(separatorText);
            consecutiveDigits = 0;
        }
    }
    result.SetIntegerBoundary(text.GetLength());
```

```
    //  Now add the decimal point if we have decimal places or we always show it
    if (places > exponent  || GetDecimalWithInteger())
    {
        TText decimalSeparator;
        GetDecimalSeparator(decimalSeparator);
        text += decimalSeparator;
    }

    //  Add the decimal places
    consecutiveDigits = 0;
    for (i = exponent; i < places; i++)
    {
        theDigit = (i >= numDigits ? 0 : digits[i]);
        ConvertToNumeral(theDigit, uc);
        text += uc;

        if (GetFractionSeparator()
            && ++consecutiveDigits == GetSeparatorSpacing()
            && i < places - 1)
            {
                // more digits coming
                TText separatorText;
                GetDigitGroupSeparator(separatorText);
                text += separatorText;
                consecutiveDigits = 0;
            }
    }

    result.SetDigitSequenceEnd(text.GetLength());

    delete [] digits;
}
```

Implementing
TNumberFormatLocale

TNumberFormatLocale is the most Windows-specific class in our framework. It
sets up the number formatters to match the settings it extracts from the Windows
locale information.

CreateCurrencyFormatter member function

CreateCurrencyFormatter creates a currency formatter that correctly formats
currency for the current locale by making calls to the Windows function
GetLocaleInfo and then modifying a TFloatingPointNumberFormatter object's
settings to match the Windows information.

```
// table to determine properties for negative currency format
// returned by Windows via LOCALE_INEGCURR
static bool pLocaleCurrFmtTable[16][5] = {
    // 0,        1,         2,        3,          4
    // useParens,prefixCurr,prefixSign,signFirst,currSpace
    { true,     true,      false,    false,     false },   // 0
    { false,    true,      true,     true,      false },   // 1
    { false,    true,      true,     false,     false },   // 2
    { false,    true,      false,    false,     false },   // 3
    { true,     false,     false,    false,     false },   // 4
    { false,    false,     true,     false,     false },   // 5
    { false,    false,     false,    true,      false },   // 6
    { false,    false,     false,    false,     false },   // 7
    { false,    false,     true,     false,     true },    // 8
    { false,    true,      true,     true,      true },    // 9
    { false,    false,     false,    false,     true },    // 10
    { false,    true,      false,    false,     true },    // 11
    { false,    true,      true,     false,     true },    // 12
    { false,    false,     false,    true,      true },    // 13
    { true,     true,      false,    false,     true },    // 14
    { true,     false,     false,    false,     true }     // 15
};

TNumberFormatter* TNumberFormatLocale::CreateCurrencyFormatter() const
{
    unsigned character lcBuf[255];
    TText decimalSep, thousandsSep, currencySym, posSym, negSym;
    long thousandsSepGrouping, currencyDigits;
    TText prefix, suffix;
    long plusMode, negMode;

    // get positive & negative currency modes
    GetLocaleInfo(LOCALE_USER_DEFAULT,LOCALE_ICURRENCY,lcbuf,sizeof(lcBuf));
    plusMode = atoi(lcbuf);
    GetLocaleInfo(LOCALE_USER_DEFAULT,LOCALE_INEGCURR,lcbuf,sizeof(lcBuf));
    negMode = atoi(lcbuf);

    // make a formatter
    TFloatingPointNumberFormatter* formatter = new TFloatingPointNumberFormatter;

    // get currency info from windows
    GetLocaleInfo(LOCALE_USER_DEFAULT,LOCALE_SCURRENCY,lcbuf,sizeof(lcBuf));
    currencySym = lcbuf;
```

```
// set up positive suffixes
// first, we get old prefix and suffix, since we're only going to change one
// or the other but not both.
GetLocaleInfo(LOCALE_USER_DEFAULT,LOCALE_SPOSITIVESIGN,lcbuf,sizeof(lcBuf));
posSym = lcbuf;
formatter->GetPlus(prefix,suffix);
bool useSpace = true;
switch (plusMode)
{
    case 0:
        useSpace = false;
        // fall through...
    case 1:
    default:
        prefix = currencySym;
        if (useSpace)
            prefix += ' ';
        break;
    case 2:
        useSpace = false;
        // fall through...
    case 3:
        if (useSpace)
            suffix = ' ';
        else suffix.del(0,suffix.length());
        suffix += currencySym;
        break;
}
SetPlus(prefix,suffix);

// set up negative suffixes
GetLocaleInfo(LOCALE_USER_DEFAULT,LOCALE_SNEGATIVESIGN,lcbuf,sizeof(lcBuf));
negSym = lcbuf;
// look up settings in table
bool useParens = pLocaleCurrFmtTable[negMode][0];
bool currPrefix = pLocaleCurrFmtTable[negMode][1];
bool signPrefix = pLocaleCurrFmtTable[negMode][2];
bool signFirst = pLocaleCurrFmtTable[negMode][3];
useSpace = pLocaleCurrFmtTable[negMode][4];

// set up string based on settings
if (useParens)
{
    // no Windows api to get parens from locale, so we
    // hard-code!
    prefix = '(';
    suffix = ')';
}
else
{
    prefix.del(0,prefix.length);
    suffix.del(0,prefix.length);
}
```

```
if (signFirst)
{
    // signFirst == true implies that sign and currency are next to each other
    if (signPrefix)
    {
        prefix += negSym;
        if (useSpace)
          prefix += ' ';
        prefix += currencySym;
    }
    else
    {
        suffix += negSym;
        if (useSpace)
          suffix += ' ';
        suffix += currencySym;
    }
}
else
{
    if (currPrefix)
    {
        prefix += currencySym;
        if (useSpace)
          prefix += ' ';
        prefix += negSym;
    }
    else
    {
        if (useSpace)
          suffix += ' ';
        suffix += currencySym;
        suffix += negSym;
    }
}
SetMinus(prefix,suffix);

GetLocaleInfo(LOCALE_USER_DEFAULT,LOCALE_SMONDECIMALSEP,lcbuf,sizeof(lcBuf));
decimalSep = lcbuf;
formatter->SetDecimalSeparator(decimalSep);

GetLocaleInfo(LOCALE_USER_DEFAULT,LOCALE_SMONTHOUSANDSEP,lcbuf,sizeof(lcBuf));
thousandsSep = lcbuf;
formatter->GetDigitGroupSeparator(thousandsSep);

GetLocaleInfo(LOCALE_USER_DEFAULT,LOCALE_SMONGROUPING,lcbuf,sizeof(lcBuf));
TText tmpBuf(lcbuf);
long idx = tmpBuf.index(';');
// strip off any trailing text
if (idx > 0)
  tmpBuf.del(0,tmpBuf.length());
// now convert string to number and set the spacing
thousandsSepGrouping = atoi(tmpBuf.chars());
formatter->SetSeparatorSpacing(thousandsSepGrouping);
```

```
    GetLocaleInfo(LOCALE_USER_DEFAULT,LOCALE_ICURRDIGITS,lcbuf,sizeof(lcBuf));
    currencyDigits = atoi(lcbuf);
    formatter->SetMinFractionDigits(currencyDigits);
    formatter->SetMaxFractionDigits(currencyDigits);

    return formatter;
}
```

CreateFloatingPointFormatter member function

CreateFloatingPointFormatter's implementation is similar to that of
CreateCurrencyFormatter, but because it doesn't have to address the issues of
sign and currency symbol formatting, it is slightly simpler.

```
TNumberFormatter* TNumberFormatLocale::CreateFloatingPointFormatter() const
{
    TCHAR lcBuf[255];
    TText decimalSep, thousandsSep;
    long thousandsSepGrouping;
    TText prefix, suffix;
    TText plusMode, negMode;

    // make a formatter and set it up
    TFloatingPointNumberFormatter* formatter = new TFloatingPointNumberFormatter();

    GetLocaleInfo(LOCALE_USER_DEFAULT,LOCALE_SDECIMAL,lcbuf,sizeof(lcBuf));
    decimalSep = lcbuf;
    formatter->SetDecimalSeparator(decimalSep);

    GetLocaleInfo(LOCALE_USER_DEFAULT,LOCALE_STHOUSAND,lcbuf,sizeof(lcBuf));
    thousandsSep = lcbuf;
    formatter->SetDigitGroupSeparator(thousandsSep);

    GetLocaleInfo(LOCALE_USER_DEFAULT,LOCALE_SGROUPING,lcbuf,sizeof(lcBuf));
    TText tmpBuf(lcbuf);
    long idx = tmpBuf.index(';');
    // strip off any trailing text
    if (idx > 0)
      tmpBuf.del(0,tmpBuf.length());
    // now convert string to number and set the spacing
    thousandsSepGrouping = atoi(tmpBuf.chars());
    formatter->SetSeparatorSpacing(thousandsSepGrouping);

    GetLocaleInfo(LOCALE_USER_DEFAULT,LOCALE_IDIGITS,lcbuf,sizeof(lcBuf));
    currencyDigits = atoi(lcbuf);
    formatter->SetMinFractionDigits(currencyDigits);
    formatter->SetMaxFractionDigits(currencyDigits);

    return formatter;
}
```

UPDATING THE SPREADSHEET DATA OBJECTS

It's now time to update the application to use the framework we've created.

Note that we needed to alter almost nothing in the Windows-specific application code to accommodate these new classes. In other words, WinMain, WndProc, and ProcessFocusChange remain identical to the versions we wrote in Chapter 5 for the first version of the application.

Our second sample, the application with the new framework added, does not add any new formatting features: we need only modify some of the internals of the classes used by the application.

Updating NumberCell

The majority of modifications required to accommodate the framework classes occur in the NumberCell class. Note that the various clients of NumberCell (for example, WndProc, ProcessFocusChange, and the NumberGrid class) were unaffected; their interface to NumberCell is unchanged. The new NumberCell class declaration is shown here. For the original version of the class, refer to "NumberCell class design" on page 76.

```
class NumberCell
{
public:
                    NumberCell(HINSTANCE hInst, HWND hwndParent,
                            int xPos = 0, int yPos = 0,
                            int width = 0, int height = 0);
                    ~NumberCell();

    //=======================================================================
    // Getter member functions

    // get the edit handle of the enclosed edit control
    HWND            GetEditHandle();
    // get the child id of the enclosed edit control
    WORD            GetID();
    // get the cell format
    NumberFormat&   GetFormat();
    // get the error status
    BOOL            GetFormatErrorStatus();
    // return the edit status of the cell
    BOOL            HasBeenAltered();

    //=======================================================================
    // Setter member functions

    // change the altered status of the cell
    BOOL            SetAlteredStatus(BOOL newStatus);
    // set the cell format
    void            SetFormat(const NumberFormat &nf);
    // set the cell to the general format
    void            SetToGeneralFormat(TNumberFormatter* tnf);
    // Set the format error status flag.
```

```
void            SetFormatErrorStatus(BOOL errorStatus);

//=====================================================================
// Cell operations

// move the cell to x,y
void            Move(int x = 0, int y = 0, int w = 0, int h = 0);
// set to general format, edit
void            Edit();
// format a cell based on current format
int             Update();

static FARPROC fLpfnOldEditProc, fLpfnNewEditProc;

private:
    HWND                 fHwndEditControl;// enclosed edit control handle
    TFormattableNumber   fNumber;         // enclosed formattable number
    TNumberFormatter*    fFormatter;      // pointer to cell's formatter
    NumberFormat         fMyFormat;       // the NumberFormat for this cell
    BOOL                 fErrorInFormat;  // error status
    BOOL                 fAltered;        // altered status
    static int           fCellNumber;     // unique cell identifier
};
```

On the surface, only a few differences exist between the two versions of our NumberCell class. We'll explore the significance of these differences as we continue analyzing this version of the application.

Note that in the new version of NumberCell we replaced the FormattableNumber data member, fNumber, with a TFormattableNumber from the number formatting framework. We also added a new data member, fFormatter, that contains a pointer to a TNumberFormatter object. Lastly, we moved the NumberFormat data member from the old FormattableNumber class to the new version of NumberCell. The NumberFormat object describes the specific format attributes that the user selects through the Format Number dialog box. It is *not* part of the framework—it exists only to keep track of the user interface settings.

NumberCell also has two new member functions, GetFormat and SetFormat, that provide access to the NumberFormat object.

We'll take a closer look at how these new data members are handled by the NumberCell class. As described in Chapter 5, the application constructs a NumberGrid which then constructs an array of NumberCell objects. In the current version of the application, that remains unchanged, but the new NumberCell constructor has been modified to accommodate its new data members.

```
NumberCell::NumberCell(HINSTANCE hInst, HWND hwndParent, int xPos, int yPos,
                    int width, int height) : fNumber()
{
    fHwndEditControl = CreateWindow("edit", NULL,
                    WS_CHILD | WS_VISIBLE | WS_BORDER | ES_LEFT | ES_AUTOHSCROLL,
                    xPos, yPos, width, height,
                    hwndParent, fCellNumber++,
                    hInst, NULL );

    if (!fLpfnNewEditProc)        // create a single thunk for the new edit proc
      fLpfnNewEditProc = MakeProcInstance((FARPROC) EditWndProc, hInst );

    // subclass the old edit proc
    fLpfnOldEditProc = (FARPROC) GetWindowLong(fHwndEditControl, GWL_WNDPROC);
    SetWindowLong(fHwndEditControl, GWL_WNDPROC, (LONG) fLpfnNewEditProc);

    // store handle to enclosing NumberCell in the edit control property list
    SetProp(fHwndEditControl, (LPSTR) KNUMBERCELLPROP, (HANDLE) this);
    fAltered = FALSE;                  // new cell, has never been altered
    fErrorInFormat = FALSE;           // default format is OK
    fMyFormat = NumberFormat::GetGeneralNumberFormat();// default NumberFormat
    fFormatter = (TNumberFormatter *) NULL;
}
```

The new and old NumberCell constructors are identical, with two small
exceptions that you'll find in the last two statements of the constructor. The
constructor initializes its TNumberFormatter pointer, fFormatter, to NIL. (We'll
get into the initialization of this pointer in the next section, "Using the
framework to handle cell updates.") The new NumberCell constructor also
initializes its NumberFormat data member with default settings using a call to the
static member function NumberFormat::GetGeneralNumberFormat.
GetGeneralNumberFormat returns a copy of a NumberFormat, initialized to the
default (general) settings.

```
NumberFormat NumberFormat::GetGeneralNumberFormat()
{
  NumberFormat nf;
  nf.fPrecision = kDefaultPrecision;
  nf.fThousandsDelimitted = FALSE;
  nf.fCurrency = FALSE;
  nf.fIntSeparator = kCommaChar;
  nf.fDecSeparator = kPeriodChar;
  nf.fCurrencySymbol = kDollarSignChar;
  nf.fFormatType = kFloatingPointFormat;
  return nf;
}
```

This completes the modifications we need to make to the NumberCell
constructor.

Using the framework to handle cell updates

We really gain access to the power of these added framework classes through the Update member function, and it's here that we'll find the greatest number of modifications to our original NumberCell class design.

✅ NOTE   Refer to "Implementing ProcessFocusChange" on page 87 for a detailed discussion of the ProcessFocusChange function. This function is responsible for calling the NumberCell::Update member function.

```
int NumberCell::Update()
{
    char szBuffer[KBUFSIZE],
    char* endPtr;
    double dTemp;
    TText theString;

    if (!fAltered)  // if the cell has not been changed, exit
        return 1;

    // if the cell is empty
    if (!GetWindowText(fHwndEditControl, szBuffer, sizeof(szBuffer)))
    {
        fErrorInFormat = FALSE;// cell empty so, format is OK,
        fAltered = FALSE;// successfully updated, starts fresh/not altered, and
        return 1;
    }
    dTemp = strtod(szBuffer, &endPtr);// attempt conversion
    if (!*endPtr)                     // if endPtr is NULL, conversion was successful
    {
        fNumber.SetNumber(dTemp);// update TFormattableNumber value member
        if (!fFormatter)       // First time cell entry, set the format
            SetFormat(fMyFormat);
        fFormatter->Format(fNumber, theString);  // Create a formatted string

        //set the edit cell to that format
        SetWindowText(fHwndEditControl, (LPSTR) tx.chars());
        fErrorInFormat = FALSE;
        fAltered = FALSE;// successfully updated, starts fresh/not altered.
        return 1;
    }

    // Record that the user has typed-in a bad numeric format
    fErrorInFormat = TRUE;
    // Signal an error
    MessageBeep(0);
    MessageBox(fHwndEditControl, "Invalid Numeric Format",
        "Number Cell Error", MB_ICONEXCLAMATION)4;
    return 0;                              // unsuccessful update
}
```

The Update member function is very similar to the implementation in the first version of this application, described in Chapter 5. The one significant difference is in NumberCell's use of its TNumberFormatter member, fFormatter, approximately midway into the function. In these statements, we first set the NumberCell's TFormattableNumber to the value the user entered into the NumberCell's EditControl. This value is read from the EditControl and converted to a double in the same manner used by the previous version of Update.

Next, Update formats the number, but note the primary difference between this and our previous version of the NumberCell class. In the earlier version, the formatting of the number was carried out by the FormattableNumber object. In the new version, the TFormattableNumber is handed to the TNumberFormatter which then creates a properly formatted text string and stores it in the TText argument. This is accomplished with the statement

```
fFormatter->Format(fNumber, theString); // Create a formatted string
```

where fFormatter is the NumberCell's pointer to its TNumberFormatter, fNumber is the NumberCell's TFormattableNumber, and theString is a local TText object.

Note that before invoking its Format function, the Update member function checks whether fFormatter is NIL. The NumberCell's constructor initializes fFormatter to NIL, and fFormatter remains NIL until the user chooses a specific format using the application's Format Number dialog box. If, however, the Update member function is invoked before the user has explicitly selected a display format, the following statement from the Update member function ensures that the TNumberFormatter is reinitialized to the default, generic display format.

```
if (!fFormatter)    // First time cell entry, set the format
    SetFormat(fMyFormat);
```

The remainder of this version of the Update member function is identical to that described in Chapter 5.

Handling changes to the format of a NumberCell

It may be helpful to examine the SetFormat member function that gets called in the preceding code. SetFormat's primary task is to set various attributes of the TNumberFormatter, based on the settings of the NumberFormat object passed into the function.

```
void NumberCell::SetFormat(const NumberFormat& nf)
{
    // new entry or format has changed
    if (!fFormatter || (fMyFormat.GetFormatType() != nf.GetFormatType()))
    {
        delete fFormatter;

        // create a floating-point formatter
        if (nf.IsCurrency())
            fFormatter =
                TNumberFormatLocale::GetUserLocale().CreateCurrencyFormatter()
        else fFormatter =
                TNumberFormatLocale::GetUserLocale().CreateFloatingPointFormatter();
    }

    // set the precision and thousands delimtter:
    fFormatter->SetIntegerSeparator(nf.IsThousandsDelimitted());

    // set cell to the new format
    fMyFormat = nf;
}
```

FRAMEWORK BENEFITS

We now have a complete, international-friendly application. The framework handles all the details of number formatting, without requiring any significant changes to the application's existing user interface code. Just as importantly, the framework is extensible, which will yield additional benefits in future versions of the application that we might want to implement, including reduced maintenance effort and more end-user features.

Let's examine the effort it took to convert the application to its current form. As it turns out, the text utility classes we used (but didn't have to write) in our framework contained a number of member functions. We've split these classes out of the analysis so that we have a more accurate account of the additional code we had to create for the framework.

	Classes	Member Functions	Lines of Code
Nonframework-based application	4	57	1257
Text utility classes	3	236	2254
Framework-based application	11	389	4724
Framework Delta	**4**	**96**	**1213**

As you can see, we had to write four additional classes and approximately 100 additional member functions. Most of those additional member functions are very short accessor member functions, though, so we had to write only 1213 additional lines of code. Considering how much extra functionality we got and how well the framework positions our application for future enhancement, this is a small amount of code to write. Most of our effort went into designing the framework, not implementing it.

CHAPTER 7

EXTENDING THE FRAMEWORK ON WINDOWS

Now that we have a working version of our framework-based application, it's time to see whether all our framework creation effort has paid off. Let's assume we've been asked to add support for a new display format: displaying rational numbers (that is, fractions). Very few modifications are required to add this feature to the application using our framework, in contrast to the amount of work that would have been necessary to implement this feature using the original, nonframework-based version of the application we created in Chapter 5. This chapter describes the necessary updates, giving you a fairly accurate idea of what is involved in extending the number formatting framework for other uses.

DESIGNING A RATIONAL NUMBER FORMATTER CLASS

We'll spend most of the effort required to update the application developing a new rational number formatting subclass of TNumberFormatter and a simple rational number class it uses. The new subclass, TRationalNumberFormatter, overrides TNumberFormatter's Format member function to format the number as text. The new helper class, TRationalNumber, handles the conversion of TFormattableNumber data into a rationalized form. The class hierarchy for the new classes is as follows:

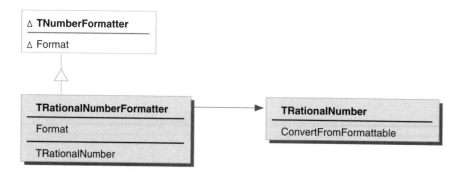

RATIONAL NUMBER FORMATTING CLASS HIERARCHY

Design of TRationalNumberFormatter

As we did when designing TFloatingPointNumberFormatter, we want to make sure the formatting code is as flexible as possible. Thus, we need to ensure that TRationalNumberFormatter lets the caller have a great deal of control over its formatting algorithm. The caller should be able to modify the following properties of the formatter:

- Which string to use as a separator between the numerator and denominator of the fraction
- Which string to use as a separator for the integer part of the rational number (for example, the space after the "3" in "3 2/5")
- Whether to print the rational number as a proper fraction (where the integer part, if any, is printed separately as, for example, in "12 1/4"") or as an improper one (as, for example, in "49/4")
- Whether to print the numerator or denominator first

TRationalNumberFormatter must provide accessors to get and set these parameters.

When TRationalNumberFormatter prints the integer part of the rational number, it should have the same level of localized, user-customizable control over the format as did TFloatingPointNumberFormatter. Rather than duplicate the functionality of that class inside TRationalNumberFormatter, TRationalNumberFormatter has an adopted TNumberFormatter, which it uses to format the integer parts of the rational number.

Finally, TRationalNumberFormatter has to override TNumberFormatter's Format function to actually do the work of using all these parameters to convert a TFormattableNumber into text and return a TFormatResult.

The class definition for our TRationalNumberFormatter class is as follows:

```
class TRationalNumberFormatter : public TNumberFormatter {
public:
    enum EFractionPropriety { kProperFraction, kImproperFraction };
    enum EFractionDirection { kNumeratorFirst, kDenominatorFirst };

    //=====================================================================
    // constructors, destructor, and standard C++ member functions
                TRationalNumberFormatter();
                TRationalNumberFormatter(EFractionPropriety thePropriety,
                    EFractionDirection theFractionDirection = kNumeratorFirst);
                TRationalNumberFormatter(const TRationalNumberFormatter&);
    virtual     ~TRationalNumberFormatter();
    TRationalNumberFormatter& operator=(const TRationalNumberFormatter&);

    //=====================================================================
    // TNumberFormatter overrides
    virtual void    FormattableNumberToText(const TFormattableNumber& num,
                            TText& text, TNumberFormatResult& result);

    //=====================================================================
    // accessors
    virtual void    GetFractionSpace(TText&) const;
    virtual void    SetFractionSpace(const TText&);

    virtual void    GetFractionSign(TText&) const;
    virtual void    SetFractionSign(const TText&);

    virtual EFractionPropriety GetFractionPropriety() const;
    virtual void    SetFractionPropriety(EFractionPropriety);

    virtual EFractionDirection GetFractionDirection() const;
    virtual void    SetFractionDirection(EFractionDirection);

    virtual TNumberFormatter* GetIntegerFormatter() const;
    virtual void    AdoptIntegerFormatter(TNumberFormatter*);

private:
    TText               fFractionSpace;
    TText               fFractionSign;
    EFractionPropriety  fFractionPropriety;
    EFractionDirection  fFractionDirection;
    TRationalNumber     fRationalNumber;
    TNumberFormatter*   fIntegerFormatter;
};
```

**TRationalNumber
helper class**

The design of TRationalNumber is very simple. It represents a rational number
as an integer part, a numerator, and a denominator. The core of this class is the
ConvertFromFormattable member function, which analyzes a
TFormattableNumber and converts it into a fraction. This member function is
called by the TRationalNumberFormatter to handle the mathematical portion of
the formatting operation.

```
class TRationalNumber {
public:
                TRationalNumber(long i = 0, long n = 0, long d = 0);
                TRationalNumber(const TFormattableNumber& fpNum);

    long    GetInteger();
    void    SetInteger(long integerPart);

    long    GetNumerator();
    void    SetNumerator(long numeratorPart);

    long    GetDenominator();
    void    SetDenominator(long denominatorPart);

    void    ConvertFromFormattable(const TFormattableNumber& number);

private:
    long    fInteger;
    long    fNumerator;
    long    fDenominator;
};
```

IMPLEMENTING THE FRAMEWORK SUBCLASSES

Now that we've designed the new subclasses for the framework, we can begin to implement them.

Implementing TRationalNumberFormatter

As a subclass of TNumberFormatter, TRationalNumberFormatter hooks into the framework by overriding the number conversion routines called by TNumberFormatter's Format member function.

Constructors, destructor, standard C++ member functions, and accessors

TRationalNumberFormatter's constructors, destructor, and standard C++ member functions are not shown here, but are fairly straightforward. We've also omitted the data accessor member functions shown earlier in the class declaration. The complete source code of the application is available on the accompanying CD-ROM.

Creating the fractional text

The FormattableNumberToText member function, overridden from TNumberFormatter, converts a TFormattableNumber into a textual representation, using the parameters set by the caller. We can implement this behavior with the following algorithm:

1. Use TRationalNumber::ConvertFromFormattable to separate the number into its integer, numerator, and denominator parts.

2. Use the TNumberFormatter specified in fIntegerFormatter to format the integer part (if any, and only if the user asked for a proper fraction) into the output text, followed by the space string stored in fFractionSpace.

3. Write the numerator and denominator in the order specified by fFractionDirection, separated by the specified fFractionSign string. The numerator and denominator are also formatted using the TNumberFormatter specified in fIntegerFormatter.

The implementation of FormattableNumberToText is as follows:

```
void TRationalNumberFormatter::FormattableNumberToText(
                     const TFormattableNumber& num,
                     TText& text, TNumberFormatResult& result)
{
    TNumberFormatResult tempResult;

    if (!num.IsInfinity() && !num.IsNan())
    {
        fRationalNumber.ConvertFromFormattable(num);

        Boolean doNegative = fRationalNumber.GetInteger() < 0 ||
                        fRationalNumber.GetNumerator() < 0;
        if (fRationalNumber.GetInteger() || !fRationalNumber.GetNumerator())
        {
            TFormattableNumber theformattable;
            theformattable.SetNumber(fRationalNumber.GetInteger());
            GetIntegerFormatter()->Format(theformattable, text, tempResult);
            result.SetCanNormalize(tempResult.GetCanNormalize());
            result.SetOutOfBoundsError(tempResult.GetOutOfBoundsError());
            doNegative = FALSE;
            result.SetIntegerBoundary(text.GetLength());
            if (fRationalNumber.GetNumerator())
            {
                TText fractionSpace;
                GetFractionSpace(fractionSpace);
                text += fractionSpace;
                result.SetCanNormalize(FALSE);
            }
        }
        else result.SetIntegerBoundary(0);

        if (fRationalNumber.GetNumerator())
        {
            result.SetCanNormalize(FALSE);

            if (fRationalNumber.GetNumerator() < 0 && !doNegative)
                fRationalNumber.GetNumerator() = -fRationalNumber.GetNumerator();

            TText numeratorText, denominatorText, fractionText;

            TFormattableNumber theFormattable(fRationalNumber.GetNumerator());
            GetIntegerFormatter()->Format(theFormattable,
                                numeratorText, tempResult);
            if (tempResult.GetOutOfBoundsError())
                result.SetOutOfBoundsError(TRUE);

            theFormattable.SetNumber(fRationalNumber.GetDenominator());
            GetIntegerFormatter()->Format(theFormattable,
                                denominatorText, tempResult);
            if (tempResult.GetOutOfBoundsError())
                result.SetOutOfBoundsError(TRUE);
```

```
                    GetFractionSign(fractionText);
                    if (GetFractionDirection() == TRationalNumberFormatter::kNumeratorFirst)
                    {
                        fractionText.prepend(numeratorText);
                        fractionText += denominatorText;
                    }
                    else
                    {
                        fractionText.prepend(denominatorText);
                        fractionText += numeratorText;
                    }
                    text += fractionText;
                }
                result.SetDigitSequenceEnd(text.GetLength());

                result.SetConfidence(TFormatResult::kPerfect);
            }
        }
```

Implementing TRationalNumber	Based on its design, TRationalNumber's implementation is fairly straightforward. Most of its complexity is in the ConvertFromFormattable function.
	TRationalNumber provides the usual constructors, destructor, and data member accessors. Because these functions are all fairly basic for C++ programmers, their implementations are not shown here.
Calculating the numerator and denominator	ConvertFromFormattable takes a TFormattableNumber as input and separates it into integer, numerator, and denominator by finding the greatest common divisor (GCD) of the numerator and denominator. Getting the GCD of floating-point numbers is difficult, so we need to find a way to generate the numerator and denominator as long integers. We'll do this by first using the standard C library routine frexp to convert the number into a mantissa and an integral power of two. The frexp routine guarantees that the mantissa is in the range

$$0.5 <= |m| < 1.0$$

Now we use the resulting integral exponent to generate integral numerators and denominators. To do so, we'll calculate the numerator by multiplying the mantissa by a power of two, (1 << multiplierBits), that will be just big enough to fill up a long integer.

Next, we need to calculate the denominator using the formula $2^{(multiplierBits-exp)}$, where *exp* is the exponent value returned by frexp. As a result, we get a numerator and denominator with large integral values, returning a numeric value nearly identical to the original floating-point number when the numerator is divided by the denominator.

At this point, we can extract the integer part of the number, if any, leaving a proper fraction. We then reduce the proper fraction by finding any common denominator and removing it. The denominator is calculated by the CalcGCD member function, described in the next section.

The source code for ConvertFromFormattable is as follows:

```
void TRationalNumber::ConvertFromFormattable(const TFormattableNumber& number)
{
    int exp;
    int multiplierBits;
    double theFloat = number.GetNumber();

    // use frexp to convert float to a mantissa (0.5 <= |x| < 1.0)
    // and an integral power of 2
    double m = frexp(theFloat,&exp);

    // now we need to make sure that we can fit the numerator and denominator
    // in a long.
    const kBitsPerByte = 8;
    if (exp >= 0)
    {
        if (exp > (sizeof(long)*kBitsPerByte-2))
          cerr << "illegal exponent value";
        multiplierBits = (sizeof(long)*8-2);
    }
    else {
        multiplierBits = exp+(sizeof(long)*kBitsPerByte-2);
        if (multiplierBits < 0)
          cerr << "illegal value";
    }

    // we make the numerator and denominator as large a multiple as we can
    // while preserving ratio between them. This gives us best accuracy.
    fNumerator = (long) (m * ((long) 1 << multiplierBits));
    fDenominator = (long) 1 << ((long) multiplierBits - (long) exp);

    // if number has integer part, separate it out
    if (fNumerator > fDenominator)
      {
        fInteger = fNumerator/fDenominator;
        fNumerator = fNumerator - (fInteger * fDenominator);
      }
    else fInteger = 0;

    // reduce fraction part
    long d1 = CalcGCD(fNumerator, fDenominator);
    if (d1 != 1)
      {
        fNumerator /= d1;
        fDenominator /= d1;
      }
}
```

Calculating the greatest common denominator

The CalcGCD member function, called by ConvertFromFormattable, is another straightforward function. The algorithm is from the National Institute of Health (NIH) class library.

```
long TRationalNumber::CalcGCD(long uu, long vv)
{
    /* gcd -- binary greatest common divisor algorithm - NIHCL Algorithm B, p. 321.
    */
    long u = labs(uu), v = labs(vv);
    long k = 0;
    long t;

    if (u == 0)
      return v;
    if (v == 0)
      return u;

    // get rid of any common multiples of 2
    while ((u & 1) == 0 && (v & 1) == 0)
      {
        u >>= 1;
        v >>= 1;
        k++;
      }

    if (u & 1)
        { t = -v; goto B4; }
    else t = u;

    do {
B4:     while ((t & 1) == 0) t /= 2;
        if (t > 0) u = t;
        else v = -t;
        t = u-v;
    } while (t != 0);

    return u<<k;
}
```

✅ NOTE   Generally, using goto statements is considered poor programming style. In this case, the benefits of reusing a well-tested, public domain library such as the one shown here far outweigh the design issues involved.

This completes our examination of TRationalNumber.

UPDATING THE APPLICATION

Now that we've implemented the new formatting classes, we'll need to update the spreadsheet application to support it.

Updating NumberCell's SetFormat function

Update is called by the application to reformat a cell. In the previous two versions of the sample, this function calls SetFormat to create a TNumberFormatter whenever one does not already exist or the user has altered the format specification for the cell since the last time the cell was formatted. The new version of SetFormat has been modified to support the rational number format. Notice that the type of number formatter created depends on the cell's display format specification, which for this sample can be either a floating-point (inclusive of currency format) or rational number representation.

```
void NumberCell::SetFormat(const NumberFormat& nf)
{
    if (!fFormatter ||  fMyFormat.GetFormatType() != nf.GetFormatType())
    {
        // format type has changed, delete the old formatter
        delete fFormatter;
        if ( nf.GetFormatType() == NumberFormat::kFloatingPointFormat )
        {
            // create a floating-point formatter
            if (nf.IsCurrency())
                fFormatter =
                    TNumberFormatLocale::GetUserLocale().CreateCurrencyFormatter()
            else fFormatter =
                    TNumberFormatLocale::GetUserLocale().CreateFloatingPointFormatter();
        }
        else fFormatter = new TRationalNumberFormatter();

        // set cell to the new format
        fMyFormat = nf;
    }
}
```

✅ NOTE   The implementation of this function illustrates a weakness in the framework's current design. The hardcoded if statements determine the kind of TNumberFormatter subclass we create. A more extensible approach would allow new types of formats to be added dynamically, perhaps by using a dictionary to map between the format types returned by the TNumberFormat object and the corresponding TNumberFormatter object.

Updating the Format Cell dialog box

The modifications needed to add an additional format choice to the Format Cell dialog box are minor. The WndProc function contains two switch statements. The "case IDM_NUMBERCELL:" within the innermost switch is responsible for displaying the Format Cell dialog box using a call to the NumberFormatDlgProc function. An excerpt of the WndProc code is as follows:

```
case IDM_NUMBERCELL:
    // if the cell does not contain a valid numeric string
    // ... Refer to previous chapter for details ...

    // valid numeric format
    // display the format number cell dialog
    lpfnNumberFormatDlgProc =
        (DLGPROC) MakeProcInstance((FARPROC) NumberFormatDlgProc, hInst);
    DialogBox(hInst, MAKEINTRESOURCE(DIALOG_1), hwnd,
        lpfnNumberFormatDlgProc);
    FreeProcInstance(lpfnNumberFormatDlgProc);
    return 0;
```

To include the new rational number format choice in the dialog box, we need to add another line to the function responsible for initializing the dialog box. This function, InitializeAndCenterDialog, is invoked as a direct result of the DialogBox function call in the preceding case statement. Each of the various SendDlgItemMessage function calls results in the display of one format choice.

```
void InitializeAndCenterDialog( HWND hDlg )
{
    HWND hwndOwner;
    RECT rc, rcDlg, rcOwner;

    // Set up initial dialog format listbox entries
    SendDlgItemMessage(hDlg, IDC_LISTBOX1, WM_SETREDRAW, FALSE, 0L);
    SendDlgItemMessage(hDlg, IDC_LISTBOX1, LB_ADDSTRING, 0,
                        (DWORD)(LPSTR) "####");
    SendDlgItemMessage(hDlg, IDC_LISTBOX1, LB_ADDSTRING, 0,
                        (DWORD)(LPSTR) "#,###");
    SendDlgItemMessage(hDlg, IDC_LISTBOX1, LB_ADDSTRING, 0,
                        (DWORD)(LPSTR) "####.#");
    // ... Five other format choices here ...
    // ... Our newly added rational number format choice follows ...
    SendDlgItemMessage(hDlg, IDC_LISTBOX1, LB_ADDSTRING, 0,
                        (DWORD)(LPSTR) "### ###/###");
    SendDlgItemMessage( hDlg, IDC_LISTBOX1, WM_SETREDRAW, TRUE, 0L );

    // Center the dialog box
    // ...
}
```

Using extensibility to deliver features faster

These are all of the modifications to the application required to support our new rational number formatter. The application has added support for a new feature, with no modifications to the framework and very few modifications to the user interface code. A typical engineer could develop this feature in a relatively short amount of time.

Adding this feature to the original version of the application developed in Chapter 5 would have been much more difficult and time-consuming. Clearly, using a well-designed framework has a direct benefit as programs are enhanced over time.

APPLYING FRAMEWORKS ON OS/2

CHAPTER 8

CREATING THE APPLICATION FOR OS/2

In Chapter 4, we created a specification for the initial version of the application. In this chapter, we convert that specification into a functioning piece of code.

The application, like most OS/2 applications, begins with a main function and a window message handler. Because the Presentation Manager directly calls these functions, and OS/2 does not support the use of C++ member functions as handlers, these routines are written as standard C functions. To take advantage of the C++ object-oriented features, we'll use these global functions as a liaison between the Presentation Manager API and the application's classes. Thus, the application can be roughly divided into two parts: a Presentation Manager application layer, and a set of classes that allows the user to see and edit the spreadsheet data.

DESIGNING THE PRESENTATION MANAGER APPLICATION LAYER

We'll begin by designing the Presentation Manager application layer, which provides two key pieces of functionality: a main function and a window message handler.

Initializing the application

The primary function of the application, main, is responsibility for initializing the application. The main function must create the window and handle message dispatching.

Presentation Manager message dispatcher

WindowSA1WndProc is called when a message is sent to the application's window. WindowSA1WndProc's function is to dispatch these messages to the appropriate piece of code within the application. As the primary dispatch function, WindowSA1WndProc acts as the interface between the application layer and the spreadsheet classes that manipulate the application's data.

Other functions

The application layer also includes functions needed by other parts of the program, such as a message handler routine for the Format Cell dialog box. We'll discuss the design and implementation of these functions as they are needed by other parts of the application.

DESIGNING THE SPREADSHEET CLASSES

The spreadsheet classes are divided into two distinct sets. The first set provides the user interface for our application and handles the messages that WindowSA1WndProc delegates to them. The second set is responsible for converting numbers into text.

User interface objects

Because the spreadsheet's user interface models a grid of cells, the first class to create is a NumberGrid. NumberGrid maintains a list of cells and keeps track of the currently selected cell for the user.

We also need to create a class, NumberCell, that represents a single cell. NumberCell manages the editing and display of the cell's contents.

Number formatting objects

Next, we need to create a class to handle the formatting process. Because our design goal is to separate data representation from the user interface as much as possible, we'll make a class, FormattableNumber, that represents a number that knows how to format itself as text, but that doesn't perform any display or editing operations.

Many variables affect the formatting process. To allow these variables to be manipulated as a set, we create a NumberFormat class that keeps track of the number format. FormattableNumber uses a NumberFormat object to perform the formatting operation.

The class hierarchy of the spreadsheet classes appears in the following figure.

✅ NOTE   The notation used for the class hierarchy diagrams appearing in this book is described in "Appendix A: Reading notation diagrams."

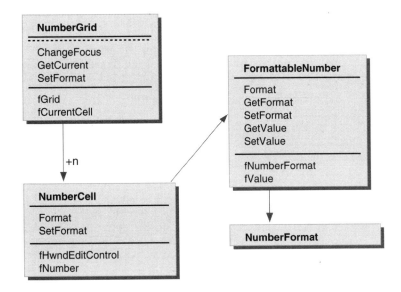

SPREADSHEET CLASS HIERARCHY

**NumberGrid
class design**

The NumberGrid object must create and maintain a two-dimensional array of pointers to NumberCells. The number of rows and columns of cells a grid should contain is specified when a grid is constructed. The NumberGrid constructor allocates, via operator new, the m-row by n-column array of NumberCell pointers. Next, the constructor allocates the actual NumberCells and stores pointers to those NumberCells in the two-dimensional array. Whenever the grid needs to access a particular cell, it uses standard array indexing syntax to retrieve a NumberCell. From this discussion, the NumberGrid appears to be a simple class.

Data members

NumberGrid provides three sets of member functions:

- Standard C++ member functions, including the constructor and destructor
- Cell editing functions, which handle basic user interface operations
- Data accessor functions, which allow you to manipulate the state of the NumberGrid

Let's look at the declarations of each of these sets of functions.

**Standard C++
Member Functions**

The class declaration begins with the constructor and destructor. The NumberGrid constructor takes the arguments needed to create the spreadsheet grid, including the number of rows, number of columns, and the column width (in characters) of each cell.

```
class NumberGrid {
public:
    //-------------------------------------------------------------------------
    // Standard C++ member functions

    // constructor and destructor
        NumberGrid(HINSTANCE hInst, HWND hwnd , int xPos = 0, int yPos = 0,
                int rows = 0, int cols = 0, int nCharsPerCell = 0);
    virtual ~NumberGrid();
```

Editing member functions

The most important member functions in NumberGrid handle our user interface functions. These functions are typically called by the application's user interface code.

```
// Format current cell according to a format code set by the user
// from the main menu
virtual void        FormatCurrentCell(int nFormatCode);

// Re-format a cell in the grid according to its current user-specified format.
virtual int         UpdateCell(int nCellNo);

// Change the focus to cell number nCellNo.
virtual int         ChangeFocus(int nCellNo);

// Does nCellNo contain a valid numeric string?
virtual BOOL        IsValidEntry(int nCellNo);

// Move the upper-left corner of the grid to a new x,y position
virtual void        Move(int x = 0, int y = 0);

// Center the grid in the client area.
virtual void        Center(HWND hwnd);
```

Accessor member functions

The remaining member functions provide access to the state of the cell grid. Convenience member functions are provided to make it easier to perform common operations on the current cell. These functions are usually called by the framework itself, rather than by clients.

```
// access the currently selected cell's id
virtual int         GetCurrentCell();
virtual int         SetCurrentCell(int nCurrent);

// set the format of the specified cell
virtual int         SetFormat(int nCellNo, const NumberFormat& nf);

// Get the Windows edit handle to nCellNo.
virtual HWND        GetHandle(int nCellNo);

// Get the edit contol's enclosing NumberCell.
virtual NumberCell* GetCell(int nCellNo);
```

Data members

The class declaration concludes with the class's private data member declarations. Of these data members, the two worth noting are fGrid, which is a pointer to our array of cells, and fCurrentCell, which keeps track of the current cell.

```
private:
    NumberCell***   fGrid;          // Pointer to the 2D grid of NumberCells.
    int             fNRows, fNCols; // Number of rows, cols in grid.
    int             fTop, fLeft;    // Position of top, left corner of grid
    int             fCellWidth, fCellHeight;
    int             fCurrentCell;   // The cell index of the current cell
};
```

**NumberCell
class design**

The NumberCell class is more complicated than NumberGrid. A NumberCell serves as a kind of pivot-point: it associates a C++ object (a cell) with a critical Presentation Manager user interface element, and it shuttles the raw and formatted user input data between this Presentation Manager user interface element and the C++ class responsible for formatting.

What is the "critical Presentation Manager user interface element"? For the application to display a NumberCell, the cell must encapsulate some user interface element that the Presentation Manager understands. Presentation Manager knows nothing about the NumberCell object. Because we expect the user to select a cell (using the mouse) and enter a number (using the keyboard), it seems logical to have the NumberCell class be a "wrapper" for a Presentation Manager edit control. (An edit control is a text-entry user interface element with built-in, simple editing functions such as select, append, insert, and delete.)

For reasons that will become apparent, we also need to design a two-way communication path between NumberCell and its encapsulated edit control. It's easy to see how a NumberCell could access its edit control: we make the edit control a data member of the NumberCell. But how does a Presentation Manager edit control access its NumberCell? That's more complex. We'll discuss that when we implement the NumberCell class in "Implementing NumberCell" on page 171.

NumberCell is also pivotal in its role of shuttling raw and formatted user input values between the edit control and the class that's actually responsible for formatting, but we have not yet described that formatting class. In Chapter 4, you saw how the user of the application specifies a display format for a particular spreadsheet cell by first selecting the cell (actually, the cell's edit control), then choosing a format from the Format Cell dialog box. Although, from the user's perspective, it appears that the chosen format is applied directly to the cell, we opted to less closely couple the NumberCell and its display format, which is stored in a FormattableNumber.

Designing some distance between the cell and its format creates a buffer of independence, which improves the potential for reuse. This makes each of the two classes, NumberCell and FormattableNumber, more reusable because it separates the cell's functions for handling actions such as keyboard input and display updating from the functions responsible for formatting the cell input value.

Standard member functions

As usual, the class declaration begins with the constructor and destructor. The hInst and hwndParent parameters are passed to the constructor by the NumberGrid object when it creates the grid of cells.

```
class NumberCell
{
public:
                    NumberCell(HINSTANCE hInst, HWND hwndParent,
                            int xPos = 0, int yPos = 0,
                            int width = 0, int height = 0);
        virtual     ~NumberCell();
```

Editing member functions

To support editing operations, NumberCell provides member functions to move the cell, update the cell's value based on the EditControl text, and redraw the cell's text.

```
// Move the cell to x,y with width w and height h
void            Move(int x = 0, int y = 0, int w = 0, int h = 0);
// Set the cell format to the edit format.
void            Edit();
// Reformat the cell based on its new format.
int             Update();
```

Accessor member functions

NumberCell also provides a number of accessor member functions to access the state of the cell.

```
void            SetFormat(const NumberFormat &nf);

HWND            GetEditHandle();
WORD            GetID();

BOOL            GetFormatErrorStatus();
void            SetFormatErrorStatus(BOOL errorStatus);

BOOL            HasBeenAltered();
BOOL            SetAlteredStatus(BOOL newStatus);
```

Data members

Lastly, NumberCell declares its private data members, including a handle to its EditControl, the FormattableNumber, and a dirty flag.

NumberCell also declares several static data members. It keeps track of the last cell ID number used in the static data member fCellNumber, ensuring that each edit control object has a unique ID. NumberCell also tracks the edit control's overridden and original message handler to help implement the application's customized edit control.

```
private:
    HWND                fHwndEditControl;    // Handle to the enclosed edit control.
    FormattableNumber   fNumber;             // Formattable number enclosed in the cell.
    BOOL                fErrorInFormat;      // Error status flag.
    BOOL                fAltered;            // Altered status flag.

    static int          fCellNumber;         // last cell id used
    static PFNWP        fLpfnOldEditProc;
};
```

FormattableNumber class design

FormattableNumber translates a number into formatted text. Its key member function is Format, which does the actual work of converting the FormattableNumber object's current value and format options into a text string. FormattableNumber also provides functions to access the format options and the value.

```
class FormattableNumber {
public:
    // Standard member functions
                    FormattableNumber(double d = 0.0);
                    FormattableNumber(double d, const NumberFormat& nf);
    virtual         ~FormattableNumber() {};

    virtual FormattableNumber&
                    operator=(const FormattableNumber &fn);
    virtual FormattableNumber&
                    operator=(double v);

    // Formatting member function
    virtual void    Format(char* fresult);

    // Accessor member functions
    virtual double  GetValue();
    virtual void    SetValue(double d) const;

    virtual const NumberFormat&
                    GetFormat();
    virtual void    SetFormat(const NumberFormat& nf) const;
private:
    double          fValue;     // Value part.
    NumberFormat    fFormat;    // Current format.
};
```

✅ NOTE   This version of the application is not fully usable in countries other than the U.S., because in the GetGeneralNumberFormat function, it hard-codes the values of the currency, decimal, and thousands separator characters to correspond to those used in the U.S. As we'll discuss in Chapter 9, correcting this deficiency is a major framework design task for the next version of this application.

NumberFormat class design

The design of NumberFormat is straightforward. It provides accessors to allow the caller to get and set the values of its various formatting data members. It also provides a static member function GetGeneralNumberFormat that you can use to set a NumberFormat to the defaults for the current locale.

```
class NumberFormat {
public:
    // Standard C++ member functions
            NumberFormat(int prec = KDEFAULTPRECISION,
                         BOOL delimtd = TRUE, BOOL curncy = FALSE,
                         char intSep = ',', char decSep = KPERIOD,
                         char curncySym = KDOLLARSIGN);
            NumberFormat(const NumberFormat &nf);
            NumberFormat& operator=(const NumberFormat& nf);
            ~NumberFormat()  { };

    // Accessor member functions
    void    Set(int prec = KZEROPRECISION,
                BOOL delimtd = FALSE, BOOL curncy = FALSE,
                char intSep = KCOMMA, char decSep = KPERIOD,
                char curncySym = KDOLLARSIGN);

    int     GetPrecision() const;

    BOOL    IsThousandsDelimitted() const;
    BOOL    IsCurrency() const;

    char    GetIntSeparator() const;
    char    GetDecSeparator() const;
    char    GetCurrencySymbol() const;

    // utility member function: creates a basic number format
    static NumberFormat
            GetGeneralNumberFormat();

private:
    int     fPrecision;
    BOOL    fThousandsDelimitted;
    BOOL    fCurrency;
    char    fIntSeparator;
    char    fDecSeparator;
    char    fCurrencySymbol;
};
```

IMPLEMENTING THE PRESENTATION MANAGER INTERFACE

Now that the basic application design is in place, we can implement the application. We'll begin with the Presentation Manager interface code.

As with all standard C programs for Presentation Manager, main is the initial entry point for the first sample program. The main function does very little before it drops into a message dispatch loop that is responsible for retrieving and dispatching messages directed at the application. Among other messages, the message loop receives notification of keyboard and mouse events and directs them to the appropriate window procedure (event handler code) where the events are processed.

A style often used in Presentation Manager programming appends WndProc as a suffix to a string identifying a pseudo class name for windows whose events are handled by this window procedure. For example, the window procedure used in our application (named "Sample 1") is called WindowSA1WndProc. Window procedures are often referred to as callback procedures, because they are called by system code, rather than called directly from user code.

Implementing main

The main function, the initial entry point for our spreadsheet application, performs the following actions:

1 Registers window classes.

2 Creates the window.

3 Enters message dispatch loop.

4 Closes the window and cleans up when the application is asked to quit.

The source code for main is as follows:

```
int main (int argc, CHAR *argv)
{
  QMSG qMsg;                    /* MSG structure to store messages */
  PID  idProcess;
  TID  idThread;
  CHAR szWindowSA1Title[30];

hAB = WinInitialize(0);
if (hAB == NULLHANDLE)
    return (-3);
  hMQ = WinCreateMsgQueue(hAB, 0);
  if (hMQ == NULLHANDLE)
    return (-4);

  /* Load program name string */
  WinLoadString (hAB, hModFRAMEWRK, IDS_APP_NAME,
                 sizeof(szAppName), szAppName);

/* Step 1. Register window classes  */
  if (cwRegisterClasses() == false)
    return (-5);

/* Display welcome dialog */
  if ( !WinDlgBox (HWND_DESKTOP, HWND_DESKTOP,   (PFNWP)PanelWELCOMEDlgProc,
                 NULLHANDLE,  ID_PANELWELCOME, (PVOID)(&hWndDeskTop)) )
  {
    DosExit (EXIT_THREAD, 1);
  }

/* Load window title string */
  WinLoadString (hAB, hModFRAMEWRK, IDS_WINDOWSA1_TITLE,
                 sizeof(szWindowSA1Title), szWindowSA1Title);

/* Step 2. Create the window */
  hWndWindowSA1 = cwCreateWindow (HWND_DESKTOP,
                                  HWND_DESKTOP,
                                  (PVOID) &hWndDeskTop,
                                  szAppName,
                                  szWindowSA1Title,
                                  FCF_TITLEBAR    |
                                  FCF_SYSMENU     |
                                  FCF_MINBUTTON   |
                                  FCF_MAXBUTTON   |
                                  FCF_SIZEBORDER  |
                                  FCF_MENU        |
                                  FCF_ICON        |
                                  FCF_SHELLPOSITION,
                                  0L,
                                  0, 0,
                                  0, 0,
                                  ID_WINDOWSA1,
                                  SWP_SHOW );
    if (hWndWindowSA1 == NULLHANDLE)
      return (false);
```

```
/* Add application to Task Manager List */
WinQueryWindowProcess (hWndMain, &idProcess, &idThread);
Swctl.hwnd          = hWndMain;
Swctl.idProcess     = idProcess;
Swctl.uchVisibility = SWL_VISIBLE;
Swctl.fbJump        = SWL_JUMPABLE;
strcpy(Swctl.szSwtitle, szWindowSA1Title);
hSwitch = WinAddSwitchEntry(&Swctl);

/* Step 3. Enter message dispatch loop */
while (WinGetMsg(hAB, &qMsg, 0, 0, 0))
  WinDispatchMsg(hAB, &qMsg);

/* Step 4. Close window, clean up memory */
if (hWndFRAMEWRKHelp != NULLHANDLE)
{
  WinDestroyHelpInstance(hWndFRAMEWRKHelp);
  hWndFRAMEWRKHelp = NULLHANDLE;
}

WinDestroyWindow(hWndMain);
hWndWindowSA1 = NULLHANDLE;
WinDestroyMsgQueue(hMQ);
WinTerminate(hAB);
return (0);
}
```

Implementing cwCreateWindow

The main function creates the application window by calling the cwCreateWindow utility function. The cwCreateWindow function creates a window and sets its initial size and position. A simplified outline of cwCreateWindow follows. Code not critical to understanding the basic purpose of cwCreateWindow has been omitted. The full source code appears in SAMPLE1.CPP.

```
HWND cwCreateWindow (
     HWND   hWndParent,    /* Handle to parent of the window to be created */
     HWND   hWndOwner,     /* Handle to owner  of the window to be created */
     PVOID  pWindowData,   /* Pointer to window data                       */
     PSZ    szClassName,   /* Class name of the window                     */
     PSZ    szTitle,       /* Title of the window                          */
     ULONG  FrameFlags,    /* Frame control flags for the window           */
     ULONG  flStyle,       /* Frame window style                           */
     INT    x,             /* Initial horizontal and vertical location     */
     INT    y,
     INT    cx,            /* Initial width and height of the window        */
     INT    cy,
     USHORT ResID,         /* Resource id value                            */
     USHORT uSizeStyle)    /* User defined size and location flags         */
```

```
{
  HPS         hPS;              /* handle to a presentation space       */
  SWP         swp;
  HWND        hWndFrame;        /* Frame window handle                  */
  HWND        hWndClient;       /* Client window handle                 */
  USHORT      rc;               /* accepts return codes from function calls */
  USHORT      SizeStyle;        /* local window positioning options     */
  FRAMECDATA  CtlData;          /* Frame-control data                   */
  FONTMETRICS FontMetrics;      /* Font metrics data                    */
  float       Xmod, Ymod;

  //... Local variables initilized (code omitted)
  hWndFrame = WinCreateStdWindow(HWND_DESKTOP,
                                 WS_VISIBLE,
                                 (PULONG) &(CtlData.flCreateFlags),
                                 (PSZ)szClassName,
                                 (PSZ)szTitle,
                                 WS_VISIBLE,
                                 (HMODULE)NULL,
                                 ResID,
                                 &hWndClient);
  if (hWndFrame == NULLHANDLE) { ErrorBox(); return (NULLHANDLE); }
  if (hWndClient == NULLHANDLE) { ErrorBox(); return (NULLHANDLE); }

  // ... Set size options (code omitted)
  rc = WinSetWindowPos (hWndFrame, HWND_TOP,
                        (SHORT)(x  * Xmod),
                        (SHORT)(y  * Ymod),
                        (SHORT)(cx * Xmod),
                        (SHORT)(cy * Ymod),
                        SizeStyle);
  if (rc != true)
  {
    // ... Display error message (code omitted)
    return (NULLHANDLE);
  }
  // return handle of newly created window
  return (hWndFrame);
}
```

**Implementing
WindowSA1WndProc**

WindowSA1WndProc is the core of the spreadsheet application. It handles several different types of messages, including window manipulation messages, menu commands, and some special number formatting messages generated by the application.

**Window manipulation
messages**

If you are familiar with Presentation Manager programming, you can easily separate the case clauses used in typical applications from those inserted specifically for our spreadsheet application. The following event cases are handled by typical Presentation Manager programs.

```
switch (Message) {
    // ...
    case WM_CONTROL:
    case WM_CREATE:
    case WM_SIZE:
    case WM_COMMAND:
        switch (SHORT1FROMMP(Param1)) {
            // ... Handle menu selections
        }
    case WM_PAINT:
    case WM_CLOSE:
    // ...
}
```

Generally, WindowSA1WndProc handles these messages by calling the appropriate routines from the Presentation Manager API.

**Application-specific
message handlers**

The following event cases are specific to our spreadsheet application.

```
switch (Message) {
    // ...
    case WM_FORMATCELL:
    case WM_FORMATERROR:
    case WM_COMMAND:
        switch (SHORT1FROMMP(Param1)) {
            case IDM_WINDOWSA1_FORMAT_CELL:
            case IDM_HELP_USINGHELP:
            case IDM_HELP_PRODINFO:
        }
    // ...
}
```

The outline of application-specific event handler code is critical to analyzing the behavior of user-defined windows. Looking at the code inside these case clauses and dissecting functions called by this code reveals the essential features of the spreadsheet example.

For now, if you ignore the code designed to handle user requests for help, you can narrow the preceding outline to three case clauses that require further analysis.

```
case WM_FORMATCELL:
case WM_FORMATERROR:
case WM_COMMAND:
    switch (SHORT1FROMMP(Param1)) {
        case IDM_WINDOWSA1_FORMAT_CELL:
    }
```

Menu command messages

The responses to menu items are processed by the WM_COMMAND message, which is sent so that a control can notify its owner (the application window) about a particular event. The Param1 argument to WindowSA1WndProc contains the ID of the window or control sending the command message.

```
case WM_COMMAND:
{
    switch (SHORT1FROMMP(Param1))
    {
        case IDM_WINDOWSA1_FORMAT_CELL:
        {
            HWND hWndPanel = NULLHANDLE;
            if ( ! theGrid.IsValidEntry( theGrid.GetCurrent() ) )
            {
                        // ... Error-handling code omitted.
                        // Set the error status to true for the
                        // currently selected NumberCell.  Open
                        // error dialog to warn user.
                    break;  // Return without opening Format Cell dialog.
            }
            // Create the dialog box named "PanelCELLFORM"
            hWndPanel = WinLoadDlg (HWND_DESKTOP,         // Parent
                                    hWndMain,            // Owner
                                    PanelCELLFORMDlgProc, // Message Proc
                                    hModFRAMEWRK,
                                    ID_PANELCELLFORM,     // Resource ID
                                    (PVOID) &hWnd);       // hWndCaller
            if (hWndPanel != NULLHANDLE)
            {
              USHORT rc;
              rc = WinProcessDlg (hWndPanel); // Call the modal dialog
            }
        }
        break;
        // ...
    }                       // end switch on Param1
}                           // end case WM_COMMAND
```

Essentially, this code creates and invokes a dialog box similar to the one shown in the following figure.

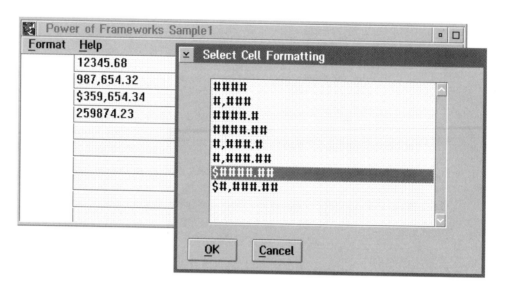

FORMAT CELL DIALOG BOX

The call to WinLoadDlg creates a new window object, which is a dialog box. The message-handling window procedure for this window is PanelCELLFORMDlgProc, specified as the third argument. The dialog box is not actually opened until WinProcessDlg is called. The message-handling code within PanelCELLFORMDlgProc is explained in "Handling cell formatting" on page 164.

Application-defined formatting messages

At certain points in the execution of the application, it can be difficult to update the user interface directly by calling application routines. Presentation Manager programs allow applications to create and send their own custom message types to tell the user interface to perform special actions. You use this technique in the program in two ways:

- WM_FORMATCELL messages are generated by the Format Cell dialog box when the user clicks the OK button or double-clicks a format in the dialog box's scrolling list. The dialog box message handler sends this message back to the application to tell the main program to update the cell's format.

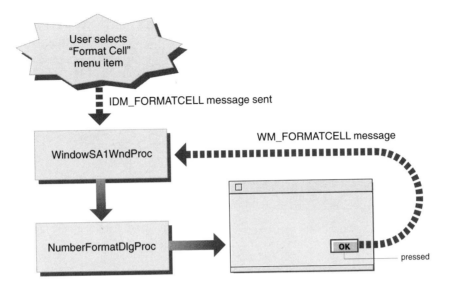

FORMAT CELL COMMAND PROCESSING

- WM_FORMATERROR messages are generated during focus-change operations if the user entered an illegal number. When this message is processed, it forces the focus to return to the cell containing the error, allowing the user to correct the error.

The code for WindowSA1WndProc, which handles the WM_FORMATCELL and WM_FORMATERROR messages, is as follows:

```
switch (Message) {
    // ...
    case WM_FORMATCELL:        // Sent in response to choosing
    {                          // OK in Format Cell dialog.
                               // Reformat and display the cell text
                               // using the new format.
        theGrid.FormatCell((int)Param2);
    }
    break;
    case WM_FORMATERROR:    // Format error, reset
    {                       // focus to cell with error.
        WinSetFocus(HWND_DESKTOP,  (HWND)Param2);
        // ...
    }
    break;
    // ...
}
```

Handling cell formatting

When WindowSA1WndProc receives an IDM_WINDOWSA1_FORMAT_CELL message, it handles the message by displaying the Format Cell dialog box. This dialog box, like most Presentation Manager dialog boxes, has a custom message handler. In this case, the message handler is PanelCELLFORMDlgProc. The portion of WindowSA1WndProc responsible for the IDM_WINDOWSA1_FORMAT_CELL message is as follows:

```
case IDM_WINDOWSA1_FORMAT_CELL:
{
    HWND hWndPanel = NULLHANDLE;
    hWndPanel = WinLoadDlg (HWND_DESKTOP,          // Parent
                            hWndMain,              // Owner
                            PanelCELLFORMDlgProc,  // Message Proc
                            hModFRAMEWRK,
                            ID_PANELCELLFORM,      // Resource ID
                            (PVOID) &hWnd);        // hWndCaller
    USHORT rc = WinProcessDlg (hWndPanel);  // Call the modal dialog
}
```

The message-handling procedure for this dialog box is the third argument to WinLoadDlg. A dialog box is a window just like an application window. Therefore, a dialog box has a message-handling window procedure as do other Presentation Manager controls. The control-flow structure of PanelCELLFORMDlgProc is similar to WindowSA1WndProc.

```
MRESULT EXPENTRY PanelCELLFORMDlgProc (HWND    hWnd,
                                       ULONG   Message,
                                       MPARAM  Param1,
                                       MPARAM  Param2)
{
    switch (Message) {
        case WM_INITDLG:
        case WM_CONTROL:
        case WM_COMMAND: {
            switch (SHORT1FROMMP(Param1)) {    // Push button id
                case IDOK:                     // Push button "~OK"
                    case IDCANCEL:             // Push button "~Cancel"
                }
            }
            case WM_CLOSE:
            default:
        }
        return ((MRESULT) false);
}
```

WM_INITDLG is invoked when the dialog box is first initialized. In addition to handling menu commands, WM_COMMAND responds to push button events such as when the user clicks the OK or Cancel button. WM_INITDLG sets up dialog box controls: it adds appropriate format strings to the list box control inside the Format Cell dialog box.

```
case WM_INITDLG:
{
    char *formats[] = { "####", "#,###", "####.#", "####.##", "#,###.#",
                        "#,###.##", "$####.##", "$#,###.##" };
    int  i;
    if (hWndFRAMEWRKHelp != NULLHANDLE)
        WinAssociateHelpInstance (hWndFRAMEWRKHelp, hWnd);
    for (i = 0; i < 8 ; ++i)
        nSel = WinInsertLboxItem( hwndListbox, LIT_END, formats[i] );
    WinSendMsg( hwndListbox, LM_SELECTITEM, (MPARAM)0, (MPARAM)true );
    cwCenter (hWnd, WinQueryWindow (hWnd, QW_OWNER));
}
break;
```

Eight format strings are added as specified in the formats array. After the strings
are added to the list box control, the first list box item is selected. Finally, the
dialog box is centered.

The controls used and the text displayed in the dialog box are specified in the
resource file for this application. The following code is found in SAMPLE1.RC.

```
DLGTEMPLATE ID_PANELCELLFORM LOADONCALL MOVEABLE DISCARDABLE
BEGIN
   DIALOG "Select Cell Formatting", ID_PANELCELLFORM, 77, 31, 235, 116,
            WS_VISIBLE | WS_CLIPSIBLINGS | WS_SAVEBITS | FS_DLGBORDER,
            FCF_TITLEBAR | FCF_SYSMENU
      BEGIN
        LISTBOX lbCELLFORMAT, 25, 26, 180, 80, WS_VISIBLE | WS_TABSTOP
        PUSHBUTTON "~OK", IDOK, 7, 4, 40, 14, WS_VISIBLE | WS_TABSTOP
        PUSHBUTTON "~Cancel", IDCANCEL, 57, 4, 40, 14, WS_VISIBLE | WS_TABSTOP
      END
END
```

The most important part of PanelCELLFORMDlgProc is the WM_COMMAND
clause, especially the code invoked when the user clicks the OK button after
selecting a format string.

```
// ...
static int nSel;
// ...
case WM_COMMAND: {
    switch (SHORT1FROMMP(Param1)) {
        case IDOK:
        {
            nSel = WinQueryLboxSelectedItem( hwndListbox );
            WinSendMsg(WinQueryWindow (hWnd, QW_OWNER),
                    WM_FORMATCELL, (MPARAM)0, (MPARAM)nSel);
            WinDismissDlg (hWnd, true);
            return ((MRESULT) false);
        }
    }
}
```

The index of the selected string is saved in nSel. Next, a user-defined message, WM_FORMATCELL, is sent to the window that owns the Format Cell dialog box. The WM_FORMATCELL message is sent back to sample1's main message loop, where it is dispatched to the application's window procedure, WindowSA1WndProc. How WindowSA1WndProc handles this message is described later. First, consider what happens if the user cancels the dialog box.

If the user clicks Cancel instead of OK, the dialog box is dismissed without sending any notification message to its owner, the main application window.

```
case WM_COMMAND: {
    switch (SHORT1FROMMP(Param1)) {
        case IDCANCEL:
        {
            WinDismissDlg (hWnd, false);
            return ((MRESULT) false);
        }
    }
}
```

Similarly, a close event (possibly generated by the dialog's system menu, if it has one) shuts the dialog box without taking action.

```
case WM_CLOSE:
{
    WinDismissDlg (hWnd, false);
    break;
}
```

Any unrecognized events are handled by the default case clause.

```
default:
{
    DefResult = WinDefDlgProc (hWnd, Message, Param1, Param2);
    return (DefResult);
}
```

When the user chooses a format string for the currently selected NumberCell and clicks OK, the dialog box sends the following notification message to the main application window:

```
WinSendMsg(
    WinQueryWindow (hWnd, QW_OWNER), // arg 1, window handle of owner
    WM_FORMATCELL,          // arg 2, message identifier
    (MPARAM)0,              // arg 3, extra message parameter (ignored)
    (MPARAM)nSel);          // arg 4, index of selected item in list box
```

This message is put in the message queue for the main application (determined by the call to WinQueryWindow). When the message is removed from the queue by the application's message dispatch loop, it is directed to the application's window procedure, WindowSA1WndProc. Eventually the message is caught by the WM_FORMATCELL case in the Message switch of the application's window procedure.

The application's handler code for the WM_FORMATCELL message looks like:

```
MRESULT EXPENTRY WindowSA1WndProc (HWND    hWnd,
                                   ULONG   Message,
                                   MPARAM Param1,
                                   MPARAM Param2)
{
  //...
  switch (Message)
  {
    //...
    case WM_FORMATCELL:    // sent by Format Cell dialog
    {
          // Reformat the current NumberCell.
          // Display text using the selected format.
          theGrid.FormatCell((int)Param2);
    }
    //...
  }
}
```

The variable theGrid is an instance of NumberGrid declared as a static variable inside the window procedure.

```
static NumberGrid theGrid(hInst, hWnd,
                          0, 0, KNROWS, KNCOLS,
                          KNCHARSPERCELL);
```

This code creates and initializes the 2-by-10 grid of NumberCells used by the applications. Because theGrid is accessed only by event handler code inside the window procedure (WindowSA1WndProc), it is declared as a local variable. Declaring theGrid as static assures that it is initialized only once rather than on each call to WindowSA1WndProc.

The call

```
theGrid.FormatCell((int)Param2);
```

in WindowSA1WndProc takes the second parameter of the WM_FORMATCELL
message (the index of the selected number format string) and invokes
NumberGrid::FormatCell. FormatCell creates a new NumberFormat object and
sets the parameters of the grid's currently selected NumberCell from the format
code passed as an argument.

```
void NumberGrid::FormatCell( int nFormatCode )
{
  NumberFormat nf;
  // ...
  // set parameters of nf based on nFormatCode
  // set format of current NumberCell to nf
  // edit and update display of current NumberCell
}
```

The details of the constructor for theGrid (NumberGrid::NumberGrid) are
covered in "Implementing NumberGrid" on page 169. The full source code for
NumberGrid::FormatCell also appears in "Formatting the currently selected cell"
on page 170 and can be found in NGRID.CPP. The declaration for the
NumberGrid class is in NGRID.H.

Changing input focus

The ProcessFocusChange function is called whenever the user selects a new
NumberCell for editing by pointing to the cell and clicking the left mouse
button. One of the main side effects of calling ProcessFocusChange is a call to
NumberGrid::SetCurrent. SetCurrent changes an instance variable inside the
NumberGrid object to remember the currently selected cell for the spreadsheet.

```
void ProcessFocusChange( HWND hwnd, MPARAM lParam, NumberGrid * grid )
{
    // ...
    grid->SetCurrent( SHORT1FROMMP(lParam) );
    // ...
}
```

So far we've been able to look at the implementations of our Presentation
Manager layer functions in order, without discussing too many of the details of
the interface between the Presentation Manager application layer and the
spreadsheet classes. We won't discuss ProcessFocusChange here, because its
implementation is much easier to understand once we've had an in-depth look at
the implementations of NumberGrid and NumberCell. We'll pick up the full
analysis of ProcessFocusChange in "Implementing ProcessFocusChange" on
page 174.

IMPLEMENTING THE SPREADSHEET CLASSES

Now that most of the Presentation Manager application layer is in place, we can implement our spreadsheet classes.

Implementing NumberGrid

We'll start by implementing the NumberGrid class.

NumberGrid constructor

NumberGrid's constructor sets up the application's default font, creates a grid of cells, and initializes the selection to point to the first cell.

```
NumberGrid::NumberGrid( HINSTANCE hInst, HWND hwnd , int xPos, int yPos,
                              int rows, int cols, int nCharsPerCell )
{
    int i, j;
    int xChar, yChar;
    FONTMETRICS fm;
    HPS hps;

    hps = WinGetPS(hwnd);
    GpiQueryFontMetrics(hps, (LONG) sizeof fm, &fm);
    WinReleasePS(hps);
    xChar = (int) fm.lAveCharWidth;
    yChar = (int) (fm.lEmHeight + fm.lExternalLeading + fm.lEmHeight / 2);

    // create the grid cells:
    fCellHeight = yChar;
    fCellWidth = nCharsPerCell * xChar;
    fNRows = rows;
    fNCols = cols;
    fGrid = new NumberCell ** [rows];
    for ( i = 0; i < rows; ++i )
            fGrid[i] = new NumberCell* [cols];
    for ( i = 0; i < rows; ++i )
        for ( j = 0; j < cols; ++j )
            fGrid[i][j] = new NumberCell( hInst, hwnd,
                                        (xPos + ((j * fCellWidth)+0)),
                                        (yPos + ((i * fCellHeight)+0)),
                                        fCellWidth, fCellHeight );
    fCurrentCell = 0;    // Select the first cell in
                         // the grid as the current cell.
}
```

Because each NumberCell is also a Presentation Manager edit control, it makes sense to identify each cell with a unique integer. This is the reason that the currently selected cell (saved in fCurrentCell) is remembered as an integer rather than as a point or a similar two-element structure. This decision requires your code to map integer cell identifiers to row and column coordinates expected by fGrid. The following example of this mapping is extracted from NumberGrid::FormatCell.

```
fGrid[fCurrentCell/fNCols][fCurrentCell % fNCols]->Update();
```

Understanding how this mapping works will make it easier to understand how NumberGrid works.

Formatting the currently selected cell

The implementation for NumberGrid::FormatCell is found in NGRID.CPP. This code includes several expressions that map fCurrentCell to the appropriate row and column values for fGrid.

```
// Change the format of the currently selected cell
// according to the format code selected by the user.
void NumberGrid::FormatCell( int nFormatCode )
{
  NumberFormat nf;
  switch ( nFormatCode )
  {
        case 0:
              nf.Set( 0, false, false, KCOMMA, KPERIOD );
              break;
        case 1:
              nf.Set( 0, true, false, KCOMMA, KPERIOD );
              break;
        case 2:
              nf.Set( 1, false, false, KCOMMA, KPERIOD );
              break;
        case 3:
              nf.Set( 2, false, false, KCOMMA, KPERIOD );
              break;
        case 4:
              nf.Set( 1, true, false, KCOMMA, KPERIOD );
              break;
        case 5:
              nf.Set( 2, true, false, KCOMMA, KPERIOD );
              break;
        case 6:
              nf.Set( 2, false, true, KCOMMA, KPERIOD );
              break;
        case 7:
              nf.Set( 2, true, true, KCOMMA, KPERIOD );
              break;
  }
  // set the current cell to the appropriate format
  fGrid[fCurrentCell/fNCols][fCurrentCell % fNCols]->SetFormat( nf );
  // update it
  fGrid[fCurrentCell/fNCols][fCurrentCell % fNCols]->Edit();
  fGrid[fCurrentCell/fNCols][fCurrentCell % fNCols]->Update();
}
```

NumberGrid::FormatCell is called from the WM_FORMATCELL clause of the
WindowSA1WndProc window procedure, which is invoked whenever a user
selects a format string from the Format Cell dialog. This code appeared in the
previous section.

```
MRESULT EXPENTRY WindowSA1WndProc (HWND   hWnd,
                                   ULONG  Message,
                                   MPARAM Param1,
                                   MPARAM Param2)
{
  //...
  switch (Message)
  {
    //...
    case WM_FORMATCELL:   // sent by Format Cell dialog
    {
          // Reformat the current NumberCell.
          // Display text using the selected format.
          theGrid.FormatCell((int)Param2);
    }
    //...
  }
}
```

Implementing NumberCell

NumberCell's implementation is more complicated than that of NumberGrid,
due mostly to its interactions with its edit control.

Creating Presentation Manager control subclasses

NumberCells are implemented as Presentation Manager edit controls. More
precisely, NumberCells have an instance variable that refers to the edit control
used to edit and display the text for each of the spreadsheet cells. This makes
NumberCell's constructor more complicated than other constructors presented
in this chapter. You've already reviewed the techniques and code used to
implement most of the constructor for NumberCell objects.

The following discussion focuses on the role of various instance variables within
NumberCell. For reference, the private instance variables inside NumberCell are:

```
class NumberCell
{
    // ...
private:
    HWND fHwndEditControl;      // Handle to the enclosed edit control.
    FormattableNumber fNumber;  // Formattable number enclosed in the cell.
    bool fErrorInFormat;        // Error status flag.
    bool fAltered;              // Altered status flag.
    static int fCellNumber;     // Cell number in a grid.
};
```

The key to understanding NumberCell's constructor is in knowing how to modify
the behavior of a standard Presentation Manager edit control. Modifying the
behavior of a standard window control is referred to as "subclassing the control."
You must define and register a new class of window. This new class is, in effect, a

subclass of an existing window, usually a standard control provided by
Presentation Manager. You must create a new window procedure to handle event
messages for your new control. You must also save a pointer to the old window
procedure for the existing control. Saving the old procedure and calling it from
your own window procedure is what distinguishes creating a window subclass
from creating an entirely new window control.

In "NumberCell class design" on page 152, the basic technique for subclassing
window controls was mentioned. As stated, a NumberCell object is primarily a
wrapper for an edit control and a number.

The technique for subclassing windows in both Windows and Presentation
Manager programming is borrowed directly from object-oriented programming.
The environment provides windows (in this case, an edit control) that already
exhibit most of the behavior you want. You want to modify this behavior only
slightly by doing some processing either before or after the original window
procedure for the control is invoked.

You must save the pointer to the old window procedure someplace where it can
be accessed whenever the window procedure for the new window is invoked. The
logical place to store the pointer to the edit control message handler is as a class
variable (declared as a static inside a C++ class) inside NumberCell. The saved
window procedure is called by our customized window procedure, EditWndProc.

```
// This window procedure is used to subclass the edit control
// used inside of NumberCell objects.
// The new edit procedure intercepts keystrokes and marks
// the NumberCell as altered.
MRESULT EXPENTRY EditWndProc(HWND hwnd, ULONG message, MPARAM Param1,
                             MPARAM Param2)
{
    switch ( message )
    {
        case WM_CHAR:                       // The user has typed a character
                                            // in an edit control.
            ((NumberCell*) GetProp(hwnd, (LPSTR) "nc"))->
                SetAlteredStatus(true);  // Mark cell as altered.
            break;
    }
    // Call the old window procedure for the edit control.
    return (NumberCell::fLpfnOldEditProc) (hwnd, message, Param1, Param2 );
}
```

The main reason for creating subclasses for the existing control is to intercept
keystroke events from the user. Whenever a key is pressed inside an active edit
control for a NumberCell, the cell is marked as altered by calling
NumberCell::SetAlteredStatus. After this call, the keystroke event is passed on to
the old window procedure to be handled normally.

Note how the NumberCell object is retrieved from the edit control handle for
which EditWndProc was invoked.

```
( (NumberCell*) GetProp( hwnd, (LPSTR) "nc") )
```

This code casts the value returned by GetProp as a pointer to a NumberCell. This cast makes it possible to get at a NumberCell object from the window handle for the control. With the pointer to the appropriate NumberCell, SetAlteredStatus can be called by the new window procedure.

```
((NumberCell*) GetProp( hwnd, (LPSTR) "nc"))->SetAlteredStatus(true);
```

GetProp and SetProp are global interface functions (defined in SAMPLE1.CPP) that implement the concept of properties for edit controls. Using the extra bytes facility available to all windows, GetProp and SetProp treat the string "nc" as a key to store and retrieve pointers to NumberCell objects. GetProp allows you to get to the NumberCell from the edit control's window handle. This is the Presentation Manager analog of storing a pointer to the edit window control as a private instance variable inside all NumberCell objects.

NumberCell constructor

NumberCell's constructor creates the edit control object and changes its window procedure to its own custom version, EditWndProc, which keeps track of whether the format text has changed. The constructor then stores a pointer to this NumberCell object in a named property of the EditControl. Finally, NumberCell initializes its data members as usual.

```
NumberCell::NumberCell( HINSTANCE hInst, HWND hwndParent , int xPos, int yPos,
                        int width, int height ) : fNumber()
{
      // Create the edit control
      fHwndEditControl =
      WinCreateWindow (hwndParent,      // Parent
                    WC_ENTRYFIELD,      // Control Class
                    "",                 // Control Text
                    (WS_VISIBLE
                     | ES_LEFT
                     | ES_MARGIN),      // Control Style
                    xPos,               // Control X position
                    yPos,               // Control Y position
                    width,              // Control Width
                    height,             // Control Height
                    hwndParent,         // Owner
                    HWND_BOTTOM,
                    fCellNumber++,      // Control ID
                    0,                  // No Control Data
                    0 );                // No Pres Params
      // Subclass the edit control's window procedure
      fLpfnOldEditProc = WinSubclassWindow(fHwndEditControl, EditWndProc);
      // store the handle to the enclosing NumberCell in the
      // edit control property list
      SetProp( fHwndEditControl, (LPSTR) "nc", (HANDLE) this );
      fAltered = false;                 // new cell, has never been altered
      fErrorInFormat = false;           // default format is OK
}
```

IMPLEMENTING PROCESSFOCUSCHANGE

Now that you have a better understanding of the NumberGrid, NumberCell, and NumberFormat classes, you are ready to work with ProcessFocusChange. As mentioned, ProcessFocusChange is called whenever the user selects a new NumberCell for editing

The entire definition for ProcessFocusChange indicates that a lot of bookkeeping is involved. You need to save references to the old cell losing input focus. You also need to get pointers to the NumberCells associated with the old edit control handle and the new edit control handle.

This aside, ProcessFocusChange formats the display text for the old cell before allowing input focus to be changed to the new cell. If a formatting error occurs, the change of focus is aborted and an error message (WM_FORMATERROR) is sent to the main application window. WindowSA1WndProc handles this message by setting input focus back to the cell that caused the format error.

```
MRESULT EXPENTRY WindowSA1WndProc (HWND    hWnd,
                                   ULONG   Message,
                                   MPARAM  Param1,
                                   MPARAM  Param2)
{
    switch (Message) {
        // ...
        case WM_FORMATERROR:    // Format error, reset focus to cell with error
        {
            WinSetFocus(HWND_DESKTOP,  (HWND)Param2);
        }
        break;
        // ...
    }
}
```

The following pseudocode of ProcessFocusChange should make the actual
definition easier to understand.

```
void ProcessFocusChange( HWND hwnd, MPARAM lParam, NumberGrid * grid )
{
    // hwnd is the edit control receiving input focus
    // SHORT1FROMMP(lParam) contains Control id
    // SHORT2FROMMP(lParam) contains Notification Code
    Get a pointer to the NumberCell from the edit control (hwnd).
    If  Notification Code is EN_SETFOCUS
    {
        The edit control is receiving input focus.
        Remember the old cell (the one losing focus).
        If the old cell already has a format error
            Send a WM_FORMATERROR application with old cell handle as Param2
            RETURN from this procedure without changing current cell.
        Call NumberCell::Update for the old cell.
        If Update produces a format error for the old cell
            Send a WM_FORMATERROR application with old cell handle as Param2
            RETURN from this procedure without changing current cell.
        Success (we have not returned).
            Change the currently selected cell.
            Turn OFF highlighting for OLD cell.
            Turn ON highlighting for NEW cell.
    }
}
```

This is the actual definition of ProcessFocusChange, which you should be able
to read now. You have already seen most of the individual statements in one
form or another.

```
void ProcessFocusChange( HWND hwnd, MPARAM lParam, NumberGrid * grid )
{
    int nOldCurrent;        // NumberCell id of cell losing the focus
    HWND hwndOldCurrent;  // Windows handle of edit control losing the focus
    // hwnd is the edit control receiving input focus
    // SHORT1FROMMP(lParam) contains Control id
    // SHORT2FROMMP(lParam) contains Notification Code
    // Get a pointer to the enclosing NumberCell
    NumberCell * ncp = (NumberCell*) GetProp(
        WinWindowFromID(hwnd, SHORT1FROMMP(lParam)), (LPSTR) "nc");
    // process a focus change
    if ( SHORT2FROMMP( lParam )  == EN_SETFOCUS )
    {
        // the edit control has received input focus
        // save the cell number of the cell losing the focus
        nOldCurrent = grid->GetCurrent();
        // get a handle to the edit control losing the focus
        hwndOldCurrent = grid->GetHandle( grid->GetCurrent() );
        // get a handle to the NumberCell enclosing the edit control
        NumberCell * ncpOldCurrent = (NumberCell*) GetProp(
            hwndOldCurrent, (LPSTR) "nc");
```

```
                    // if there's already a numeric format error
                    if ( ncpOldCurrent->GetFormatErrorStatus() )
                    {
                        // return to the cell to edit it
                        WinPostMsg( hwnd, WM_FORMATERROR, 0, (MPARAM) hwndOldCurrent  );
                        ncpOldCurrent->SetFormatErrorStatus( false );  // try again
                        return;
                    }
                    // Call to Update sets format error status, if any.
                    ncpOldCurrent->Update();
                    if ( ncpOldCurrent->GetFormatErrorStatus() )
                    {
                        // format error produced by update
                        // return to the cell and edit it
                        WinPostMsg( hwnd, WM_FORMATERROR, 0, (MPARAM)hwndOldCurrent  );
                        return;
                    }
                    // OK update, highlight the new current cell
                    // set the current cell number to the cell receiving the focus
                    grid->SetCurrent( SHORT1FROMMP(lParam) );
                    // invalidate (the rectangle) of the edit control losing the input focus
                    WinInvalidateRect( grid->GetHandle( nOldCurrent ), NULL, true );
                    // force old cell to paint, turns OFF highlighting for this cell
                    WinSendMsg( grid->GetHandle( nOldCurrent ), WM_PAINT, 0, 0L );
                    WinInvalidateRect( grid->GetHandle( grid->GetCurrent() ), NULL, true );
                    // force current cell to paint, turns ON highlighting for this cell
                    WinSendMsg( grid->GetHandle( grid->GetCurrent() ), WM_PAINT, 0, 0L );
                    ncp->Edit();
                }
            }
```

Handling format errors

Various errors can occur when you are formatting a cell, and various events can trigger a format. The next if statement in ProcessFocusChange handles formatting errors that might have already occurred, but have not been cleared from an edit prior to this invocation of ProcessFocusChange.

In such a case, a WM_FORMATERROR is sent to the control receiving input focus and the format error status flag of the old NumberCell. The function then aborts through an early return.

```
// if there's already a numeric format error
if ( ncpOldCurrent->GetFormatErrorStatus() )
{
    //  return to the cell to edit it
    WinPostMsg( hwnd, WM_FORMATERROR, 0, (MPARAM) hwndOldCurrent  );
    ncpOldCurrent->SetFormatErrorStatus( false );  // try again
    return;
}
```

If no format error is detected, the next several statements format the number in the cell losing input focus. Similar error recovery code is also included here for errors resulting from the call to Update.

```
// Call to Update sets format error status, if any.
ncpOldCurrent->Update();
if ( ncpOldCurrent->GetFormatErrorStatus() )
{
    // format error produced by update
    // return to the cell and edit it
    WinPostMsg( hwnd, WM_FORMATERROR, 0, (MPARAM)hwndOldCurrent  );
    return;
}
```

As before, a format error resulting from Update causes a WM_FORMATERROR to be placed in the application's message queue. This message is processed by the WM_FORMATERROR case clause of WindowSA1WndProc.

**Updating the
NumberCell**

The role of NumberCell::Update is to format a NumberCell's current value according to the format the user selected from the Format Cell dialog box.

```
int NumberCell::Update()
{
    char szBuffer[32];
    char *endPtr;
    double dTemp;
    if ( ! fAltered )
        return 1;
    if ( !WinQueryWindowText( fHwndEditControl,
            sizeof(szBuffer), szBuffer ) )  // is the cell empty?
    {
        fErrorInFormat = false;             // if so, format is OK,
        fAltered = false;                   // set altered to false
        return 1;                           // successfully updated
    }
    if ( fErrorInFormat )                   // bad numeric format,
        return 0;                           // abandon update
    dTemp = strtod( szBuffer, &endPtr );    // attempt conversion
    if ( !*endPtr )                         // if endPtr is NULL,
    {                                       // conversion was successful
        fNumber = dTemp;                    // update FormattableNumber value
        fNumber.Format( szBuffer );         // generate new format string
        WinSetWindowText( fHwndEditControl,
            (LPSTR) szBuffer );             //set the edit cell's text to
        fErrorInFormat = false;             // the formatted string
        fAltered = false;                   // set altered to false
        return 1;                           // successfully updated
    }
    // Record that the user has typed-in a bad numeric format
    fErrorInFormat = true;
    // Signal an error
    MessageBeep( 0 );
    MessageBox( fHwndEditControl, "Invalid Numeric Format",
            "Number Cell Error", MB_ICONEXCLAMATION );
    return 0;                                      // ERROR: unsuccessful update
}
```

NumberCell::Update will return immediately if the cell has not been altered since it was last formatted. Update will also return early if the cell's edit control is empty. Otherwise, Update attempts to convert the cell's current edit control text to a double using the ANSI library function strtod. If the conversion fails, Update sets the cells fErrorInFormat instance variable to true, beeps, and displays a warning dialog box to the user. When the user closes this dialog box, Update returns the value 0, indicating a failure condition.

If conversion is successful, Update assigns the double to the fNumber instance variable of the NumberCell.

```
fNumber = dTemp;                    // update FormattableNumber value
```

Next FormattableNumber::Format is called with the edit controls text string as an argument.

```
fNumber.Format( szBuffer );         // generate new format string
```

Format takes the generic number representation in szBuffer and converts it to the format selected for the cell by the user. The string in szBuffer is modified by Format; then the display text for the edit control is set to the modified string.

```
WinSetWindowText( fHwndEditControl,
    (LPSTR) szBuffer );             //set the edit cell's text to
```

The format error and cell-altered flags are cleared before returning a value of 1, indicating a successful update of the NumberCell.

```
fErrorInFormat = false;             // the formatted string
fAltered = false;                   // set altered to false
return 1;                           // successfully updated
```

Implementing FormattableNumber

FormattableNumber is responsible for converting numbers to text. The bulk of the class's implementation consists of accessor members.

As with the other classes in the application, FormattableNumber provides accessor member functions that allow its format and numeric value to be manipulated. The code for the format state accessors is:

```
const NumberFormat& FormattableNumber::GetFormat() const
{
    return fMyFormat;
}

void FormattableNumber::SetFormat(const NumberFormat &nf)
{
    fMyFormat = nf;
}
```

Format function

The most important member function in FormattableNumber is Format, which is responsible for converting the value and format into a string. To perform this conversion, Format first divides the numeric value into its component parts by calling the standard library function fcvt.

It then creates a formatted string by applying the sign, currency character, and thousands separators to the number as needed. Notice that the positioning of these characters in the number is fixed in this version of the application, which make it unusable in some other countries.

```cpp
void FormattableNumber::Format( char *fresult )
{
    int  decimal, sign;
    char *buffer;
    char outbuf[BUFFLEN];
    ostrstream ostrstr(outbuf, BUFFLEN);
    // source = int(source);
    buffer = fcvt( fValue, fMyFormat.GetPrecision(), &decimal, &sign );
    if (sign)    // negative sign?
        ostrstr << "-";
    if ( fMyFormat.IsCurrency() )    // Currency?
        ostrstr << "$";
    // print the decimal part:
    for ( char *p = buffer; p < ( buffer + decimal ); ++p )
    {
        ostrstr << *p;
        if ( fMyFormat.IsThousandsDelimitted() )     // delimited integer format?
            // not the end and comma?
            if ( ( p < ( buffer + decimal - 1 ) ) &&
                ( ( buffer + decimal - p - 1 ) / sizeof(char) ) % 3 == 0 )
                ostrstr << fMyFormat.GetIntSeparator();
    };
    if ( fMyFormat.GetPrecision() > 0 ) // there's a decimal point
        ostrstr << ".";
    while ( *p )  // print the decimal part
        ostrstr << *p++;
    ostrstr << '\0';    // append a NULL
    strcpy( fresult, outbuf );
}
```

Format uses a standard floating point to string conversion utility from the ANSI library, fcvt. The fcvt function converts the fValue instance variable of the FormattableNumber into a character string using the precision attribute of fMyFormat (an instance of NumberFormat). Format then determines the sign of the number and whether the user wants to format the value entered as currency. This version of Format always uses a $ symbol for currency. Note that you are using a standard C++ output stream for a working buffer.

Format starts building up the integer part of the string representation checking to see whether the user wants to display a thousands separator. If so, Format notes the digit positions and inserts the delimiter in the appropriate places. Next Format checks whether the representation calls for a decimal point by again testing the precision attribute of fMyFormat. If required, a decimal point is inserted into the output stream.

Now the decimal part of the number is inserted. A NULL character is inserted into the stream to mark the end of the character buffer. The work buffer now contains a properly formatted string representing the number. This string is copied to the buffer passed in by the caller. In this case, the caller is NumberCell::Update, which uses the returned string to set the text of the edit control to the formatted number.

PUTTING THE APPLICATION TOGETHER

This version of the application is now complete. We have a simple but serviceable spreadsheet, one that the user can edit and format. Even though the application has some problems with international formatting, its design lays the foundation for a version that handles these issues correctly.

CHAPTER 9

DESIGNING A NUMBER FORMATTING FRAMEWORK FOR OS/2

At this point, we have a workable, if somewhat simplistic, OS/2 application, which we will run through the usual process of testing and then shipping to customers.

As customers use the product, they report bugs and submit feature requests. Some of the feature requests are minor (using a different font, and so on), while others are more complex. Of the feature requests we receive, two of the most common are the ability to format numbers as fractions (to display stock prices) and the ability to use the program in other countries. We decide to concentrate on adding support for other countries first, but we also want to make sure that it's possible to add support for fractions later without having to redesign or rewrite a lot of code.

Our current implementation of the program has room for improvement. Even though we've divided the problem into a set of objects, adding support for international number formatting to the existing application forces us to make significant changes to the design and implementation of our NumberCell and NumberFormat classes.

However, because the application wasn't designed to be extensible, we can see that these types of problems will probably appear again the next time we have to add features.

Rather than just do a patch on the existing design, we decide to develop a general solution to the number formatting problem: creating a number formatting framework. We'll still be able to reuse, with substantial editing, much of the code created for the first version of the sample, including virtually all the existing code for the user interface.

DESIGNING THE FRAMEWORK

In the current implementation of the application, the FormattableNumber class is responsible for building the formatted number string. While having a single object that can format itself seemed reasonable at the time, it poses a few problems now. For example, to add support for displaying fractions to the FormattableNumber, we'll need to add case and if statements to many different formatting routines.

We also want to be able to add new number formatting capabilities to the application later, without adding new classes or revisiting existing ones. Thus, the core of the framework should be a class that formats numbers generically, TNumberFormatter. We'll create subclasses of TNumberFormatter to format numbers in more specific ways. For example, to format floating-point numbers, we'll add a TFloatingPointFormatter class to the framework.

Because the current application design allows only the double value kept by FormattableNumber to be used, we also want to provide a more general way of passing numbers to TNumberFormatter. Therefore, the framework provides a more general TFormattableNumber class, which can be passed to any TNumberFormatter object. Like the old NumberFormatter class, TNumberFormatter uses a double to represent the number being formatted.

Unlike NumberFormatter, this design lets us create a subclass of TFormattableNumber to represent new data types, which in turn lets us format numeric data types about which the framework itself knows nothing. A future version of the application could use a Binary-Coded Decimal (BCD) class for its calculations, and by using a TFormattableBCDNumber class, the application would be able to format these values without modifying the underlying framework.

This kind of flexibility is one of the keys to good framework design. The framework provides reasonable default behavior that lets us format floating-point numbers, but it also allows for future extensibility without affecting the underlying framework design and implementation.

We also need a way to communicate formatting errors to framework clients. Correctly designed classes usually respond to error conditions by throwing exceptions or returning error codes, either of which is appropriate when there are no shades of grey in the success or failure of a particular operation.

However, when formatting a number, error conditions are not always so clear. Number formatting operations rarely fail outright, but it is possible that the result won't serve the client's needs. For example, the space available to display the number might be fixed in width, and you might want to display the number in a different format (such as scientific notation) to allow it to fit into the allocated space. To address this issue, we need to create a class that allows us to return more detailed results to the client. This class, TFormatResult, includes error information and more general information about the formatting results.

Finally, we need a TNumberFormatLocale class, which stores the common formatter types used for a given area of the world. This class is used to isolate the international dependencies from the rest of the framework.

The class hierarchy of the framework is shown in the following figure.

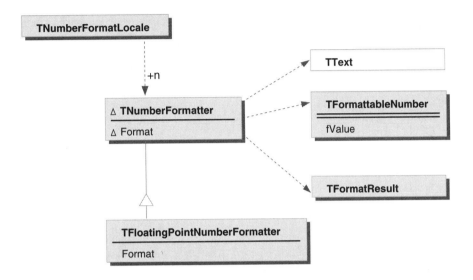

CLASS HIERARCHY OF THE NUMBER FORMATTING FRAMEWORK

This method of formatting offers advantages over the previous technique we used. For one, the TFormattableNumber object does not have to carry specialized functions to format itself. It's "just" data. Formatting knowledge is kept in the TNumberFormatter class hierarchy. This makes an efficient separation for the use, maintenance, and extension of these classes.

Using these classes in the application requires minor revisions to the NumberCell class, described in "Updating NumberCell" on page 205.

✅ NOTE   The framework also uses a TText class, which represents a standard C string. Because its implementation is straightforward, the design and implementation of this class is not shown in the book. The source code for this class is included on the accompanying CD-ROM.

Now that our basic design is in place, we'll begin filling out the design of the framework's classes.

Designing TNumberFormatter

The first class we need to design is TNumberFormatter. TNumberFormatter's primary function is to "remember" a formatting style and to convert a numeric value into a textual representation using that style.

Format member functions

The Format member functions are the core of the TNumberFormatter class, and are the primary functions called by clients of the framework. They take a TFormattableNumber, convert it to text according to the format set in the TNumberFormatter, and return the text to the caller, along with an optional TFormatResult object that provides additional information about the conversion process.

```
virtual bool    Format(const TFormattableNumber& num, TText& resultText);
virtual bool    Format(const TFormattableNumber& num, TText& resultText,
                    TFormatResult& result);
```

Formatting support member functions

The Format member function relies on two protected member functions, SetUpFormattableNumber and FormattableNumberToText, to handle most of its formatting efforts. SetupFormattableNumber tells TFormattableNumber how it should process the numeric properties of its value. FormattableNumberToText does the actual work of converting the numeric properties of the TFormattableNumber into text. Subclasses of TNumberFormatter need to override these member functions to provide more specialized behavior. The default versions of these functions implemented by TNumberFormatter can handle only simple floating-point numbers without exponents.

```
virtual void    SetUpFormattableNumber(TFormattableNumber& num);
virtual void    FormattableNumberToText(const TFormattableNumber& num,
                    TText& text, TNumberFormatResult& result);
```

Accessor member functions

TNumberFormatter also provides a set of accessor member functions that allow the formatting of the number to be controlled. TNumberFormatter doesn't know whether the number should be formatted as a floating-point number or as an integral number, so it can control only the formatting of the sign of the number. Note that TNumberFormatter also provides accessors that control the setting of prefix and suffix strings for both positive and negative numbers, allowing TNumberFormatter to show negative numbers with parentheses.

```
virtual void    GetPlus(TText& prefix, TText& suffix) const;
virtual void    SetPlus(const TText& prefix, const TText& suffix);
virtual void    GetMinus TText& prefix, TText& suffix) const;
virtual void    SetMinus(const TText& prefix, const TText& suffix);
virtual bool    GetShowPlusSign() const;
virtual void    SetShowPlusSign(bool);
```

Miscellaneous member functions and data members

The remainder of the member functions for the class consists of standard C++ constructors and an assignment operator. The data members store the suffix and prefix strings, along with a flag that keeps track of whether we display the positive sign prefix and suffix to the user.

```
TNumberFormatter&   operator=(const TNumberFormatter&);

protected:
                    TNumberFormatter(const TNumberFormatter& format);
                    TNumberFormatter();

private:
    TText           fPlusPrefix;
    TText           fPlusSuffix;
    TText           fMinusPrefix;
    TText           fMinusSuffix;
    bool            fShowPlusSign;
};
```

Designing TFormattableNumber

TFormattableNumber's primary role is to provide the input number to the TNumberFormatter, along with information about the number's properties. Its class declaration is as follows:

```
class TFormattableNumber {
public:
                    TFormattableNumber();
                    TFormattableNumber(const double number);
                    TFormattableNumber(const TFormattableNumber& copy);
    virtual         ~TFormattableNumber();

    virtual TFormattableNumber& operator=(const TFormattableNumber& toCopy);

    typedef unsigned char Digit;
    enum  { kNoSignificandDigit = 253 };

    //-----------------------------------------------------------------------
    // Accessors for number's properties
    //-----------------------------------------------------------------------

    // access the value of the number
    virtual double  GetNumber() const;
    virtual void    SetNumber(double);

    // Is the number negative
    virtual bool    IsNegative() const;
```

In addition to storing the number as a double, TFormattableNumber provides access to the individual digits of the number for use by the text converter. It does so using a string of byte-encoded digits (with "0" having a numeric value of zero), called the *significand*. The implicit decimal point appears after the first digit in the string as in scientific notation. Special values exist for infinity, illegal numeric values (NaNs), and zero.

Before retrieving the significand, the user must allocate storage for the significand buffer that is at least as large as GetSignificandLength multiplied by the size of a Digit.

```
virtual void    GetSignificand(Digit* theSignificand) const;
virtual size_t  GetSignificandLength() const;

// Exponent represents powers of 10.
virtual long    GetExponent() const;

// bool tests for Infinity, NaN and Zero (sign irrelevant)
virtual bool    IsZero();
virtual bool    IsInfinity();
virtual bool    IsNan();
```

Setting conversion parameters

These accessor functions provide information about the properties of the number. Determining these properties requires an analysis of the value, and TFormattableNumber provides routines to control the number of significant digits to preserve when doing this analysis.

```
// Get/SetDigitsFromDecimalPoint controls rounding to a fixed number of
// digits from the decimal point in the significand string when converting.
virtual short           GetDigitsFromDecimalPoint() const ;
virtual void            SetDigitsFromDecimalPoint(short digitsFromDecimalPoint);
```

Numeric analysis member functions

As part of TFormattableNumber's protected interface, we provide routines to analyze the numeric properties of the number and set its internal fields. The setters are protected virtual functions; therefore they can be overridden if necessary by a subclass that fine-tunes the analysis process.

```
protected:
    // analyze the numeric value to determine its properties, using the
    // rounding and precision settings of the number. Called automatically whenever
    // the number value or any of the rounding/precision values is changed.
    virtual void    AnalyzeValue();

    // set the properties of the number (used by analyzer routine)
    virtual void    SetAnalysisDirtyFlag(bool flag = true);
    virtual void    SetSignBit(bool signIsMinus);
    virtual void    SetSignificand(Digit significand[], size_t length);
    virtual void    SetExponent(long theExponent);
    virtual void    SetInfinity();
    virtual void    SetNan(unsigned short nanCode);
```

The class declaration concludes with the definition of TFormattableNumber's private data members, which keep track of the number and its properties.

```
private:
    enum     {kBufferLength = 122};
    enum     {kInfinityDigit = 254};
    enum     {kNaNDigit = 255};

    double           fNumber;
    bool             fIsSignMinus;
    long             fExponent;
    size_t           fSignificandLength;
    Digit            fSignificand[kBufferLength+2];
    unsigned short   fTotalDigitCount;
    unsigned short   fDigitsFromDecimalPoint;
    double           fRoundToMultiple;
    bool             fAnalysisDirtyFlag;
};
```

Designing TFloatingPointNumber Formatter

The TFloatingPointNumberFormatter class adds the ability to format floating-point numbers to the basic formatting capabilities provided by TNumberFormatter.

The class declaration begins with the definitions of types and enumerations that define some of the allowable formatting parameters that can be set by the user.

```
class TFloatingPointNumberFormatter : public TNumberFormatter {
public:
    typedef unsigned short DigitCount;
    enum ESign { kMinusSign = -1, kNoSign = 0, kPlusSign = 1 };
```

The following are the standard constructors, destructor, and assignment operator for this class.

```
    TFloatingPointNumberFormatter();
    TFloatingPointNumberFormatter(const TFloatingPointNumberFormatter& format);
    virtual ~TFloatingPointNumberFormatter();
    TFloatingPointNumberFormatter&
            operator=(const TFloatingPointNumberFormatter&);
```

TNumberFormatter formatting overrides

The numeric conversion routines SetupFormattableNumber and FormattableNumberToText, originally defined by TNumberFormatter, are overridden by TFloatingPointNumberFormatter. These routines do the actual work of formatting the text string, using the current format state. The overridden FormattableNumberToText function calls two new protected functions, FormattableNumberToExponentText and FormattableNumberToDecimalText, to handle the formatting of the exponent and decimal portions of the number.

```
virtual void    SetUpFormattableNumber(TFormattableNumber& num);

virtual void    FormattableNumberToText(const TFormattableNumber&, TText&,
                                TNumberFormatResult&);
virtual void    FormattableNumberToExponentText(const TFormattableNumber&,
                                  TText&, TNumberFormatResult&);
virtual void    FormattableNumberToDecimalText(const TFormattableNumber&,
                                TText&, TNumberFormatResult&);
```

Formatting control accessor functions

The remainder of the class is made up of accessors, that control the formatting of floating-point numbers.

```
public:
    //=======================================================================
    // Getters and setters.

    // in text 1,234,567, the digit group separator text is ",",
    // the separator spacing is 3.
    // Call SetIntegerSeparator(true) if the digit group separator
    // is to be shown for the integer part.
    virtual void       GetDigitGroupSeparator(TText&) const;
    virtual void       SetDigitGroupSeparator(const TText&);
    virtual DigitCount  GetSeparatorSpacing() const;
    virtual void       SetSeparatorSpacing(DigitCount);
    virtualbool        GetIntegerSeparator() const;
    virtualvoid        SetIntegerSeparator(bool);

    // minDigitCount is the minimum number of digits to display when formatting
    // a number as text. Also known as zero-padding.
    virtual DigitCount  GetMinIntegerDigits() const;
    virtual void       SetMinIntegerDigits(DigitCount);

    virtual void       GetNanSign(TText&) const;
    virtual void       GetInfinitySign(TText&) const;
    virtual void       SetNanSign(const TText&);
    virtual void       SetInfinitySign(const TText&);

    // SetDecimalSeparator sets the text to be used to separate the integer
    // and the fraction parts of numbers. It defaults to a space
    virtual void       GetDecimalSeparator(TText&) const;
    virtual void       SetDecimalSeparator(const TText&);

    // SetDecimalWithInteger indicates if the decimal point should be
    // displayed for integer numbers.
    virtual bool       GetDecimalWithInteger() const;
    virtual void       SetDecimalWithInteger(bool);
```

```
// SetFractionSeparator indicates if the digit group separator text,
// which is set through TNumberFormatter::SetDigitGroupSeparator,
// should be displayed for the fraction part. It defaults to false.
virtual bool    GetFractionSeparator() const;
virtual void    SetFractionSeparator(bool);

// SetExponentSeparatorText indicates the text to be used for
// the exponent separator. The default is 'E'.
virtual void    GetExponentSeparatorText(TText&) const;
virtual void    SetExponentSeparatorText(const TText&);

virtual DigitCount  GetMinFractionDigits() const;
virtual void        SetMinFractionDigits(DigitCount);
virtual DigitCount  GetMaxFractionDigits() const;
virtual void        SetMaxFractionDigits(DigitCount);

 // == 1 for scientific, 3 for engineering formats
virtual DigitCount  GetExponentPhase() const;
virtual void        SetExponentPhase(DigitCount);

virtual double  GetUpperExponentThreshold() const;
virtual void    SetUpperExponentThreshold(double);
virtual double  GetLowerExponentThreshold() const;
virtual void    SetLowerExponentThreshold(double);
```

Despite their simplicity, these functions are important to the design of the
framework because they provide control over how numbers are formatted. In
fact, they provide more control than is strictly necessary for this sample program.
This is a common by-product of the framework design process: we have to do
more design and implementation work up front to make the framework truly
general. The alternative, of course, is to develop a framework that is not truly
general, and we end up having to redesign and reimplement everything
whenever we want to add new functionality.

Is the cost of adding all this generality worth it? It is if we would have to do most
of the work involved in designing the framework anyway. The previous version of
the program wouldn't work in countries other than the U.S., and it only
supported a limited number of number formats. Adding support for these
features to the previous version of the framework would require us to add a
similar amount of code to achieve the same level of functionality.

The remainder of the class consists of the data members needed to store all of this state.

```
private:
    TText            fNanSign;
    TText            fInfinitySign;
    TText            fDigitGroupSeparator;    // e.g. thousands separator ","
    DigitCount       fMinIntegerDigits;       // 0-pad at least this many digits
    DigitCount       fSeparatorSpacing;       // digit group length for separator
    bool             fHasIntegerSeparator;
    TText            fDecimalSeparator;       // '.' in 1.23
    TText            fExponentSeparator;      // 'E' in 1E-3
    double           fExponentUpperThreshold;// when to switch to E notation
    double           fExponentLowerThreshold;
    DigitCount       fExponentPhase;          // multiples of exponent to show
    DigitCount       fMinFractionDigits;      // 0-pad to fill
    DigitCount       fMaxFractionDigits;
    bool             fDecimalWithInteger;
    bool             fHasFractionSeparator;   // use digit group separator?
    bool             fHasExponentSeparator;   // use digit group separator?
    bool             fSignedExponent;
    EMantissaType    fMantissaType;
    EShowBaseType    fShowBaseType;
};
```

Designing TNumberFormatLocale

The TNumberFormatLocale class provides a number of member functions to create default formatters for both currency and floating-point formats. One default locale corresponds to the user's location, and it can be accessed by calling GetUserLocale.

```
class TNumberFormatLocale {
public:
                        TNumberFormatLocale();
                        TNumberFormatLocale(const TNumberFormatLocale&);
    virtual             ~TNumberFormatLocale();

    // member functions to create standard formatters for the current locale.
    virtual TNumberFormatter*   CreateCurrencyFormatter() const;
    virtual TNumberFormatter*   CreateFloatingPointFormatter() const;

    static const TNumberFormatLocale& GetUserLocale();

protected:
    virtual void  HandleSymbols(bool csPrecedes,
                        bool useSpace, bool useSign, bool signFirst,
                        TText& currSym, TText& signSym,
                        TText& prefix, TText& suffix);

private:
    static TNumberFormatLocale* gUserLocale;
};
```

We use this class to isolate the locale dependencies from the rest of the framework. The current design supports accessing the current locale only. Future enhancements might include the addition of support for setting the locale under program control, and the use of the locale object to support access to other localized classes. For this example, the current design is sufficient.

Implementing TNumberFormatter

Now that the design of the framework's classes is in place, it's time to implement the framework. Since it is assumed that you are familiar with constructors and destructors, and because the getter and setter functions are so simple, not every step of the implementation process is described here. The complete source code is available on the CD-ROM that accompanies this book. This discussion concentrates on the key member functions of the framework.

The key function of TNumberFormatter is the Format member function. Format takes a TFormattableNumber and converts it to text using the current settings of TNumberFormatter.

```
void TNumberFormatter::Format(const TFormattableNumber& value, TText& theText,
                              TNumberFormatResult& result)
{
    theText.del(0,theText.length());
    SetUpFormattableNumber(value);

    FormattableNumberToText(value, theText, result);

    TText prefix;
    TText suffix;

    bool isNegative;
    isNegative = value.GetSignBit();
    if (isNegative)
        GetMinus(prefix, suffix);
    else if (GetShowPlusSign())
        GetPlus(prefix, suffix);

    theText += suffix;
    theText.prepend(prefix);

    result.SetIntegerBoundary(result.GetIntegerBoundary() + prefix.GetLength());
    result.SetDigitSequenceEnd(result.GetDigitSequenceEnd() + prefix.GetLength());
}
```

FormattableNumber setup and conversion functions

The Format member function calls two member functions to handle most of the number formatting operation. The first of these, SetUpFormattableNumber, sets up the analysis parameters of the TFormattableNumber object. Subclasses of TNumberFormatter can override this member function to customize the behavior of the TFormattableNumber, as we do later when we describe the implementation of TFloatingPointNumberFormatter.

```
void TNumberFormatter::SetUpFormattableNumber(TFormattableNumber& num)
{
    num.SetDigitsFromDecimalPoint(TFormattableNumber::kNoSignificantDigit);
}
```

The second of these member functions is FormattableNumberToText. FormattableNumberToText does most of the work of formatting for the Format member function, and it's usually overridden by subclasses. The default version supplied by TNumberFormatter handles thousands separators, but prints numbers without exponents, filling with zeroes as needed.

```
void TNumberFormatter::FormattableNumberToText(const TFormattableNumber& num,
                                    TText& text, TNumberFormatResult& result)
{
    char uc;

    // delete any existing text
    text.Delete(TTextRange(TTextOffset(0), text.GetLength()));

    if (!num.IsInfinity() && !num.IsNan())
    {
        int numDigits = num.GetSignificandLength();
        if (numDigits <= 0)
        {
            ConvertToNumeral(TFormattableNumber::Digit(0),uc);
            text.prepend(uc);
            return;
        }

        // first, determine and allocate the correct size digit buffer
        // must be at least as big as FormattableNumber returns, but
        // may need extra space for leading zeros.
        int n = num.GetExponent() + 1;
        int exponent = n;
        long places = ( exponent > numDigits ? exponent : numDigits );
        TFormattableNumber::Digit* digits = new
                            TFormattableNumber::Digit[places];
        num.GetSignificand(digits);

        // fill with zeros at end
        if (exponent > numDigits)
            for (int i = numDigits; i < exponent; i++)
                digits[ i ] = TFormattableNumber::Digit(0);
```

```
// work back through number, filling in digits
int consecutiveDigits = 0;
int digit = 0;
for (int theDigit = exponent - 1; theDigit >= 0; theDigit--)
{
    ConvertToNumeral(digits[theDigit], uc);
    text.prepend(uc);
    if (GetIntegerSeparator()
            && ++consecutiveDigits == GetSeparatorSpacing()
            && (theDigit < exponent - 1)
            && (theDigit > 0))
    {
        TText separatorText;
        GetDigitGroupSeparator(separatorText);
        text.prepend(separatorText);
        consecutiveDigits = 0;
    }
}

// zero pad integral portion as needed
TPositionalNumberFormatter::DigitCount minIntegerDigits =
                    GetMinIntegerDigits();
if ((minIntegerDigits > 0) && (minIntegerDigits > n))
{
    ConvertToNumeral(0, uc);
    for (int i = n; i < minIntegerDigits; i++)
    {
        text.prepend(uc);
    }
}

result.SetIntegerBoundary(text.length());
result.SetDigitSequenceEnd(text.length());

delete [] digits;

// it currently just sets the confidence to be kPerfect.
result.SetConfidence(TNumberFormatResult::kPerfect);
}
}
```

Implementing TFormattableNumber

TFormattableNumber contains a large number of accessor functions used to retrieve information about the number, including its exponent, its sign, and so on. Whenever a member function that returns analysis results is called, TFormattableNumber checks a dirty flag to see whether it should reanalyze the number's properties, as shown in the IsNegative member function:

```
bool TFormattableNumber::IsNegative() const
{
    if (fAnalysisDirtyFlag)
        AnalyzeValue();
    return fIsSignMinus;
}
```

Similarly, when a member function is called that might change the analysis results, TFormattableNumber sets the dirty flag in that member function, as shown in the SetNumber member function:

```
void TFormattableNumber::SetNumber(double number)
{
    fNumber = number;
    SetAnalysisDirtyFlag(true);
}
```

The AnalyzeValue member function analyzes the number and extracts its numeric properties, using the conversion settings provided. It uses the ANSI C standard function fcvt to convert the number into its components.

```
void TFormattableNumber::AnalyzeValue()
{
    int  decimal, sign;
    Digit* buffer;
    int siglen = 0;
    long digits = fDigitsFromDecimalPoint;
    if (digits > 12)
      digits = 12;

    // fcvt determines the exponent, mantissa, and sign for us,
    // but it uses ascii characters, which isn't very general, so we
    // convert them to our internal Digit format.
    buffer = (Digit*) fcvt(fNumber, digits, &decimal, &sign);
    siglen = strlen(buffer);
    for (int i = 0; i < siglen; i++)
      buffer[i] = buffer[i] - '0';

    SetSignBit(( sign != 0 ? true: false));
    SetSignificand((Digit*) buffer, siglen);
    SetExponent((long) decimal - 1);

    SetAnalysisDirtyFlag(false);
}
```

**Implementing
TFloatingPointNumber
Formatter**

The key member functions of TFloatingPointNumberFormatter are the two overridden member functions of TNumberFormatter, SetUpFormattableNumber and FormattableNumberToText.

**Implementing
SetUpFormattableNumber**

The SetUpFormattableNumber member function sets up the conversion parameters of the formattable number that the class has been asked to format. The overridden implementation first calls the SetUpFormattable member function it inherited from TNumberFormatter and then overrides the setting that controls the number of decimal points to match the maximum permitted digits parameter of TFloatingPointNumberFormatter.

```
void TFloatingPointNumberFormatter::SetUpFormattableNumber(TFormattableNumber& num)
    {
        TNumberFormatter::SetUpFormattableNumber(num);

        num.SetDigitsFromDecimalPoint(GetMaxFractionDigits());
    }
```

FormattableNumberToText

TFloatingPointNumberFormatter overrides the FormattableNumberToText member function to handle both scientific and engineering notation for floating-point numbers. It delegates the work to two new member functions, FormattableNumberToExponentText and FormattableNumberToDecimalText.

```
    void TFloatingPointNumberFormatter::FormattableNumberToText(
                    const TFormattableNumber& num,
                    TText& text, TNumberFormatResult& result)
    {
        if (!num.IsInfinity() && !num.IsNan())
        {
            // get absolute value of number
            double number = num.GetNumber();
            if (number < 0)
                number = -number;

            // determine whether to print as scientific notation or not, using
            // the exponent threshold parameters.
            if (number != 0.0 && (number < GetLowerExponentThreshold() ||
                            number > GetUpperExponentThreshold()))
                FormattableNumberToExponentText(num, text, result);
            else FormattableNumberToDecimalText(num, text, result);

            // we currently just set the confidence to be kPerfect.
            result.SetConfidence(TNumberFormatResult::kPerfect);
        }
        else
        {
            // let the TNumberFormatter take care of the edge cases
            TNumberFormatter::FormattableNumberToText(num,text,result);
        }
    }
```

FormattableNumberToExponentText

FormattableNumberToExponentText generates a text string in scientific notation. Rather than duplicate all the code to print a basic number, it uses a TNumberFormatter to format the exponent as though it were a whole number and then calls FormattableNumberToDecimalText to format the mantissa. Using the appropriate separator text, it subsequently puts the two numbers together.

```
void TFloatingPointNumberFormatter::FormattableNumberToExponentText(
        const TFormattableNumber& num, TText& text, TNumberFormatResult& result)
{
    long exponent = num.GetExponent();
    long exponentAdjuster = 0;// used later to process mantissa
    long phase = (long) GetExponentPhase();
    if (phase > 1)
        {
            // we round the exponent down using the phase value
            // for engineering notation, phase is 3, so we get an
            // exponent value rounded down to the nearest multiple
            // of 3
            long idealExponent;
            if (exponent < 0)
                idealExponent = (((-1 - exponent) / phase) * -phase) - phase;
            else idealExponent = (exponent / phase) * phase;

            exponentAdjuster = exponent - idealExponent;
            exponent = idealExponent;
        }

    // first we format the exponent, using a basic TNumberFormatter which
    // we handily initialize with this object's settings
    TNumberFormatter exponentFormat(*this);
    TText exponentText;
    TNumberFormatResult exponentResult;
    TFormattableNumber formattableExponent((double) exponent);
    exponentFormat.Format(formattableExponent, exponentText, exponentResult);

    // now we format the integral part of our number
    // we make a new number which reflects only the mantissa, with the correct
    // number of digits to match the exponent we've already printed
    TFormattableNumber formattableMantissa(num.GetNumber() /
                            pow(10.0, exponentAdjuster));
    FormattableNumberToDecimalText(num, text, result);

    TText exponentSeparator;
    GetExponentSeparatorText(exponentSeparator);
    text += exponentSeparator;
    text += exponentText;

    result.SetDigitSequenceEnd(text.GetLength());
}
```

FormattableNumberToDecimalText

FormattableNumberToDecimalText is responsible for formatting a floating-point number in the standard (nonscientific) format. Its implementation is similar to that of TNumberFormatter::FormattableNumberToText, but it provides more control over the formatting.

```
void TFloatingPointNumberFormatter::FormattableNumberToDecimalText(
                        const TFormattableNumber& num,
                        TText& text, TNumberFormatResult& result)
{
    double number = 0.0;
    TFormattableNumber::Digit theDigit;
    char uc;

    if (!num.IsInfinity() && !num.IsNan())
        number = num.GetNumber();

    long numDigits = num.GetSignificandLength();
    TFormattableNumber::Digit* digits = new TFormattableNumber::Digit[numDigits];
    num.GetSignificand(digits);
    long exponent = num.GetExponent() + 1;
    long minPlaces = exponent + GetMinFractionDigits();
    long maxPlaces = exponent + GetMaxFractionDigits();

    long places = numDigits;

    if (places < minPlaces)   places = minPlaces;
    if (places > maxPlaces)   places = maxPlaces;

    // First the stuff to the left of the decimal place
    long consecutiveDigits = 0;
    for (long i = exponent - 1; i >= 0; i--)
    {
        theDigit = (i >= numDigits ? 0 : digits[i]);
        ConvertToNumeral(theDigit, uc);

        text.prepend(uc);
        if (GetIntegerSeparator()// i.e., insert ","
            && ++consecutiveDigits == GetSeparatorSpacing() // insert it here
            && i < exponent - 1
            && i > 0)
        {
            // more digits coming
            TText separatorText;
            GetDigitGroupSeparator(separatorText);
            text.prepend(separatorText);
            consecutiveDigits = 0;
        }
    }
    result.SetIntegerBoundary(text.GetLength());
```

```
    //  Now add the decimal point if we have decimal places or we always show it
    if (places > exponent  || GetDecimalWithInteger())
    {
        TText decimalSeparator;
        GetDecimalSeparator(decimalSeparator);
        text += decimalSeparator;
    }

    //  Add the decimal places
    consecutiveDigits = 0;
    for (i = exponent; i < places; i++)
    {
        theDigit = (i >= numDigits ? 0 : digits[i]);
        ConvertToNumeral(theDigit, uc);
        text += uc;

        if (GetFractionSeparator()
            && ++consecutiveDigits == GetSeparatorSpacing()
            && i < places - 1)
        {
            // more digits coming
            TText separatorText;
            GetDigitGroupSeparator(separatorText);
            text += separatorText;
            consecutiveDigits = 0;
        }
    }

    result.SetDigitSequenceEnd(text.GetLength());

    delete [] digits;
}
```

Implementing TNumberFormatLocale

TNumberFormatLocale is the most OS/2-specific class in our framework. It sets up the number formatters to match the settings it extracts from the OS/2 Presentation Manager's locale.

CreateCurrencyFormatter member function

CreateCurrencyFormatter creates a currency formatter that correctly formats currency for the current locale by making calls to the OS/2 function localeconv and then modifying a TFloatingPointNumberFormatter object's settings to match the locale information.

```
TNumberFormatter* TNumberFormatLocale::CreateCurrencyFormatter() const
{
    TText prefix, suffix;
    bool signFirst = false;
    bool useSign = true;

    // make a formatter
    TFloatingPointNumberFormatter* formatter = new TFloatingPointNumberFormatter();

    // get locale info from OS/2
    lconv* localeInfo = localeconv();
```

```
// set positive currency info
switch (localeInfo->p_sign_posn)
{
    case 0:
        // enclose in parens
        // no localized parens available, so we hardcode
        prefix += '(';
        HandleSymbols(localeInfo->p_cs_precedes,
                      localeInfo->p_sep_by_space, false, false,
                      localeInfo->currency_symbol,
                      localeInfo->positive_sign,
                      prefix, suffix);
        suffix += ')';
        break;
    case 1:
        // sign precedes quantity and currency symbol
        prefix += localeInfo->positive_sign;
        HandleSymbols(localeInfo->p_cs_precedes,
                      localeInfo->p_sep_by_space, false, false,
                      localeInfo->currency_symbol,
                      localeInfo->positive_sign,
                      prefix, suffix);
        break;
    case 2:
        // sign follows quantity and currency symbol
        HandleSymbols(localeInfo->p_cs_precedes,
                      localeInfo->p_sep_by_space, false, false,
                      localeInfo->currency_symbol,
                      localeInfo->positive_sign,
                      prefix, suffix);
        suffix += localeInfo->positive_sign;
        break;
    case 3:
        // sign precedes currency symbol
        signFirst = true;
        // fall through...
    case 4:
        // sign follows currency symbol
        HandleSymbols(localeInfo->p_cs_precedes,
                      localeInfo->p_sep_by_space, true, signFirst,
                      localeInfo->currency_symbol,
                      localeInfo->positive_sign,
                      prefix, suffix);
        break;
    default:
        // don't print sign at all
        break;
}
```

```
// set the formatter's positive prefix and suffix
SetPlus(prefix,suffix);

// set up negative suffixes
prefix.del(0,prefix.length());
suffix.del(0,suffix.length());
signFirst = false;
switch (localeInfo->n_sign_posn)
{
    case 0:
        // enclose in parens
        // no localized parens available, so we hardcode
        prefix += '(';
        HandleSymbols(localeInfo->n_cs_precedes,
                      localeInfo->n_sep_by_space, false, false,
                      localeInfo->currency_symbol,
                      localeInfo->negative_sign,
                      prefix, suffix);
        suffix += ')';
        break;
    case 1:
        // sign precedes quantity and currency symbol
        prefix += localeInfo->negative_sign;
        HandleSymbols(localeInfo->n_cs_precedes,
                      localeInfo->n_sep_by_space, false, false,
                      localeInfo->currency_symbol,
                      localeInfo->negative_sign,
                      prefix, suffix);
        break;
    case 2:
        // sign follows quantity and currency symbol
        HandleSymbols(localeInfo->n_cs_precedes,
                      localeInfo->n_sep_by_space, false, false,
                      localeInfo->currency_symbol,
                      localeInfo->negative_sign,
                      prefix, suffix);
        suffix += localeInfo->negative_sign;
        break;
    case 3:
        // sign precedes currency symbol
        signFirst = true;
        // fall through...
    case 4:
        // sign follows currency symbol
        HandleSymbols(localeInfo->n_cs_precedes,
                      localeInfo->n_sep_by_space, true, signFirst,
                      localeInfo->currency_symbol,
                      localeInfo->negative_sign,
                      prefix, suffix);
        break;
    default:
        // don't print sign at all
        break;
}
```

```
    // set the formatter's negative prefix and suffix
    SetMinus(prefix,suffix);

    // set up grouping and separators
    formatter->SetDecimalSeparator(localeInfo->decimal_point);
    formatter->SetDigitGroupSeparator(localeInfo->mon_thousands_sep);
    // OS/2 allows setting spacing of each set of digits separately.
    // Our framework only allows one spacing, so we just use
    // the first grouping
    formatter->SetSeparatorSpacing(localeInfo->mon_grouping[0]);
    formatter->SetMinFractionDigits(localeInfo->frac_digits);
    formatter->SetMaxFractionDigits(localeInfo->frac_digits);

    return formatter;
}
```

CreateCurrencyFormatter calls HandleSymbols, a protected member function of
TNumberFormatLocale, to do most of the work of setting up the prefix and
suffix strings.

```
void  TNumberFormatLocale::HandleSymbols(bool csPrecedes,
                             bool useSpace, bool useSign, bool signFirst,
                             TText& currSym, TText& signSym,
                             TText& prefix, TText& suffix)
{
    if (csPrecedes)
    {
        if (useSign && signFirst)
            prefix += sign;
        prefix += currSym;
        if (useSign && !signFirst)
            prefix += sign;
        if (useSpace)
            prefix += ' ';
    }
    else
    {
        if (useSpace)
            suffix = ' ';
        if (useSign && signFirst)
            suffix += sign;
        suffix += currSym;
        if (useSign && !signFirst)
            suffix += sign;
    }
}
```

CreateFloatingPointFormatter member function

CreateFloatingPointFormatter's implementation is similar to that of
CreateCurrencyFormatter, but because it doesn't have to address the issues of
sign and currency symbol formatting, it is much simpler.

```
TNumberFormatter* TNumberFormatLocale::CreateFloatingPointFormatter() const
{
    TText prefix, suffix;

    // make a formatter
    TFloatingPointNumberFormatter* formatter = new TFloatingPointNumberFormatter();

    // get locale info from OS/2
    lconv* localeInfo = localeconv();

    // set up grouping and separators
    formatter->SetDecimalSeparator(localeInfo->decimal_point);
    formatter->SetDigitGroupSeparator(localeInfo->thousands_sep);
    // OS/2 allows setting spacing of each set of digits separately.
    // Our framework only allows one spacing, so we just use
    // the first grouping
    formatter->SetSeparatorSpacing(localeInfo->grouping[0]);

    return formatter;
}
```

UPDATING THE SPREADSHEET DATA OBJECTS

At this point, we'll use the framework we've created to update the application.

Note that we need to alter almost nothing in the Presentation Manager–specific code to accommodate these new classes. Therefore, main, WindowSA1WndProc, and ProcessFocusChange remain identical to the versions we examined in Chapter 8.

Our second sample, the application with the new framework added, does not add any new formatting features: we need only modify some of the internals of the classes used by the application.

Updating NumberCell

The majority of modifications required to accommodate the framework classes occur in the NumberCell class. Note that the various clients of NumberCell (for example, WindowSA1WndProc, ProcessFocusChange, and the NumberGrid class) were unaffected; their interface to NumberCell is unchanged. The new NumberCell class declaration is as follows. For the original version of the class, refer to "NumberCell class design" on page 152.

```
class NumberCell
{
public:
                    NumberCell(HINSTANCE hInst, HWND hwndParent,
                               int xPos = 0, int yPos = 0,
                               int width = 0, int height = 0);
                    ~NumberCell();

    //=====================================================================
    // Getter methods

    // get the edit handle of the enclosed edit control
    HWND            GetEditHandle();
    // get the child id of the enclosed edit control
    WORD            GetID();
    // get the cell format
    NumberFormat&   GetFormat();
    // get the error status
    bool            GetFormatErrorStatus();
    // return the edit status of the cell
    bool            HasBeenAltered();
```

```
//========================================================================
// Setter methods

// change the altered status of the cell
bool            SetAlteredStatus(bool newStatus);
// set the cell format
void            SetFormat(const NumberFormat &nf);
// set the cell to the general format
void            SetToGeneralFormat(TNumberFormatter* tnf);
// Set the format error status flag.
void            SetFormatErrorStatus(bool errorStatus);


//========================================================================
// Cell operations

// move the cell to x,y
void            Move(int x = 0, int y = 0, int w = 0, int h = 0);
// set to general format, edit
void            Edit();
// format a cell based on current format
int             Update();

static FARPROC fLpfnOldEditProc, fLpfnNewEditProc;

private:
    HWND                fHwndEditControl;// enclosed edit control handle
    TFormattableNumber  fNumber;        // enclosed formattable number
    TNumberFormatter*   fFormatter;     // pointer to cell's formatter
    NumberFormat        fMyFormat;      // the NumberFormat for this cell
    bool                fErrorInFormat; // error status
    bool                fAltered;       // altered status
    static int          fCellNumber;    // unique cell identifier
};
```

On the surface, only a few differences exist between the two versions of our
NumberCell class. We'll explore the significance of these differences as we
continue analyzing this version of the application.

Note that in the new version of NumberCell, we replaced the
FormattableNumber data member, fNumber, with a TFormattableNumber from
the number formatting framework. We also added a new data member,
fFormatter, that contains a pointer to a TNumberFormatter object. Lastly, we
moved the NumberFormat data member from the old FormattableNumber class
to the new version of NumberCell. The NumberFormat object describes the
specific format attributes that the user selects through the Format Number
dialog box. It is *not* part of the framework—it exists only to keep track of the user
interface settings.

NumberCell also has two new member functions, GetFormat and SetFormat, that
provide access to the NumberFormat object.

We'll take a closer look at how these new data members are handled by the
NumberCell class. As described in Chapter 8, the application constructs a
NumberGrid which then constructs an array of NumberCell objects. In the
current version of the application, that much remains unchanged, but the
new NumberCell constructor has been modified to accommodate its new
data members.

```
NumberCell::NumberCell(HINSTANCE hInst, HWND hwndParent , int xPos, int yPos,
                                        int width, int height) : fNumber()
{
    // Create the edit control
    fHwndEditControl =
        WinCreateWindow(hwndParent,                 // Parent
                WC_ENTRYFIELD,                      // Control Class
                " ",                                // Control Text
                (WS_VISIBLE | ES_LEFT | ES_MARGIN),// Control Style
                xPos,                               // Control X position
                yPos,                               // Control Y position
                width,                              // Control Width
                height,                             // Control Height
                hwndParent,                         // Owner
                HWND_BOTTOM,
                fCellNumber++,                      // Control ID
                0,                                  // No Control Data
                0 );                                // No Pres Params
    // subclass the edit control window procedure
    fLpfnOldEditProc = WinSubclassWindow(fHwndEditControl, EditWndProc);
    // store the handle to the enclosing NumberCell
    // in the edit control property list
    SetProp(fHwndEditControl, (LPSTR) "nc", (HANDLE) this);
    fAltered = false;            // new cell, has never been altered
    fErrorInFormat = false;              // default format is OK
    fMyFormat = NumberFormat::GetGeneralNumberFormat();
    fFormatter = NULL;
}
```

The new and old NumberCell constructors are identical, with two exceptions in
the last two statements of the constructor:

```
fMyFormat = NumberFormat::GetGeneralNumberFormat();
fFormatter = NULL;
```

The new constructor initializes its TNumberFormatter pointer, fFormatter, to NIL. The "filling-in" of this pointer is discussed later in this chapter. The new NumberCell constructor also initializes its NumberFormat data member with default settings. This is accomplished via the call to the trivial static member function, NumberFormat::GetGeneralNumberFormat.

```
NumberFormat NumberFormat::GetGeneralNumberFormat()
{
    NumberFormat nf;
    nf.fPrecision = KDEFAULTPRECISION;
    nf.fThousandsDelimitted = false;
    nf.fCurrency = false;
    nf.fIntSeparator = KCOMMA;
    nf.fDecSeparator = KPERIOD;
    nf.fCurrencySymbol = KDOLLARSIGN;
    nf.fFormatType = kFloatingPointFormat;
    return nf;
}
```

This completes the modifications we need to make to the NumberCell constructor.

Using the framework to handle cell updates

We really gain access to the power of these added framework classes through the Update member function, and it's here that we'll find the greatest number of modifications to our original NumberCell class design.

✅ NOTE   Refer to "Implementing ProcessFocusChange" on page 174 for a detailed discussion of the ProcessFocusChange function. This function is responsible for calling the NumberCell::Update member function.

```
int NumberCell::Update()
{
    char szBuffer[KBUFSIZE], *endPtr;
    double dTemp;
    TText tx;

    if ( ! fAltered )                       // if cell has not been changed,
        return 1;                           // exit

    if ( !WinQueryWindowText( fHwndEditControl,
            sizeof(szBuffer), szBuffer ) )  // is the cell empty?
    {
        fErrorInFormat = false;             // if so, format is OK,
        fAltered = false;                   // successfully updated
        return 1;
    }
```

```
        dTemp = strtod( szBuffer, &endPtr );    // attempt conversion
        if ( !*endPtr )                         // if endPtr is NULL,
        {                                        // conversion was successful
            fNumber.SetNumber( dTemp );          // update FormattableNumber value member
            if (!fFormatter)                     // first time cell entry, set the format
                SetFormat( fMyFormat );
            fFormatter->Format(fNumber, tx);     // create a formatted string
            WinSetWindowText( fHwndEditControl,
                (LPSTR) tx.chars() );            //set the edit cell to that format
            fErrorInFormat = false;
            fAltered = false;                    // successfully updated
            return 1;
        }

        // Record that the user has typed-in a bad numeric format
        fErrorInFormat = true;
        // Signal an error
        DosBeep( 0, 0 );
        WinMessageBox(HWND_DESKTOP,
                      fHwndEditControl,
                      "Invalid Numeric Format",
                      "Number Cell Error",
                      0,
                      MB_ICONEXCLAMATION );
        return 0;                                // unsuccessful update
}
```

The Update member function is very similar to the implementation in the first
version of this application, described in Chapter 8. The one significant
difference is in NumberCell's use of its TNumberFormatter member, fFormatter,
approximately midway into the function. In these statements, we first set the
NumberCell's TFormattableNumber to the value the user entered into the
NumberCell's EditControl. This value is read from the EditControl and
converted to a double in the same manner used by the previous version of
Update.

Next, Update formats the number, but note the primary difference between this
and our previous version of the NumberCell class. In the earlier version, the
formatting of the number was carried out by the FormattableNumber object. In
the new version, the TFormattableNumber is handed to the TNumberFormatter,
which then creates a properly formatted text string and stores it in the TText
argument. This is accomplished with the statement

```
    fFormatter->Format(fNumber, theString); // Create a formatted string
```

where fFormatter is the NumberCell's pointer to its TNumberFormatter,
fNumber is the NumberCell's TFormattableNumber, and theString is a local
TText object.

Note that before invoking its Format function, the Update member function verifies whether fFormatter is NIL. The NumberCell's constructor initializes fFormatter to NIL, and fFormatter remains NIL until the user chooses a specific format using the application's Format Number dialog box. If, however, the Update member function is invoked before the user has explicitly selected a display format, the following statement from the Update member function ensures that the TNumberFormatter is reinitialized to the default, generic display format.

```
if (!fFormatter)    // First time cell entry, set the format
    SetFormat(fMyFormat);
```

The remainder of this version of the Update member function is identical to that described in Chapter 8.

Handling changes to the format of a NumberCell

It is helpful to examine the NumberCell::SetFormat member function that gets called in the preceding code. SetFormat's primary task is to set various attributes of the TNumberFormatter, based on the settings of the NumberFormat object passed into the function.

```
void NumberCell::SetFormat(const NumberFormat& nf)
{
    // new entry or format has changed
    if (!fFormatter || (fMyFormat.GetFormatType() != nf.GetFormatType()))
    {
        delete fFormatter;

        // create a floating point formatter
        if (nf.IsCurrency())
            fFormatter =
                TNumberFormatLocale::GetUserLocale().CreateCurrencyFormatter()
        else fFormatter =
                TNumberFormatLocale::GetUserLocale().CreateFloatingPointFormatter();
    }

    // set the precision and thousands delimtter:
    fFormatter->SetIntegerSeparator(nf.IsThousandsDelimitted());

    // set cell to the new format
    fMyFormat = nf;
}
```

FRAMEWORK BENEFITS

We now have a complete and international-friendly application. The framework handles all the details of number formatting, without requiring any significant changes to the application's existing user interface code. Just as importantly, the framework is extensible, which will yield additional benefits in future versions of the application that we might want implement, including reduced maintenance effort and more end-user features.

The following table reviews the effort it took to convert the application to its current form. The text utility classes we used (but didn't have to write) in our framework contained a number of member functions. We've split these classes out of the analysis so that we have a more accurate account of the additional code we had to create for the framework.

	Classes	Member Functions	Lines of Code
Nonframework-based application	4	66	2086
Text utility classes	3	236	2254
Framework-based application	10	395	5803
Framework Delta	**3**	**93**	**1463**

As you can see, we had to write three additional classes and fewer than 100 additional member functions. Most of those additional functions are very short accessor functions, though, so we had to write only 1463 additional lines of code. Considering how much extra functionality we got and how well the framework positions our application for future enhancement, this is a small amount of code to write. Most of our effort went into designing the framework, not implementing it.

CHAPTER 10

EXTENDING THE FRAMEWORK FOR OS/2

Now that we have a working version of our framework-based application, we'll determine whether all the framework creation effort has paid off. Let's assume we've been asked to add support for a new display format: displaying rational numbers (that is, fractions). Very few modifications are required to provide this feature on top of our framework, in stark contrast to the amount of work that would have been necessary to implement this feature using the original, nonframework-based version of the application we created in Chapter 8. This chapter describes the necessary updates, giving you a fairly accurate idea of what would be involved to extend the number formatting framework for other uses.

DESIGNING A RATIONAL NUMBER FORMATTER CLASS

We'll spend most of the effort required to update the application developing a new rational number formatting subclass of TNumberFormatter and a simple rational number class it uses. The new subclass, TRationalNumberFormatter, overrides TNumberFormatter's format function to format the number as text. The new helper class, TRationalNumber, handles converting TFormattableNumber data into a rationalized form. The class hierarchy for the new classes is as follows:

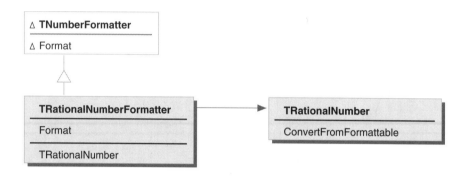

RATIONAL NUMBER FORMATTING CLASS HIERARCHY

Design of TRationalNumberFormatter

As we did when designing TFloatingPointNumberFormatter, we want to make sure the formatting code is as flexible as possible. Thus, we need to ensure that TRationalNumberFormatter lets the caller have a great deal of control over its formatting algorithm. The caller should be able to modify the following properties of the formatter:

- Which string to use as a separator between the numerator and denominator of the fraction
- Which string to use as a separator for the integer part of the rational number (for example, the space after the "3" in "3 2/5")
- Whether to print the rational number as a proper fraction (where the integer part, if any, is printed separately as, for example, in "12 1/4"") or as an improper one (as, for example, in "49/4")
- Whether to print the numerator or denominator first

TRationalNumberFormatter must provide accessors to get and set these parameters.

When TRationalNumberFormatter prints the integer part of the rational number, it should have the same level of localized, user-customizable control over the format as did TFloatingPointNumberFormatter. Rather than duplicate the functionality of that class inside TRationalNumberFormatter, TRationalNumberFormatter has an adopted TNumberFormatter, which it uses to format the integer parts of the rational number.

Finally, TRationalNumberFormatter has to override TNumberFormatter's Format function to actually do the work of using all these parameters to convert a TFormattableNumber into text and return a TFormatResult.

The class definition for our TRationalNumberFormatter class is as follows:

```
class TRationalNumberFormatter : public TNumberFormatter {
public:
    enum EFractionPropriety { kProperFraction, kImproperFraction };
    enum EFractionDirection { kNumeratorFirst, kDenominatorFirst };

    //=====================================================================
    // constructors, destructor, and standard C++ member functions
                TRationalNumberFormatter();
                TRationalNumberFormatter(EFractionPropriety thePropriety,
                    EFractionDirection theFractionDirection = kNumeratorFirst);
                TRationalNumberFormatter(const TRationalNumberFormatter&);
    virtual     ~TRationalNumberFormatter();
    TRationalNumberFormatter& operator=(const TRationalNumberFormatter&);

    //=====================================================================
    // TNumberFormatter overrides
    virtual void    FormattableNumberToText(const TFormattableNumber& num,
                                TText& text, TNumberFormatResult& result);

    //=====================================================================
    // accessors
    virtual void    GetFractionSpace(TText&) const;
    virtual void    SetFractionSpace(const TText&);

    virtual void    GetFractionSign(TText&) const;
    virtual void    SetFractionSign(const TText&);

    virtual EFractionPropriety GetFractionPropriety() const;
    virtual void    SetFractionPropriety(EFractionPropriety);

    virtual EFractionDirection GetFractionDirection() const;
    virtual void    SetFractionDirection(EFractionDirection);

    virtual TNumberFormatter* GetIntegerFormatter() const;
    virtual void    AdoptIntegerFormatter(TNumberFormatter*);

private:
    TText               fFractionSpace;
    TText               fFractionSign;
    EFractionPropriety  fFractionPropriety;
    EFractionDirection  fFractionDirection;
    TRationalNumber     fRationalNumber;
    TNumberFormatter*   fIntegerFormatter;
};
```

**TRationalNumber
helper class**

The design of TRationalNumber is very simple. It represents a rational number as an integer part, a numerator, and a denominator. The core of this class is a member function, ConvertFromFormattable, that analyzes a TFormattableNumber and converts it into a fraction. This member function is called by the TRationalNumberFormatter to handle the mathematical portion of the formatting operation.

```
class TRationalNumber {
public:
        TRationalNumber(long i = 0, long n = 0, long d = 0);
        TRationalNumber(const TFormattableNumber& fpNum);

    long    GetInteger();
    void    SetInteger(long integerPart);

    long    GetNumerator();
    void    SetNumerator(long numeratorPart);

    long    GetDenominator();
    void    SetDenominator(long denominatorPart);

    void    ConvertFromFormattable(const TFormattableNumber& number);

private:
    long    fInteger;
    long    fNumerator;
    long    fDenominator;
};
```

IMPLEMENTING THE FRAMEWORK SUBCLASSES

Now that we've designed the new subclasses for the framework, we can begin to implement them.

Implementing TRationalNumberFormatter

As a subclass of TNumberFormatter, TRationalNumberFormatter hooks into the framework by overriding the number conversion routines called by TNumberFormatter's Format member function.

Constructors, destructor, standard C++ member functions, and accessors

TRationalNumberFormatter's constructors, destructor, and standard C++ member functions are not shown here, but are fairly straightforward. We've also omitted the data accessor member functions shown earlier in the class declaration. The complete source code of the application is available on the accompanying CD-ROM.

Creating the fractional text

The FormattableNumberToText member function, overridden from TNumberFormatter, converts a TFormattableNumber into a textual representation, using the parameters set by the caller. We can implement this behavior with the following algorithm:

1. Use TRationalNumber::ConvertFromFormattable to separate the number into its integer, numerator, and denominator parts.

2. Use the TNumberFormatter specified in fIntegerFormatter to format the integer part (if any, and only if the user asked for a proper fraction) into the output text, followed by the space string stored in fFractionSpace.

3. Write the numerator and denominator, in the order specified by fFractionDirection, separated by the specified fFractionSign string. The numerator and denominator are also formatted using the TNumberFormatter specified in fIntegerFormatter.

The implementation of FormattableNumberToText is as follows:

```
void TRationalNumberFormatter::FormattableNumberToText(
                        const TFormattableNumber& num,
                        TText& text, TNumberFormatResult& result)
{
    TNumberFormatResult tempResult;

    if (!num.IsInfinity() && !num.IsNan())
    {
        fRationalNumber.ConvertFromFormattable(num);

        Boolean doNegative = fRationalNumber.GetInteger() < 0 ||
                        fRationalNumber.GetNumerator() < 0;
        if (fRationalNumber.GetInteger() || !fRationalNumber.GetNumerator())
        {
            TFormattableNumber theformattable;
            theformattable.SetNumber(fRationalNumber.GetInteger());
            GetIntegerFormatter()->Format(theformattable, text, tempResult);
            result.SetCanNormalize(tempResult.GetCanNormalize());
            result.SetOutOfBoundsError(tempResult.GetOutOfBoundsError());
            doNegative = false;
            result.SetIntegerBoundary(text.GetLength());
            if (fRationalNumber.GetNumerator())
            {
                TText fractionSpace;
                GetFractionSpace(fractionSpace);
                text += fractionSpace;
                result.SetCanNormalize(false);
            }
        }
        else result.SetIntegerBoundary(0);

        if (fRationalNumber.GetNumerator())
        {
            result.SetCanNormalize(false);

            if (fRationalNumber.GetNumerator() < 0 && !doNegative)
                fRationalNumber.GetNumerator() = -fRationalNumber.GetNumerator();

            TText numeratorText, denominatorText, fractionText;

            TFormattableNumber theFormattable(fRationalNumber.GetNumerator());
            GetIntegerFormatter()->Format(theFormattable,
                                numeratorText, tempResult);
            if (tempResult.GetOutOfBoundsError())
                result.SetOutOfBoundsError(true);

            theFormattable.SetNumber(fRationalNumber.GetDenominator());
            GetIntegerFormatter()->Format(theFormattable,
                                denominatorText, tempResult);
            if (tempResult.GetOutOfBoundsError())
                result.SetOutOfBoundsError(true);
```

```
                    GetFractionSign(fractionText);
                    if (GetFractionDirection() == TRationalNumberFormatter::kNumeratorFirst)
                    {
                        fractionText.prepend(numeratorText);
                        fractionText += denominatorText;
                    }
                    else
                    {
                        fractionText.prepend(denominatorText);
                        fractionText += numeratorText;
                    }
                    text += fractionText;
                }
                result.SetDigitSequenceEnd(text.GetLength());

                result.SetConfidence(TFormatResult::kPerfect);
        }
    }
```

Implementing TRationalNumber

Based on its design, TRationalNumber's implementation is fairly straightforward. Most of its complexity is in the ConvertFromFormattable function.

TRationalNumber provides the usual constructors, destructor, and data member accessors. Because these functions are all fairly basic for C++ programmers, their implementations are not shown here.

Calculating the numerator and denominator

ConvertFromFormattable takes a TFormattableNumber as input and separates it into integer, numerator, and denominator by finding the greatest common divisor (GCD) of the numerator and denominator. Getting the GCD of floating-point numbers is difficult, so we need to find a way to generate the numerator and denominator as long integers. We'll do this by first using the standard C library routine frexp to convert the number into a mantissa and an integral power of two. The frexp routine guarantees that the mantissa will be in the range

$$0.5 <= |m| < 1.0$$

Now we use the resulting integral exponent to generate integral numerators and denominators. We'll calculate the numerator by multiplying the mantissa by a power of two, (1 << multiplierBits), that will be just big enough to fill up a long integer.

Next, we need to calculate the denominator using the formula $2^{(multiplierBits-exp)}$, where *exp* is the exponent value returned by frexp. As a result, we get a numerator and denominator with large integral values, returning a numeric value nearly identical to the original floating-point number when the numerator is divided by the denominator.

At this point, we can extract the integer part of the number, if any, leaving a proper fraction. We then reduce the proper fraction by finding any common denominator and removing it. The denominator is calculated by the CalcGCD member function, described in the next section.

The source core for ConvertFromFormattable is as follows:

```
void TRationalNumber::ConvertFromFormattable(const TFormattableNumber& number)
{
    int exp;
    int multiplierBits;
    double theFloat = number.GetNumber();

    // use frexp to convert float to a mantissa (0.5 <= |x| < 1.0)
    // and an integral power of 2
    double m = frexp(theFloat,&exp);

    // now we need to make sure that we can fit the numerator and denominator
    // in a long.
    const kBitsPerByte = 8;
    if (exp >= 0)
    {
        if (exp > (sizeof(long)*kBitsPerByte-2))
          cerr << "illegal exponent value";
        multiplierBits = (sizeof(long)*8-2);
    }
    else {
        multiplierBits = exp+(sizeof(long)*kBitsPerByte-2);
        if (multiplierBits < 0)
          cerr << "illegal value";
    }

    // we make the numerator and denominator as large a multiple as we can
    // while preserving ratio between them. This gives us best accuracy.
    fNumerator = (long) (m * ((long) 1 << multiplierBits));
    fDenominator = (long) 1 << ((long) multiplierBits - (long) exp);

    // if number has integer part, separate it out
    if (fNumerator > fDenominator)
      {
        fInteger = fNumerator/fDenominator;
        fNumerator = fNumerator - (fInteger * fDenominator);
      }
    else fInteger = 0;

    // reduce fraction part
    long d1 = CalcGCD(fNumerator, fDenominator);
    if (d1 != 1)
      {
        fNumerator /= d1;
        fDenominator /= d1;
      }
}
```

Calculating the greatest common denominator

The CalcGCD member function, called by ConvertFromFormattable, is another straightforward function. The algorithm is from the National Institute of Health (NIH) class library.

```
long TRationalNumber::CalcGCD(long uu, long vv)
{
    /* gcd -- binary greatest common divisor algorithm - NIHCL Algorithm B, p. 321.
    */
    long u = labs(uu), v = labs(vv);
    long k = 0;
    long t;

    if (u == 0)
      return v;
    if (v == 0)
      return u;

    // get rid of any common multiples of 2
    while ((u & 1) == 0 && (v & 1) == 0)
      {
        u >>= 1;
        v >>= 1;
        k++;
      }

    if (u & 1)
        { t = -v; goto B4; }
    else t = u;

    do {
B4:     while ((t & 1) == 0) t /= 2;
        if (t > 0) u = t;
        else v = -t;
        t = u-v;
    } while (t != 0);

    return u<<k;
}
```

✅ NOTE   Generally, using goto statements is considered poor programming style. In this case, the benefits of reusing a well-tested, public domain library such as the one shown here far outweigh the design issues involved.

This completes our examination of TRationalNumber.

UPDATING THE APPLICATION

Now that we've implemented the new formatting classes, we'll need to update the spreadsheet application to support it.

Updating NumberCell's SetFormat function

Update is called by the application to reformat a cell. In the previous two versions of the sample, this function calls SetFormat to create a TNumberFormatter whenever one does not already exist or the user has altered the format specification for the cell since the last time the cell was formatted. The new version of SetFormat has been modified to support the rational number format. Notice that the type of number formatter created depends on the cell's display format specification, which for this sample can be either a floating-point (inclusive of currency format) or rational number representation.

```
void NumberCell::SetFormat(const NumberFormat& nf)
{
    if (!fFormatter ||  fMyFormat.GetFormatType() != nf.GetFormatType())
    {
        // format type has changed, delete the old formatter
        delete fFormatter;
        if ( nf.GetFormatType() == NumberFormat::kFloatingPointFormat )
        {
            // create a floating-point formatter
            if (nf.IsCurrency())
                fFormatter =
                    TNumberFormatLocale::GetUserLocale().CreateCurrencyFormatter()
            else fFormatter =
                    TNumberFormatLocale::GetUserLocale().CreateFloatingPointFormatter();
        }
        else fFormatter = new TRationalNumberFormatter();

        // set cell to the new format
        fMyFormat = nf;
    }
}
```

✔ NOTE   The implementation of this function illustrates a weakness in the framework's current design. The hardcoded if statements determine the kind of TNumberFormatter subclass we create. A more extensible approach would allow new types of formats to be added dynamically, perhaps by using a dictionary to map between the format types returned by the TNumberFormat object and the corresponding TNumberFormatter object.

Updating the Format Cell dialog box

The modifications needed to add an additional format choice to the Format Cell dialog box are minor. The WindowSA1WndProc function contains two nested switch statements. The "case IDM_WINDOWSA1_FORMAT_CELL:" within the innermost switch statement is responsible for displaying the Format Cell dialog box using a call to the PanelCELLFORMDlgProc function. An excerpt of that code from WindowSA1WndProc is as follows:

```
MRESULT EXPENTRY WindowSA1WndProc(HWND hWnd, ULONG  Message,
                              MPARAM Param1, MPARAM Param2)
{
    // ...
    switch (SHORT1FROMMP(Param1)) {
        case IDM_WINDOWSA1_FORMAT_CELL:
            HWND hWndPanel = NULLHANDLE;
            // if the cell does not contain a valid numeric string
            // ... Refer to previous chapter for details
            // This makes a call to the dialog box named "PanelCELLFORM"
            hWndPanel = WinLoadDlg (HWND_DESKTOP,              // Parent
                               hWndMain,                      // Owner
                               PanelCELLFORMDlgProc,          // Message Proc
                               hModFRAMEWRK,
                               ID_PANELCELLFORM,              // Resource ID
                               (PVOID) &hWnd);                // hWndCaller
            if (hWndPanel != NULLHANDLE)
            {
              USHORT rc;
              rc = WinProcessDlg (hWndPanel); // Modal Dialog
            }
        }
        break;
        // ...
    }
    // ...
}
```

To include the new rational number format choice in the dialog box, we need to add another line to the function responsible for initializing the dialog box. This code is found in the "case WM_INITDLG:" clause of the message switch for the dialog box's window procedure.

```
MRESULT EXPENTRY PanelCELLFORMDlgProc (HWND    hWnd,
                                       ULONG   Message,
                                       MPARAM  Param1,
                                       MPARAM  Param2)
{
    // ...
    switch (Message)
    {
        case WM_INITDLG:
        {
            char *formats[] = { "####", "#,###", "####.#", "####.##", "#,###.#",
                                "#,###.##", "$####.##", "$#,###.##","## ##/##" };
            // ...
            for (i = 0; i < 9; ++i)
                nSel = WinInsertLboxItem( hwndListbox, LIT_END, formats[i] );
            // ...
        }
        // ...
    }
    // ...
}
```

Finally, we must add an additional case to the switch statement in the FormatCell member function to add support for our new format code.

```
void NumberGrid::FormatCell(int nFormatCode)
{
    NumberFormat nf;
    switch (nFormatCode)
    {
        case 0:
            nf.Set(0, false, false, KCOMMA, KPERIOD);
            break;
        case 1:
            nf.Set(0, true, false, KCOMMA, KPERIOD);
            break;
        case 2:
            nf.Set(1, false, false, KCOMMA, KPERIOD);
                break;
        case 3:
            nf.Set(2, false, false, KCOMMA, KPERIOD);
            break;
        case 4:
            nf.Set(1, true, false, KCOMMA, KPERIOD);
            break;
        case 5:
            nf.Set(2, true, false, KCOMMA, KPERIOD);
            break;
        case 6:
            nf.Set(2, false, true, KCOMMA, KPERIOD);
            break;
```

```
        case 7:
            nf.Set(2, true, true, KCOMMA, KPERIOD);
            break;
        case 8:
            nf.Set(2, true, true, KCOMMA, KPERIOD, KDOLLARSIGN,
                    NumberFormat::kRationalNumberFormat);
            break;
    }
    fGrid[fCurrentCell/fNCols][fCurrentCell % fNCols]->Edit();
    // set the current cell to the appropriate format
    fGrid[fCurrentCell/fNCols][fCurrentCell % fNCols]->SetFormat(nf);
    // update it
    fGrid[fCurrentCell/fNCols][fCurrentCell % fNCols]->Update();

}
```

USING EXTENSIBILITY TO DELIVER FEATURES FASTER

These are all the modifications to the application required to support our new rational number formatter. The application has added support for a new feature, with no modifications to the framework and very few modifications to the user interface code. A typical developer can develop this feature in a relatively short amount of time.

Adding this feature to the original version of the application developed in Chapter 8 would have been much more difficult and time-consuming. Clearly, using a well-designed framework has a direct benefit as programs are enhanced over time.

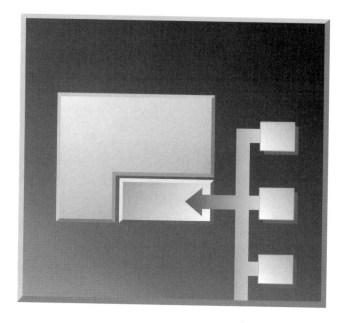

PART 3

LEVERAGING FRAMEWORKS

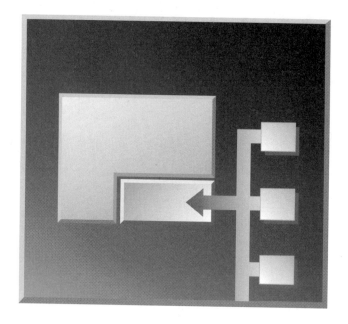

CHAPTER 11

MAXIMIZING YOUR FRAMEWORK BENEFITS

As you've seen, the benefits gained from developing frameworks are not necessarily immediate: frameworks are a long-term investment. Underlying all discussion of frameworks is the issue of time. Framework designers need more time initially to create a framework than they do to create a procedural or class library. Clients might need more time to learn to use a framework than is necessary with a procedural or class library.

Although writing your own frameworks has a number of benefits, you can get even more leverage by using frameworks that are already available from other sources, either internally in your own company or purchased from vendors who design framework solutions. Consider the advantages and disadvantages in both these approaches as you begin to work with frameworks.

WHEN TO DEVELOP, WHEN TO USE FRAMEWORKS?

When should you develop your own frameworks, and when should you use someone else's preexisting framework?

Consider writing your own framework if:

- No existing framework is available.
- You expect the framework to be reused.
- You expect the design requirements to change over time.

On the other hand, if a developer has the appropriate domain expertise and makes a framework available, consider using it if:

- The framework's design fits your needs with little or no customization required.
- You have confidence in the long-term maintainability of the code and in support from the provider.
- The framework provider has done the necessary design work to ensure a robust framework.

Frameworks are a long-term win: the cost of designing a framework is paid up front, while the benefits accrue over time.

CREATING YOUR OWN FRAMEWORKS

Chapter 3 discusses the basics of developing a framework; Part 2 takes you through the actual steps you need to create a framework. The following topics discuss issues to consider when you build, release, and maintain your framework as a product.

Explaining your frameworks

Well-commented headers, complete documentation, and sample code are a necessary part of any programming project, but they are especially important when developing frameworks. As a framework developer, you have to provide information so that your clients understand how to use the framework to produce the solution they want.

Documenting your framework

Make it clear which classes your clients can use directly, which classes they must instantiate, and which classes and member functions they must override. Clients want to know how your framework helps them solve their problems, so the details of the framework implementation itself are not as important.

When you document your framework, include the following information:

- Diagrams of the framework architecture, including design patterns
- Descriptions of the framework
- Directions for using the framework
- Limitations for framework use—what the framework does not cover as a guide for customer extensions

Including sample programs

At a minimum, provide as many sample programs as possible. In the process of developing and testing your framework, you'll have to develop applications that exercise your framework—often these applications can become the foundation for a set of sample applications. Try to provide a variety of samples that demonstrate how to use the framework in different contexts—a well-rounded set of sample programs is invaluable for clients learning your framework and essential if you do not distribute the source code for your framework. Consider designing the sample programs so that they show a progression of the architectural features of the framework.

Following common coding standards

When more than one developer works on a software project, having a common coding style becomes increasingly important. Using coding standards consistently helps to make your frameworks more understandable and can help address common design errors. Taligent has compiled lists of coding do's and don'ts in *Taligent's Guide to Designing Programs: Well-Mannered Object-Oriented Design in C++* (Taligent 1994). This book provides an excellent basis for developing coding standards for object-oriented programming projects.

Managing change

Frameworks evolve, especially as your understanding of the problem domain expands and the number of clients grows. However, once you release a framework for client use, you need to limit the changes—a constantly changing framework is difficult to use.

As a general rule, you should:

- Fix bugs immediately (clients can have difficulty working around a bug in your flow of control).
- Add new features occasionally. Add new interfaces instead of redefining existing ones.
- Change existing interfaces as infrequently as possible.

During the development of a framework, changes happen much more frequently. However, once clients start using a framework, you might still need to make changes that affect their work.

When you do update a framework, minimize the impact on your clients. It's better to add new classes instead of changing the existing class hierarchy and to add new functions instead of changing or removing existing functions. On the other hand, avoid bloating the framework with unnecessary classes and functions.

Give your clients advance notice of framework updates and allow time for them to adapt to the changes. One approach is to add the new and changed classes in an interim release and flag the old ones with obsolete warnings. This way, your clients are forewarned as to when classes they are using are going to change.

Managing dependencies

Projects can often be factored into a number of separate frameworks and assigned to small teams. If it takes more than three or four developers to produce a framework, decide whether the project can be split into a set of smaller frameworks. Teams of two to four are also more effective than one developer working alone, unless the single developer is both an experienced framework developer and a domain expert.

Working with several small teams introduces additional management challenges:

- Developers focus on one aspect of a large project and might not understand all the interrelationships and client implications.
- Architectural consistency must be maintained across teams. Determine which frameworks can best store functionality across projects.
- Dependencies between frameworks can create bottlenecks.

To alleviate these problems, you can adopt several strategies:

- Appoint a project architect who maintains the "big picture," ensuring that the frameworks ultimately work together.
- Establish and follow standard design and coding guidelines.
- Decouple the frameworks by isolating their interdependencies in intermediary classes and, if necessary, provide libraries or classes, or frameworks to tie them together.

Project architect

Having a project architect on your team who is responsible for the overall design integrity of all your software can help you keep control over your software. A good architect has enough domain expertise to understand the specific technical problems being solved by each framework, while still having a general understanding of the team's effort as a whole. The architect can enforce using frameworks over many projects and encourage framework distribution.

If you are the architect for your team, stay focused on the big picture. The best architects act as guides through the design process, leaving the details of the design and implementation to the domain experts.

Isolate interdependencies

Often when one framework requires the services of another, the connection can be implemented through an interface or server object. Then, only one object is dependent on the other framework. Until the other framework can support the necessary operations, the intermediary class provides stub code that allows you to test the dependent framework. Loosely-coupled frameworks are generally more flexible from the client's perspective as well.

For example, let's say you're working on a database query tool, and you need to use a communications framework to set up a connection to a remote database across the network. The framework provides a class that represents a network address, stream classes for reading and writing data, and various exception classes that handle network errors. You could use the framework as is, using its data types directly throughout your framework's interfaces. The downside is that your framework's interface is inextricably linked to the communications framework—changes to that framework might break your interfaces, and you are never able to use your framework on a platform where the communications framework does not exist.

A better alternative is to provide an abstract class that addresses your framework's communication needs and to use that class within your framework. You can then implement the abstract class (through a concrete subclass) using the communications framework to handle the details. This allows you to use new frameworks as they become available. If you later have to port your framework, you can reimplement the class (as a different concrete subclass) using a different underlying framework or library.

At times it is appropriate to let your dependencies show through. For example, an application's user interface module that contains platform-specific user interface code should use that platform's facilities to the fullest extent, because the portability and modularity issues don't apply. Similarly, you can expose external dependencies in a framework's interface if you know that these dependencies are unlikely to cause problems in the future.

You can use this same approach to isolate platform-dependent code or code that accesses a particular applications framework. When you use different platforms or application frameworks, you need to modify only an isolated piece of the framework. This modification does not affect your clients. You can also use intermediaries to access legacy data or nonframework services.

Publishing your framework

To get the maximum benefit—reuse—from your framework, you must distribute it to others who can use it. Whether you design your framework to use internally or to distribute outside your company, treat it as a product from the start. In addition to documenting the framework thoroughly, plan how to distribute and support the finished product for both internal and external clients.

Consider publishing your framework outside your company. Weigh the disadvantages against the advantages. One of the obvious disadvantages is that you often must continue to provide support. But the advantages can outweigh this factor. Widening the range of your framework's use correspondingly widens the range of feedback you'll receive. This leads to more robust frameworks and the opportunity to add features based on customer input. In addition, your framework can be a source of revenue for your company.

Distributing your frameworks

To ensure that other developers can use your frameworks, they need to know not only that the frameworks exist, but also how to access them. You must establish a a process for distributing your frameworks so that developers can use them. Ideally, all frameworks should be kept in a central repository, with a repository manager responsible for notifying clients about newly developed frameworks and updates to existing ones. With a large enough repository of existing frameworks, other developers can select the appropriate frameworks from which to build when developing new applications.

Encouraging reuse

There's more to reuse, though, than merely making the frameworks available: your organization must actively cultivate reusing frameworks. One way is to adjust the recognition structures—encourage and support developers who write and distribute frameworks that others can use. And, equally important, reward the developers who use them. The following ideas can help promote reuse:

- Evaluate productivity based on client functionality implemented, instead of using lines of code or other size-based metrics. The best implementation is one that gets the most done for the client, and reusing a framework is a good way to get a lot done with less effort.
- Maintain a repository of reusable code, and provide awards and/or recognition to the developers of widely reused code.

Encouraging feedback

Be sure to release your framework to your clients early in your iterative development cycle, in time to incorporate feedback. Early feedback from developers ensures that your design meets the needs of your clients. Take an active role in encouraging feedback, and be sure that your clients know that you'll respond to their feedback.

Providing support

To fully realize the benefits frameworks can provide, your organization should commit the necessary resources to support its frameworks over time. Developers will not use your frameworks unless you respond to problem reports and feature requests.

Early in its creation, a framework requires routine maintenance to fix bugs and provide new functionality. But framework support is not limited to bug fixing and minor feature additions. Over time, even a well-crafted framework needs design alterations to support client requirements as they change.

With frameworks, this is where the investment pays off. Over the lifetime of a framework, the cost of supporting it actually becomes a benefit. The cost of supporting one framework with three dependent applications is less than the cost of supporting three independent applications with duplicate code. The more applications using a framework, the bigger the savings. In the long run, using frameworks can substantially reduce support and maintenance costs.

REUSING EXISTING FRAMEWORKS

Reusing existing frameworks can make programming more productive and more rewarding, because you can concentrate your efforts on adding value to the application in your area of domain expertise instead of implementing your application's infrastructure. Before you can reuse frameworks effectively, however, you must address several issues.

Learning overhead

You have to know how a framework works to begin writing software with it. You need to understand what the various classes are and the functionality they provide. You also need to understand how these classes interact with each other, and what they expect from your code. Acquiring all this knowledge takes time.

If you start by learning the basics, and build your knowledge of the framework incrementally, you can program and debug productively with that framework. In addition, because much of the overhead comes from understanding in general how frameworks work, learning how to use one framework can often help when learning another.

Loss of flow of control

Programming using frameworks, as described by Dave Wilson (1994) has been likened to the developer being inside a box, in the dark. Occasionally the framework opens the lid of the box for a moment, yells something at the developer such as "Draw yourself!" and then slams the lid shut. You do the framework's bidding, not the other way around.

The key to overcoming uncertainty in the "don't call us, we'll call you" world of frameworks is to learn to think in terms of the responsibilities of objects—what the objects are required to do—and let the framework determine when the objects should do it. Once developers understand frameworks, they can begin to realize the enormous advantages that framework-oriented programming can deliver over other development approaches.

Preserving creativity

Getting over the loss of the flow of control is the single biggest stumbling block to becoming an accomplished framework user. Some developers believe that frameworks impose a particular canonical way of doing things, thus compromising their creativity. It is true that frameworks require that code adhere to their protocols (how else could a framework call your code?), but this misses the larger issue—in return for orthodoxy at the statement and declaration level, you are often given more power and flexibility at the design level.

The rewards of using frameworks, however, are considerable. By relinquishing flow of control, you gain the potential for substantial reuse, a large base of existing functionality, and the ability to focus on your problem's unique aspects instead of less relevant implementation details. As a consequence, your overall code size is reduced, your time to market is reduced, and your code's reliability and usability is greatly increased. Frameworks let you express your creativity where it makes the biggest impact—in the form of radically new and powerful features.

Debugging

Using frameworks that take over the flow of control can make debugging your program more difficult. Unless you are familiar with the internal structure of the framework, it is difficult to know how code was called inside the program. Consequently, the program's behavior is difficult to follow when debugging. Of course, the better designed the framework, and the more knowledge you have of its design, the less of a problem framework debugging becomes.

You can help alleviate this problem by becoming an expert at using your debugger's breakpoints. Setting a breakpoint on one of your own member functions to see where and by which code it is called can be very informative. Setting a conditional point on a member function so that it breaks only when called for a certain object helps track down difficult problems.

Finally, having a high-quality source-level debugger, and especially a debugger that understands objects, is of enormous benefit.

Coding overhead

Frameworks impose a certain amount of coding overhead: they require some "boilerplate" code to support particular protocols. A minimal CommonPoint application—the Taligent version of a "Hello world" program—works out to about 200 lines of code.

Keep in mind that a CommonPoint system version of "Hello world" has more features than a five-line version on a UNIX workstation. In the CommonPoint system, even the minimal program offers features available to all CommonPoint applications, including:

- Embedding compound documents
- Multilevel undo/redo
- Document saving and version control
- Collaboration
- Printing
- Localization
- Hypermedia linking and traversal
- Windows, panes, menus, and screen support

If you are familiar with X Window System or Windows programming, estimate the level of effort required by those systems to provide the same features as those listed for a similar "Hello world" program.

Overhead versus complexity

Developers typically don't write trivial "Hello world" sorts of programs. What they write instead are complex applications that require multiple developers and a significant investment. On conventional systems, these applications require considerable design and coding. In the CommonPoint system, however, the total amount of design and coding is greatly reduced, both because of the presence of frameworks and because of the reuse that comes from components.

The CommonPoint system often requires a higher initial overhead to implement any given component, but this is more than offset by combining components to provide more complex functionality. As the complexity of the target application increases, the cost on a CommonPoint system grows much more slowly than the cost on a traditional system, despite the higher overhead at the beginning—at some point early in the development process the two curves cross.

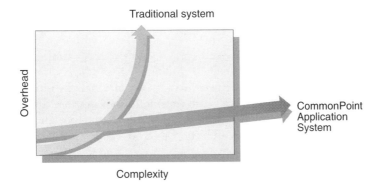

LEARNING OVERHEAD VERSUS SYSTEM COMPLEXITY

Thus, despite higher initial overhead, the average cost per delivered capability is much lower for the CommonPoint system than on other systems. This cost differential is analogous to the time and cost it takes to set up a production line versus doing custom work: while the production line is slower getting started, once it starts to produce, it quickly beats the time needed to create custom products.

In the CommonPoint system, think of the coding overhead required by the frameworks as the cost of getting the production line built. Once a wide variety of components are available, the production line can generate production-quality applications in a fraction of the time required on a conventional system.

Performance issues

Performance can also be an issue when using frameworks, especially when a generic framework is used to solve a simple problem. A generalized framework always has more runtime overhead than a hand-tailored, single-use solution. However, careful design and tuning of the framework minimizes these problems. In addition, the extensibility of the framework pays off over time, as the program gets larger. In fact, for production-quality programs (with, for example, more than 25,000 lines of code), a framework-based program normally offers size and speed benefits, because the overhead of the framework becomes less and less significant as programs become larger.

ACCRUING FRAMEWORK BENEFITS OVER TIME

Frameworks are still a new concept, even for developers used to object-oriented design and programming. Whether you choose to develop your own frameworks or use those available through other sources for your programming solutions, the productivity gains do not automatically follow the first or second use of the technology. Frameworks provide the greatest gains in productivity through multiple uses. The benefits from using and reusing frameworks are felt only over time. Once developers and organizations understand—and experience—these benefits, they accept frameworks as an important and usable approach to software development.

Object-oriented technology, using frameworks in particular:

- Makes development faster once you've mastered the initial learning curve
- Integrates maintenance into the iterative process of your development cycle
- Makes delivery and training easier

Frameworks take you a step beyond class libraries. Class libraries help one programmer create one application program one time. Two programming teams using same class library can create two application programs with similar design and structure. But if the two teams both use the same framework, the two resulting programs have very similar structure. These programs, based on a common framework, are more likely to interoperate. The two programs can be enhanced in similar ways over time. Members of one team can move to the other team and be productive. Teams can write new programs to interact with the first two. All this happens as a result of working with the framework—"the common DNA"—as the basis of the application.

To maximize the benefits of developing with frameworks, consider how best your projects and organization can use frameworks. You can take or combine two approaches:

- Develop your own frameworks.
- Use existing internal or commercially-available frameworks.

If you choose to develop your own frameworks, treat the framework as a product from the very beginning of the process:

- Develop the framework with good documentation.
- Use consistent coding standards.
- Design with methods to manage change.
- Manage your projects to use frameworks over a group of applications and promote reuse throughout your projects.
- Release the framework to internal and external customers to get feedback to improve the framework.

If you use available frameworks, consider how best to handle issues such as the following:

- Education to minimize the learning curve
- Loss of control to the framework
- Complexity issues and coding overhead
- Performance

Chapter 12

Introducing the CommonPoint application system

By now, you should have a sense of how reusing frameworks can help you create more feature-rich, maintainable, and extensible programs more efficiently than you ever could before. However, a survey of the marketplace shows that few frameworks are available for purchase, except in the category of the GUI application frameworks including Microsoft Foundation Classes (MFC), the Borland Object Windows Library, and MacApp.

Does this mean that you are going to be forced to design and implement *all* of the frameworks you need by yourself? Fortunately, the answer is no. More and more frameworks become available every day. Better still, the Taligent CommonPoint application system includes nearly 100 frameworks, designed to solve a wide variety of problems commonly faced by application and system programmers.

KEY BENEFITS OF THE COMMONPOINT APPLICATION SYSTEM

To show you how powerful framework reuse can be, the following topics provide a brief overview of the benefits, including breadth, depth, and extensibility of services provided and the high-level structure of the CommonPoint application system. For more details on the features of the CommonPoint system and the philosophy behind its design, refer to the CommonPoint developer documentation or to *Inside Taligent Technology* (Cotter with Potel 1995).

Providing services

The CommonPoint system environment provides services that cover many more areas of application programming than any preceding application system. (Virtually everything in the system is handled via object interfaces.) In addition to providing more extensive document-, view-, and command-handling mechanisms than previous generation GUI application frameworks, the CommonPoint system supplies object-oriented support for everything from multimedia and graphics, to file and database access, and even tasks and threads.

The CommonPoint system offers not only object-oriented facilities for a broad range of functionality, it also provides a great deal of depth in that functionality. The Data Access Frameworks, for example, are designed to communicate with databases through a large number of standard protocols, including ODBC. The Localization Services provide an unprecedented level of support for international text formatting and editing. All the frameworks that comprise the CommonPoint system are designed to work with as broad a range of existing systems as possible.

System extensibility

Working with established systems is necessary, but it's not enough. For a system to be truly useful, it has to work with future technologies as well. CommonPoint application system frameworks are designed to be extensible, fully leveraging the capabilities of framework design. Furthermore, this extensibility is not designed just for use by Taligent as it develops future versions of the system. The system is purposely designed so that application developers and OEMs can also provide extensions.

Portability

The CommonPoint system is a portable application system that lives on top of and cooperates with many different operating systems, including AIX®, HP-UX®, OS/2, Mac OS, Windows 95, and Windows NT. Because of the breadth and depth of the CommonPoint system functionality, you can write most application programs without making any calls to the underlying system's APIs. CommonPoint applications should port very smoothly to run on different systems, furnishing developers with an easy and cost-effective way of managing multiplatform software development.

A new user interface paradigm

The CommonPoint system design lays the foundation for a new user interface paradigm, grounded in the People, Places, and Things® metaphor and focused on Task Centered Computing™. CommonPoint applications are compound document–based, enabling unprecedented support for collaborative computing.

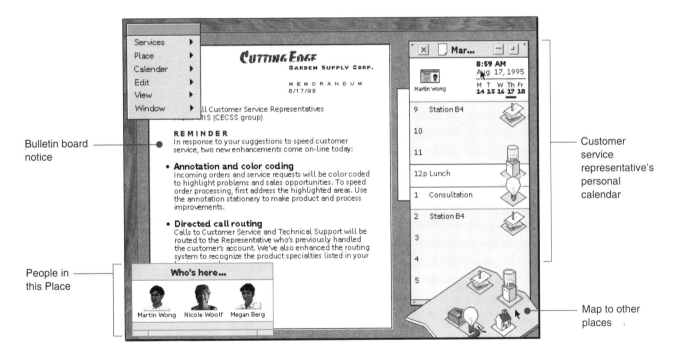

CommonPoint SYSTEM USER INTERFACE METAPHOR

A TAXONOMY OF THE COMMONPOINT APPLICATION SYSTEM

The CommonPoint application system offers the developer substantial breadth and depth of programming functionality. At its highest level, think of the system as providing two distinct sets of services:

- Application Frameworks, used to create powerful, interactive applications.
- System Services, used to manipulate data, to communicate with other computers, and to interface to the underlying operating system. These frameworks insulate applications from the underlying operating system, thus providing portability across platforms.

The following sections describe the frameworks available from Taligent in the CommonPoint system: Application Frameworks and System Services.

Application Frameworks	Embeddable Data Types		Allow viewing and editing of complex data types, with full support for linking and embedding.	
		Graphics Editing Framework	Allows structured editing of graphical objects.	
		Text Editing Framework	Allows editing of text with full support for styles and languages.	
		Document Data Access Framework	Provides an embeddable document component that represents a database query and its results.	
		Time Media User Interface Framework	Provides standard document parts that can be used to present video, audio, and other time media data.	
	Desktop Frameworks		Support the CommonPoint application model, including its user interface policy, its look and feel, and its compound document architecture.	
		Workspace Framework	Allows developers to create extensions to the Taligent People, Places, and Things user interface.	
		Presentation Framework	Unifies a number of user interface and document model mechanisms, making it easier to create fully featured, document-based CommonPoint applications.	
		Document Frameworks	Provide a document model as the basis for data representation.	
			Shared Document Framework	Allows compound documents to be used in a collaborative environment across a network.
			Compound Document Framework	Supports active linking and embedding data from other documents.
			Basic Document Framework	Supports the basic document architecture of the system, including storage and command processing.

Application Frameworks (continued)	Desktop Frameworks (continued)	User Interface Frameworks	Support the creation and use of interactive user interface elements.	
			Cursor Tools	Support creation of generic cursor tools, which can be used to manipulate many data types.
			Dialogs	Allow sets of user interface elements to be grouped together.
			Clipboard	Provides a mechanism for the user to store and retrieve data on the clipboard, within or between applications.
			Drag and Drop	Provides an abstract protocol for direct manipulation of user interface objects.
			Windows	Provide a set of basic window types and handle common window management operations, including resizing, zooming, and moving.
			Frames	Provide a selectable, manipulatable frame around a view.
			Controls	Provide a wide range of interactive user interface elements, including buttons, scroll bars, and menus.
			Views	Provide a basic mechanism for dividing a user interface into a hierarchical collection of views, each of which may have its own coordinate system, transform, and buffering mechanism.
			Actions	Allow a handler to be notified when the user performs an action.
			Input	Provides a mechanism for converting user input into user interface events.
			User Interface Utilities	Provide miscellaneous services for creating user interfaces, including support for labels and decorations.
	Application Services		Support media- and data-handling services needed to create industrial-strength, interactive applications.	
		Interoperability Services	Allow CommonPoint applications to interoperate with other systems.	
			OpenDoc and OLE Compatibility	Provides interoperability with OpenDoc and OLE.
			Graphics Converters	Provide conversion of several industry-standard graphics formats into the CommonPoint system graphics format.
			Text Converters	Supports conversion of plain and styled text into the CommonPoint system text format.
			Data Translation Framework	Provides a framework for data exchange with non-CommonPoint software.

Application Frameworks (continued)	*Application Services (continued)*	**Printing**		Supports platform- and printer-independent printing.
			Document Printing	Supports the printing of CommonPoint documents.
			Print Jobs	Support user- and printer-customizable print jobs.
			Basic Printing	Provides a model for printing pages to a printer.
			Printing Devices	Provide a hardware-independent abstraction of a printer.
		Scanning		Provides an abstract mechanism for control of scanners.
		Time Media		Supports a rich set of time media data types.
			MIDI	Allows use of MIDI devices to produce and record music.
			Audio	Supports general sound production and recording facilities.
			Telephony	Allows voice communications to be integrated into CommonPoint applications.
			Video	Supports video playback and recording.
		Localization Services		Support multilingual and localizable user interface elements and text.
			Date and Time Conversion	Supports language-sensitive conversion of dates and times into and from a textual form.
			Text Analysis	Supports language-sensitive text collation, pattern matching, and boundary searching.
			Text Input and Output	Supports transliteration, virtual keyboards, and other text I/O services.
			Text Scanning and Formatting	Supports the reading and writing of numbers and other binary data in a textual form.
			Locales	Provide a hierarchy of archived resources localized for each geographic region.
		Text		Supports styled, multilingual text data.
			Line Layout	Support for text direction, highlighting, and line-by-line display of multilingual styled text.
			Paragraph Styles	Support paragraph styles, including indents and line spacing.
			Text Styles	Support for text styles, including fonts, sizes, positioning, and color.
			Text and Style Storage Management	Provides basic support for storage of textual information, including styles, text ranges, and text positions.
			Character Sets	Support Unicode characters and other character sets via transcoding.

Application Frameworks (continued)	Application Services (continued)	Graphics		Provide a rich set of services for modeling and rendering 2-D and 3-D graphics.
			2-D Graphics	Support 2-D graphics, including geometries, attribute bundles, transforms, and high-level 2-D graphics objects.
			3-D Graphics	Support 3-D graphics, including geometries, attribute bundles, transforms, and high-level 3-D graphics objects.
			Colors	Support multiple color spaces and color matching.
			Font Support	Provides font rendering support independent of font format.
			Sprites	Support bitmap animation.
			Pixel Buffers	Provide an abstraction for onscreen and offscreen pixel buffers.
			Graphic Devices	Provide basic capabilities for graphics device drivers, including rasterization, device transforms, and color mapping.
			Displays	Provide an abstract display screen.

System Services	Enterprise Services			Provide a set of services that allow the CommonPoint application system to interoperate with other computers distributed within an enterprise.
		Data Access Framework		Allows data on local or remote databases to be accessed, queried, and modified.
		Caucus Framework		Provides multicast communications facilities for collaborative applications.
		System Management		Supports administration of computers throughout the enterprise, including software installation, system configuration, maintenance, security, and support.
			Licensing Services	Provide an abstract software licensing mechanism to control software use and distribution.
			Authentication Services	Provide an abstract authentication mechanism to help ensure system security.
		Messaging Services		Provide store-and-forward messaging services independent of platform and protocol.
		Concurrency Control and Recovery		Provides basic transaction-processing services to ensure the consistency of data accessed by multiple tasks.
		Remote Object Call Services		Provide a mechanism for invoking services of remote servers on CommonPoint and non-CommonPoint systems.

System Services	Foundation Services			Provide a fundamental set of object services that make it easier to write object-oriented programs.
		Notification		Provides a systemwide mechanism to propagate change information from one object to another.
		Identifiers		Provide several different methods for associating a textual name with other data.
			Attributes	Provide a simple mechanism for associating names with arbitrary, immutable data.
			Properties	Provide a mechanism for storing collections of named data items, with a powerful query mechanism that allows property collections to be searched.
			Tokens	Provide a lightweight wrapper for static text strings, allowing text sharing and efficient comparisons.
		Object Storage		Provides mechanisms to support the persistent storage of objects and the structuring of objects in memory.
			Archives	Allow collections of objects to be stored on disk and retrieved individually.
			Data Structures and Collections	Allow objects to be organized into various kinds of type-safe and efficient collections.
			Streams and Persistence	Provide a mechanism for converting a collection of objects into a persistent, canonical byte-encoded stream for storage on disk or for sending across a network.
			Safe Pointers	Provides several kinds of special wrapper classes that make using C++ pointers safer.
		Testing		Provides a suite of tools and services to aid in the testing of objects.
			Assertions	Provide a mechanism for asserting invariants in a program, generating exceptions when these invariants are not met.
			Test Framework	Provides a framework for executing, logging, and evaluating tests.
			User Interface Testing	Provides tools and services for driving the user interface of a CommonPoint application from a test.
			Utility Tests	Provide standard tests for common object behaviors, including hashing and streaming.
		Math and Language Libraries		Support the CommonPoint application system's math and runtime libraries.
			Numerics	Provide a high-precision numeric environment, using a CommonPoint-style object interface or the ANSI standard interface.
			Standard C and C++ Libraries	Support the ANSI C runtime libraries and the proposed ANSI C++ libraries.

System Services (continued)	**OS Services**		Provide basic support for creating programs that work across a wide variety of host operating systems and hardware platforms.
		Communications	Support local and remote communications.
			Directory Services — Provide a homogeneous view of the network's name spaces, including support for DNS, X.500, AOCE, and DCE.
			Service Access Framework — Provides a mechanism for identifying and accessing network services.
			Message Streams — Provide a consistent mechanism for sending data between tasks on local or remote machines, independent of the underlying protocol.
			Protocols — Support various standard communications protocols, including TCP/IP, AppleTalk®, and Novell Netware.
		File System	Provides an object abstraction for manipulating volumes, directories, and files.
		Time Services	Provide a hardware-independent, customizable model of time.
		Object Runtime Services	Support the CommonPoint application system's object runtime.
			Memory Heaps — Provide a multithread-safe way to allocate memory.
			Exceptions — Provide runtime support for C++ exceptions and a set of common exception types for use by the CommonPoint application system.
			Shared Libraries — Provide a mechanism for packaging code and data into dynamically loadable shared libraries.
			Metadata — Provides a mechanism for accessing information about the type of an object and allows dynamic instantiation of an object at run time.
		Microkernel Services	Provide an abstract interface to the microkernel facilities necessary for the CommonPoint application system to run, independent of the host operating system.
			Tasks and Threads — Provide abstractions for creating and managing tasks and threads.
			Interprocess Communication — Provides a mechanism for sending messages to tasks and threads on the local machine.
			Synchronization Services — Provide semaphores, monitors, and other services to synchronize multiple tasks and threads.
			Virtual Memory Management — Provides a set of services that allow virtual memory segments to be created and managed.
			System Shutdown — Provides a staged, well-defined protocol for shutting down the CommonPoint application system.

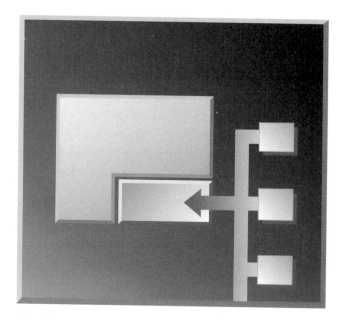

CHAPTER 13

CREATING AN APPLICATION USING COMMONPOINT FRAMEWORKS

Now that you've been introduced to the key features of the CommonPoint application system, it's time to see how easy it is to develop an application using the frameworks provided by the CommonPoint system instead of the framework we developed in Part 2. As you review the implementation of the application, note that many of the details of CommonPoint programming have been omitted because they go beyond the scope of this book. Instead, view the sample code as a guide to the basic principles of CommonPoint programming and compare the total program size and complexity with that of the samples we developed earlier. When you consider how much extra functionality the CommonPoint application provides, the advantages of reusing CommonPoint system frameworks are evident.

CommonPoint system development tools ease application development

The application code shown in this chapter was developed without the use of any special development tools. Taligent has several such tools, which can make application development substantially easier than we've shown here.

The first of these tools, *cp*Constructor™, allows developers to create user interface elements in a graphical editing environment. *cp*Constructor stores user interface elements in fully localized archives. If we had used *cp*Constructor to create the user interface elements of our application, much of the window and menu management code in the application would have been replaced with code that accessed the archived user interface elements, greatly simplifying the application.

The second of these tools, CodeAuthor, generates the source code for a CommonPoint application using a user-interface archive created in *cp*Constructor as input. If we were to use CodeAuthor to generate our application, the amount of code we would have to write would drop to nearly none.

The third of CommonPoint's development tools, *cp*Professional™, is a full-featured, object-oriented development environment. With true incremental compiling and linking, turnaround times are much lower than those of traditional development tools. The *cp*Professional browsers and editors make the creation and modification of C++ programs much easier. Although using *cp*Professional would not have a

direct effect on the amount of code we'd have to write for our application, it would make the development process faster and more enjoyable.

These tools weren't used to create the CommonPoint system version of the application because that would have made the code so small and simple that it would have made a comparison between the CommonPoint application and the Windows or OS/2 application meaningless. Creating our CommonPoint application using C++ exclusively lets us see everything needed to create a CommonPoint application.

If you create your own CommonPoint application, these development tools deserve a serious look.

NUMBER FORMATTING REVISITED

CommonPoint includes a number formatting framework which bears a close resemblance to the framework we developed earlier in the book. Instead of writing your own number formatting framework, you can use the Text Scanning and Formatting Framework supplied with the CommonPoint application system, saving yourself a great deal of effort.

The Text Scanning and Formatting Framework is more sophisticated than the number formatting framework we developed in Part 2, so a brief overview of its design is in order.

The Text Scanning and Formatting Framework's protocol is as follows:

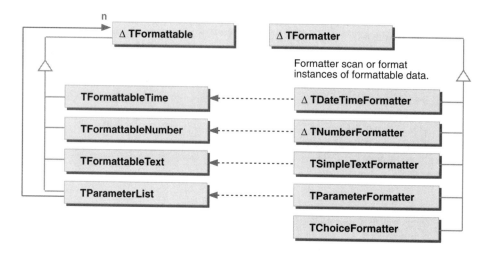

TEXT SCANNING AND FORMATTING FRAMEWORK CLASS DIAGRAM

TFormattable

TFormattable classes provide a wrapper for a specific data type, allowing it to be manipulated by the formatter for that type of data. Data types are provided for numbers, time, text, and for lists of TFormattable parameters.

TFormatter

TFormatter classes perform the actual conversions, with a specific TFormatter subclass working with a particular type of TFormattable data. Several different types of TFormatter subclasses are provided:

- TNumberFormatter is the abstract base class for classes that format and scan numeric data, much like the number formatting framework we designed in Part 2.
- TDateTimeFormatter is the abstract base class for a family of classes that format and scan time data.
- TSimpleTextFormatter formats and scans text strings. It is used primarily by the TParameterFormatter and TChoiceFormatter classes.
- TParameterFormatter takes a list of TFormattable data parameters and formats them into text strings (or scans text strings into a list of data parameters). This class is typically used to create variably-formatted strings for the user such as:

    As of <date>, <time>, there are <n> tasks remaining.

- TChoiceFormatter specifies a mapping between numerical values and a set of strings or TParameterFormatter instances. It is typically used in combination with TParameterFormatter to generate different forms of a string:

    There is 1 task remaining.

    There are 5 tasks remaining.

TFormatResult

TFormatResult classes return information about the conversion process, so that the results of the formatting operation can be analyzed.

Formatting numbers with the Text Scanning and Formatting Framework

As previously mentioned, the Text Scanning and Formatting Framework provides an abstract TNumberFormatter class used to scan and format numeric data. As with the simple framework we designed, this class has a number of subclasses that can format numbers a particular way. Unlike our framework, though, the Text Scanning and Formatting Framework provides full support for Arabic, Han (Chinese), and Hebrew numeric systems, and provides formatters that can output numbers as roman numerals, outline labels, and more.

The class hierarchy of the number formatting classes is as follows:

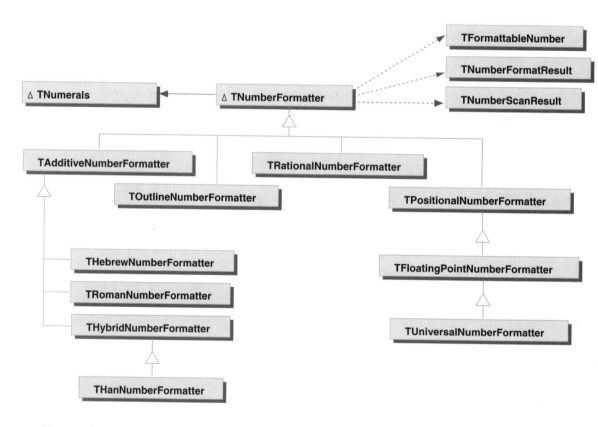

NUMBER SCANNING AND FORMATTING CLASS HIERARCHY

As you can see, the breadth of formatting functionality provided is impressive, and allows CommonPoint to support the full range of international markets. This discussion concentrates on the details of the classes that are most relevant to our application.

- TNumberFormatter provides the ability to format and scan TFormattableNumber data items to and from text. TFormattableNumber stores the numeric information as a double.

- TPositionalNumberFormatter provides the protocol for formatting numbers in a value-based system, where the total value of the number is determined by the position and value of each digit. The decimal numbering system used is an example of such a system.

- TFloatingPointNumberFormatter is a subclass of TPositionalNumberFormatter and provides the ability to format floating-point numbers into a decimal form, in either scientific or standard notation.

- TRationalNumberFormatter formats noninteger values as a ratio of two integers (a fraction). Both proper ("3 5/8") and improper ("29/8") fractions are supported.

Locales

Another aspect of number formatting our framework did not address was the ability to provide full support for multilingual applications. Although our application does use the number formatting information correctly (for example, currency symbol, thousands separator), it does so only for the current location in use.

The CommonPoint system provides full support for multilingual applications via a locale mechanism. A locale is a collection of objects that are localized for a particular geographic region and is represented by a TLocale. The classes provided by the Locale Services are shown in the following figure.

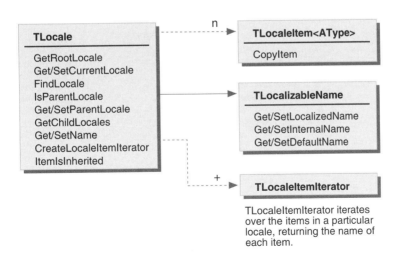

LOCALE SERVICES CLASS DIAGRAM

Each TLocale has a unique TLocalizableName object, which specifies the internal name of the locale and provides a set of names for that locale that have themselves been localized. These localized versions of the name can be used to display the correct name for a locale to the user. For example, the "English" locale's name would be displayed as "Anglais" when accessed from a French system.

Locales can contain any kind of object that you want to localize. Each item within a TLocale is wrapped by a TLocaleItem object. You can use a TLocaleItemIterator to iterate through all the TLocaleItem objects in the TLocale or retrieve individual TLocaleItem objects from a TLocale by using its internal name.

Each TLocale can, in turn, contain other TLocales. This allows a hierarchy of locales to be maintained, with each level of the hierarchy representing an increasingly fine-grained geographic region. The CommonPoint system always provides a root locale, along with locales for each language, country, and time zone supported by the system.

Locales effectively inherit items from their parents, so items can be placed in the hierarchy at the appropriate level. Item inheritance allows us to build a complete hierarchy without duplicating items within the locale hierarchy. Items in sublocales override those in the parent with the same name. A sample locale hierarchy is shown in the following figure.

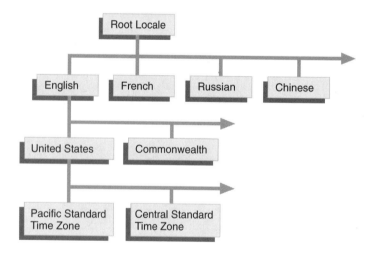

A TYPICAL LOCALE HIERARCHY

You can access the root locale using the static TLocale function GetRootLocale, and the user's current locale can be accessed using the static function GetCurrentLocale. You can find a particular TLocale object in the hierarchy by calling FindLocale. Usually, you use the current default locale, because it contains the formats the user expects to see.

The CommonPoint system's locale hierarchy always contains certain items that are needed for the system to operate. These items include the default text font, default time and date formatters, and time zone information. More importantly for our purposes, locales always include default currency and number formatters. The code to access these default formatters is straightforward:

```
// Get the current locale
TLocale currentLocale = TLocale::GetCurrentLocale();

try {
    // make a locale item
    TLocaleItem<TNumberFormatter> numberFormatterItem;

    // TDeleterFor automatically deletes the TNumberFormatter when it goes out of scope
    // The call to CopyItem creates a duplicate of the default formatter for the current
    // locale
    TDeleterFor<TNumberFormatter> numberFormatter =
        numberFormatterItem.CopyItem( TLocale::kNumberFormatID, currentLocale );
}
catch (const TArchiveException&) {
    // rethrow the exception, or create a number formatter by hand
}
```

Locales provide a powerful mechanism for multilingual application programming.

DESIGNING THE APPLICATION

Like most CommonPoint applications, our application uses the Presentation Framework as a base for its user interface and document model. The Presentation Framework is the CommonPoint framework most similar to more traditional application frameworks such as MacApp. It makes it easy to create compound document–based applications that follow the CommonPoint application system's user interface guidelines. Although a complete description of the Presentation Framework is beyond the scope of this book, a brief description can help you understand the implementation of our application.

At its simplest, creating a new application using the Presentation Framework involves creating several different classes to represent our application:

- A *model* to represent the data of the document
- A *presenter* to create the windows and menus of the program
- A *view* to allow the user to see and edit the data in the model

Taken as a whole, these classes comprise our application's ensemble, as discussed in Chapter 1, "A first look at frameworks." We provide the classes that know what a spreadsheet is, and the system provides everything else needed to create a full-featured CommonPoint application.

This application does everything our original sample application did, and more: among other capabilities, our spreadsheet data can now be embedded in another document, and can also be printed; moreover, the application supports saving and versioning of files. The following figure shows the sample application running on the CommonPoint system.

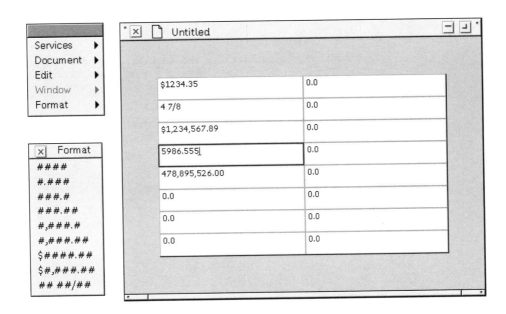

SAMPLE APPLICATION RUNNING ON THE COMMONPOINT SYSTEM

TSpreadsheetModel

Our model object, TSpreadsheetModel, is very simple. Each cell of the spreadsheet is represented by a TCell object, which is described as follows:

```
class TSpreadsheetModel : public TModel {
public:
    // Provides boilerplate overrides needed by all TModel subclasses
    ModelDeclarationsMacro(TSpreadsheetModel);

public:
                              TSpreadsheetModel();
    virtual                   ~TSpreadsheetModel();

    // These methods read and write the data of the object to a stream.
    virtual TStream&          operator>>=(TStream& toStream) const;
    virtual TStream&          operator<<=(TStream& fromStream);

    // This method returns a selection over the whole model.
    // It is used for embedding
    virtual TModelSelection*CreateSelection() const;

    // This method returns an iterator over the cells in the model in row order
    TIteratorOver<TCell>*  CreateCellIterator();
```

```
                    // grid size information accessors
                    unsigned short              GetNumberOfRows() const;
                    unsigned short              GetNumberOfColumns() const;

                    // methods to get cell at x,y and to tell the model the cell should be changed.
                    virtual TCell*              GetCellAt(unsigned short row, unsigned short col) const;
                    virtual void                CellChangedAt(unsigned short row, unsigned short col);
                    virtual void                CellChanged(TCell* cell);

                                                TSpreadsheetModel(const TSpreadsheetModel& source);
                    TSpreadsheetModel&          operator=(const TSpreadsheetModel& source);

                private:
                    // Even though we use a two-dimensional array to represent the spreadsheet
                    // to the user, its a one dimensional array internally.
                    TArrayOf<TCell>             fCells;
                    unsigned short              fNoOfRows;
                    unsigned short              fNoOfColumns;

                    enum EVersion { kOriginalVersion };
                };
```

TCell

The data stored by the model is represented by a TCell. Each cell has a TNumberFormatter and a floating-point data value. Accessor member functions, called GetValue and SetValue, are provided for these fields.

```
                class TCell
                {
                public:
                                                TCell();
                                                TCell(const TCell&);
                    virtual                     ~TCell();

                    virtual TStream&            operator>>=(TStream& toStream) const;
                    virtual TStream&            operator<<=(TStream& fromStream);

                    TNumberFormatter*           GetNumberFormatter() const;
                    void                        AdoptNumberFormatter(TNumberFormatter* theNumberFormatter);

                    double                      GetValue() const;
                    void                        SetValue(double theValue);

                private:
                    TNumberFormatter*           fNumberFormatter;
                    double                      fValue;

                    enum Version { kOriginalVersion };
                };
```

TSpreadsheetPresenter

The TSpreadsheetPresenter class is the core of our application. It creates and maintains the application's windows and menus, and it handles many of the user's actions. The key functions of TSpreadsheetPresenter are:

- HandleCreateMainView—Creates and returns the TSpreadsheetView that users use to view and edit the cell data.

- CreateViewSubMenuItem—Called by the Presentation Framework to create our Format submenu so that the user can change formats for cells.

- HandleMenuAction—Called to respond to a click on one of our custom menu items.

```
class TSpreadsheetPresenter : public TGUIPresenter
{
public:
                            TSpreadsheetPresenter(const TGUIBundle&);
                            TSpreadsheetPresenter(const TSpreadsheetPresenter&);
                            TSpreadsheetPresenter();
        virtual             ~TSpreadsheetPresenter();

        TaligentTypeExtensionDeclarationsMacro(TSpreadsheetPresenter)

        enum ENumberFormatType {
            kAllDigitsMenuItem,                             // ####
            kDigitDotDigitsMenuItem,                        // #.###
            kDigitsDotDigitMenuItem,                        // ###.#
            kDigitsDotTwoDigitsMenuItem,                    // ###.##
            kDigitsWithCommaDotDigitMenuItem,               // #,###.#
            kDigitsWithCommaDotTwoDigitsMenuItem,           // #,###.##
            kDollarDigitsDotTwoDigitsMenuItem,              // $####.##
            kDollarDigitsWithCommaDotTwoDigitsMenuItem,     // $#,###.##
            kDigitsWithFractionMenuItem                     // ## ##/##
        };

        virtual TSubMenuItem*   CreateViewSubMenuItem() const;

        virtual TView*          HandleCreateMainView(TGUIBundle*) const;
        virtual void            HandleMenuActivate(TMenu& theMainMenu);
        virtual bool            HandleMenuAction (TMenuAction& action);
        virtual bool            HandleViewAction(TViewAction& action);

private:
        void                    CreateAndAdoptMenuItem(
                                    TMenu* menu,
                                    ENumberFormatType numberFormatType,
                                    const TStandardText menuText) const;

        TFloatingPointNumberFormatter*  CreateNumberFormatter();
        TFloatingPointNumberFormatter*  CreateCurrencyFormatter();
        TRationalNumberFormatter*       CreateRationalNumberFormatter();

        TSubMenuItem*                   fgFormatMenu;
        TTextControl*                   fCurrentTextControl;
        TCell*                          fCurrentCell;
        TFloatingPointNumberFormatter*  fAnchorNumberFormatter;

        enum EVersion { kOriginalVersion };
};
```

TSpreadsheetView

TSpreadsheetView is responsible for displaying the grid of spreadsheet cells. Its implementation relies on a collection of TTextControl objects, provided by the CommonPoint application system to handle the display and editing of the cell's text. TSpreadsheetView needs only to draw a border around the cells.

```
class TSpreadsheetView : public TDocumentComponentView
{
public:
    TaligentTypeExtensionDeclarationsMacro(TSpreadsheetView)

                        TSpreadsheetView();
                        TSpreadsheetView(TGUIBundle*);
    virtual             ~TSpreadsheetView();

    // creates the text controls that are used to edit cell contents
    void                CreateControlList(long numRows, long numColumns);

    // returns an iterator over the controls in the view
    TIteratorOver<TTextControl>* CreateControlIterator();

    virtual void        DrawContents(TGrafPort&) const;

    // These methods    read and write the data of the object to a stream.
    virtual TStream&    operator>>=(TStream& toStream) const;
    virtual TStream&    operator<<=(TStream& fromStream);

private:
                        TSpreadsheetView(const TSpreadsheetView&);
    TSpreadsheetView&   operator=(const TSpreadsheetView&);

    enum EVersion { kOriginalVersion };

    TArrayOf<TTextControl>fControls;
};
```

IMPLEMENTING TSPREADSHEETMODEL

Now that we've defined the classes needed for our application, it's time to implement them. The first class we'll implement is TSpreadsheetModel, which is one of the simpler classes in our application.

TModel boilerplate

The first step is to handle a standard boilerplate needed by every Presentation Framework–based application. This boilerplate is usually created automatically by the CommonPoint system–specific development tools such as *cp*Professional, but we've shown it here because we're writing this application by hand. The ModelDefinitionsMacroOne declaration implements the standard TModel functions originally defined by the ModelDeclarationsMacro from the class definition.

```
ModelDefinitionsMacroOne(TSpreadsheetModel, kOriginalVersion, TModel);
```

Constructors and destructor

Next, we need to write the constructors, destructor, and assignment operator. The basic constructor creates the fixed-size grid of cells and stores them in the model's fCells array. The destructor reverses the process, deleting all the cell objects. The copy constructor and the assignment operator are very similar; they copy the cell data out of another TSpreadsheetModel.

```
TSpreadsheetModel::TSpreadsheetModel()
{
    fNoOfRows = 8;
    fNoOfColumns = 2;

    for (int col=0; col < fNoOfColumns; col++)
    {
        for (int row=0; row < fNoOfRows; row++)
        {
            fCells.Add (new TCell());
        }
    }
}

TSpreadsheetModel::~TSpreadsheetModel()
{
    fCells.DeleteAll();
}
```

```
TSpreadsheetModel::TSpreadsheetModel(const TSpreadsheetModel& source)
    : TModel(source)
{
    fNoOfRows = source.fNoOfRows;
    fNoOfColumns = source.fNoOfColumns;

    fCells.DeleteAll();

    TDeleterFor< TIteratorOver<TCell> > iter = source.CreateCellIterator();
    for (const TCell* theCell = iter->First();
        theCell != NIL;
        theCell = iter->Next())
    {
        TCell *newCell = ::CopyPointer(theCell);
        fCells.Add(newCell);
    }
}

TSpreadsheetModel& TSpreadsheetModel::operator=(const TSpreadsheetModel& source)
{
    if (&source != this)
    {
        TModel::operator=(source);
    }

    fNoOfRows = source.fNoOfRows;
    fNoOfColumns = source.fNoOfColumns;

    fCells.DeleteAll();

    TDeleterFor< TIteratorOver<TCell> > iter = source.CreateCellIterator();
    for (const TCell* theCell = iter->First();
        theCell != NIL;
        theCell = iter->Next())
    {
        TCell *newCell = ::CopyPointer(theCell);
        fCells.Add(newCell);
    }

    return *this;
}
```

Streaming operators

Next, we need to implement the streaming operators for our model. The CommonPoint system's persistent object model requires these functions to be written for any class that can exist across application sessions or be sent across process boundaries. In general, all your objects should implement streaming operators. In our case, the streaming operators read and write our collection of TCell objects. The TCell streaming operators (implemented later in this chapter) do all the work.

✅ NOTE   The streaming operators shown here use the global CommonPoint system functions Flatten and Resurrect to write and read objects. These functions know how to write objects polymorphically. We use them here because we want the correct kind of TNumberFormatter object to be written and resurrected, and there is no way to tell at compile time which subclass of TNumberFormatter (if any) will actually be stored in our fNumberFormatter data member.

The code for our stream-out operator is as follows:

```
const VersionInfo kOriginalVersion = 0;

TStream& TSpreadsheetModel::operator>>=(TStream& toStream) const
{
    ::WriteVersion(toStream, kOriginalVersion);

    TModel::operator>>=(toStream);

    fNoOfRows >>= toStream;
    fNoOfColumns >>= toStream;

    for (int col = 0; col < fNoOfColumns; col++)
    {
        for (int row = 0; row < fNoOfRows; row++)
        {
            TCell *cell = GetCellAt(row,col);
            ::Flatten(cell,toStream);
        }
    }

    return toStream;
}
```

Next we have the code for the stream-in operator, which reads everything back in exactly the same order in which it was written using the stream-out operator.

```
TStream& TSpreadsheetModel::operator<<=(TStream& fromStream)
{
    ::ReadVersion(fromStream, kOriginalVersion, kOriginalVersion);
    TModel::operator<<=(fromStream);

    fCells.DeleteAll();

    fNoOfRows <<= fromStream;
    fNoOfColumns <<= fromStream;

    for (int col = 0; col < fNoOfColumns; col++)
    {
        for (int row = 0; row < fNoOfRows; row++)
        {
            TCell *newCell;
            ::Resurrect(newCell,fromStream, TAllocationHeap(this));
            fCells.Add (newCell);
        }
    }

    return fromStream;
}
```

CreateSelection

We'll now need to implement the CreateSelection function. It returns a TModelSelection that represents the entire model. We actually use a prebuilt template class provided as part of the CommonPoint application to do all the work.

```
TModelSelection* TSpreadsheetModel::CreateSelection() const
{
    return new TGUIModelSelectionFor<TSpreadsheetModel>;
}
```

Cell data accessors

Finally, we reach the functions that allows the user interface to access and modify the cell data. These functions are fairly straightforward. The only point we need to emphasize is that any function that changes the data of the model must call the inherited member function NotifyOfChange to tell the model that the data needs to be saved.

```
TIteratorOver<TCell>* TSpreadsheetModel::CreateCellIterator()
{
    return fCells.CreateIterator();
}

unsigned short TSpreadsheetModel::GetNumberOfRows() const
{
    return fNoOfRows;
}

unsigned short TSpreadsheetModel::GetNumberOfColumns() const
{
    return fNoOfColumns;
}

TCell* TSpreadsheetModel::GetCellAt(unsigned short row, unsigned short col) const
{
    return fCells.At((row*fNoOfColumns)+col);
}

void TSpreadsheetModel::CellChangedAt(unsigned short row, unsigned short col)
{
    NotifyOfChange(TNotification(GetAllChangesInterest()));
}

void TSpreadsheetModel::CellChanged(TCell* cell)
{
    NotifyOfChange(TNotification(GetAllChangesInterest()));
}
```

This is the complete TSpreadsheetModel class.

IMPLEMENTING TCELL

TCell's implementation is very straightforward because it is really just a container for the cell's number formatter and value.

Constructors and destructor

First we have the constructors and destructor. Note the use of the TaligentTypeExtensionMacro at the beginning of the class implementation, which implements some special mechanisms needed by the Taligent application's object runtime.

```
TaligentTypeExtensionMacro(TCell);

TCell::TCell()
{
    TFloatingPointNumberFormatter* floatingPointNumberFormatter
                            = new TFloatingPointNumberFormatter;

    fValue = 0.0;
    fNumberFormatter = NIL;

    // Get the current locale
    TLocale currentLocale = TLocale::GetCurrentLocale();

    try {
        TLocaleItem<TNumberFormatter> numberFormatterItem;

        fNumberFormatter = numberFormatterItem.CopyItem(TLocale::kNumberFormatID,
                                                    currentLocale);
    }
    catch (const TArchiveException&) {
        // rethrow the exception, but first create a basic formatter
        fNumberFormatter = new TFloatingPointNumberFormatter;
        throw;
    }
}

TCell::TCell(const TCell& source)
{
    fNumberFormatter = ::CopyPointer(
                        (const TNumberFormatter*) source.fNumberFormatter);
    fValue = source.fValue;
}

TCell::~TCell()
{
    delete fNumberFormatter;
}
```

Streaming operators

Just as we implemented streaming operators for TSpreadsheetModel, we must implement them for TCell. The code itself is straightforward; we read or write each of our data members using the stream provided by the system.

```
const VersionInfo kOriginalVersion = 0;

TStream& TCell::operator>>=(TStream& toStream) const
{
    ::WriteVersion(toStream, kOriginalVersion);

    ::Flatten(fNumberFormatter, toStream);
    fValue >>= toStream;

    return toStream;
}

TStream& TCell::operator<<=(TStream& fromStream)
{
    ::ReadVersion(fromStream, kOriginalVersion, kOriginalVersion);

    delete fNumberFormat;
    ::Resurrect(fNumberFormatter, fromStream, TAllocationHeap(this));

    fValue <<= fromStream;

    return fromStream;
}
```

Number formatter accessors

Next, we have the functions that are used to access the number formatter associated with the cell. Note that to adopt a new TNumberFormatter, we delete the old formatter first to prevent a memory leak.

```
TNumberFormatter* TCell::GetNumberFormatter() const
{
    return fNumberFormatter;
}

void TCell::AdoptNumberFormatter(TNumberFormatter* theNumberFormatter)
{
    delete fNumberFormatter;
    fNumberFormatter = theNumberFormatter;
}
```

Value accessors

Next, we have the member functions that get and set the numeric value of the cell. These functions are self-explanatory.

```
double TCell::GetValue() const
{
    return fValue;
}

void TCell::SetValue( double& theValue )
{
    fValue = theValue;
}
```

IMPLEMENTING TSPREADSHEETPRESENTER

Most of our application is implemented in TSpreadsheetPresenter.

Constructors and destructor

As usual, the first thing to implement is the standard constructors and destructor. Because we have several different constructors, the code common to them has been broken out into a separate member function, CreateControlList, which is as follows:

```
TaligentTypeExtensionMacro(TSpreadsheetPresenter);

TSpreadsheetPresenter::TSpreadsheetPresenter(const TGUIBundle& bundle)
        : TGUIPresenter(bundle)
{
    fCurrentTextControl = 0;
    fCurrentCell = 0;
    fgViewMenu = NIL;

    fAnchorNumberFormatter = CreateNumberFormatter();
}

TSpreadsheetPresenter::TSpreadsheetPresenter()
        : TGUIPresenter()
{
    fCurrentTextControl = 0;
    fCurrentCell = 0;

    fAnchorNumberFormatter = CreateNumberFormatter();
}

TSpreadsheetPresenter::TSpreadsheetPresenter(const TSpreadsheetPresenter& source)
        : TGUIPresenter(source)
{
    fCurrentTextControl = source.fCurrentTextControl;
    fCurrentCell = source.fCurrentCell;
    fAnchorNumberFormatter = ::CopyPointer(source.fAnchorNumberFormatter);
}

TSpreadsheetPresenter::~TSpreadsheetPresenter()
{
    delete fAnchorNumberFormatter;
}
```

HandleCreateMainView

Next, we need to implement the HandleCreateMainView function. This function is called when a new presentation is being created. It creates a TSpreadsheetView objects, and then puts the TTextControl objects into the view.

```
TView* TSpreadsheetPresenter::HandleCreateMainView(TGUIBundle* bundle) const
{
    TSpreadsheetView* contentView = new TSpreadsheetView(bundle);

    const TModelPointerTo<TSpreadsheetModel> model(GetModelReference());

    contentView->CreateControlList(model->GetNumberOfRows(),
                             model->GetNumberOfColumns());
    contentView->SetAllocatedArea(TGRect(TGPoint(0,0),  TGPoint(500, 340)));

    return contentView;
}
```

Menu creation and maintenance

Next, we create the code to maintain our menus. Whenever the application is activated by the user, the Presentation Framework calls the HandleMenuActivate member function; whenever the application is deactivated, it calls the HandleMenuDeactivate member function. Notice that we check to see whether the format menu has ever been created before, and, if not, we call CreateViewSubMenuItem to create it.

```
void TSpreadsheetPresenter::HandleMenuActivate(TMenu& theMainMenu)
{
    TGUIPresenter::HandleMenuActivate(theMainMenu);
    if (fgFormatMenu == NIL) {
        fgFormatMenu = CreateViewSubMenuItem();
        theMainMenu.AdoptLast(fgFormatMenu);
    }
}
```

CreateViewSubMenuItem creates the format menu. For each format we support, it makes a menu item and adds it to the menu. Each menu item is given a unique ID, so that we can tell which format to apply when the user selects a format command.

```
TSubMenuItem* TSpreadsheetPresenter::CreateViewSubMenuItem() const
{
    TMenu* formatMenu = new TMenu;

    // #### Menu
    CreateAndAdoptMenuItem(formatMenu, kAllDigitsMenuItem,
                                        TStandardText("####"));
    // #.### Menu
    CreateAndAdoptMenuItem(formatMenu, kDigitDotDigitsMenuItem,
                                        TStandardText("#.###"));
    // ###.# Menu
    CreateAndAdoptMenuItem(formatMenu, kDigitsDotDigitMenuItem,
                                        TStandardText("###.#"));
    // ###.## Menu
    CreateAndAdoptMenuItem(formatMenu, kDigitsDotTwoDigitsMenuItem,
                                        TStandardText("###.##"));
    // #,###.# Menu
    CreateAndAdoptMenuItem(formatMenu, kDigitsWithCommaDotDigitMenuItem,
                                        TStandardText("#,###.#"));
    // #,###.## Menu
    CreateAndAdoptMenuItem(formatMenu, kDigitsWithCommaDotTwoDigitsMenuItem,
                                        TStandardText("#,###.##"));
    // $####.## Menu
    CreateAndAdoptMenuItem(formatMenu, kDollarDigitsDotTwoDigitsMenuItem,
                                        TStandardText("$####.##"));
    //  $#,###.## Menu
    CreateAndAdoptMenuItem(formatMenu, kDollarDigitsWithCommaDotTwoDigitsMenuItem,
                                        TStandardText("$#,###.##"));
    // ## ##/## Menu
    CreateAndAdoptMenuItem(formatMenu, kDigitsWithFractionMenuItem,
                                        TStandardText("## ##/##"));

    return new TSubMenuItem(formatMenu, new TTextLabel(TStandardText("Format")));
}

const TMenuDomainID gSpreadsheetPresenterDomainID("SpreadsheetPresenter");

void TSpreadsheetPresenter::CreateAndAdoptMenuItem(
                                    TMenu *menu,
                                    ENumberFormatType numberFormatType,
                                    const TStandardText& menuText) const
{
    TMomentaryMenuItem* newMenuItem =
            new TMomentaryMenuItem(new TTextLabel(menuText));

    newMenuItem->SetID(numberFormatType);
    newMenuItem->SetDomainID(gSpreadsheetPresenterDomainID);
    newMenuItem->AdoptState(
        new TMomentaryMenuActionControlState(menu, newMenuItem));

    menu->AdoptLast(newMenuItem);
}
```

HandleMenuAction

We now implement HandleMenuAction, one of the most complicated functions in our application. When the user selects one of the format commands, we perform the following steps:

1 Verify that the active cell contains a valid number.

If the number is in an illegal format, we need to handle the error. In this application, we set the value to zero and continue, but a commercial application would probably display an error dialog box.

2 Create a new number formatter that matches the format the user wants.

3 Apply the new formatter to the active cell.

4 Reset the text of the TTextControl associated with that cell.

```
bool TSpreadsheetPresenter::HandleMenuAction(TMenuAction& action)
{
    bool handled = TGUIPresenter::HandleMenuAction(action);

    if (!fCurrentCell)
        return handled;

    TNumberFormatter* theCellNumberFormatter;
    TFloatingPointNumberFormatter* numberFormatter;
    TRationalNumberFormatter* rationalNumberFormatter;

    if (!handled && (action.GetMenuItem()->GetDomainID() ==
                        gSpreadsheetPresenterDomainId))
    {
        handled = true;
        switch (action.GetMenuItem()->GetID())
        {
            case kAllDigitsMenuItem:
                numberFormatter = CreateNumberFormatter();
                numberFormatter->SetPrecision(0.5,
                        TPositionalNumberFormatter::kRoundEven);
                numberFormatter->SetMinFractionDigits(0);
                numberFormatter->SetMaxFractionDigits(0);
                theCellNumberFormatter = numberFormatter;
                break;

            case kDigitDotDigitsMenuItem:
                numberFormatter = CreateNumberFormatter();
                numberFormatter->SetExponentPhase(1);
                numberFormatter->SetUpperExponentThreshold(1E+1);
                numberFormatter->SetPrecision(0.000005,
                        TPositionalNumberFormatter::kRoundEven);
                theCellNumberFormatter = numberFormatter;
                break;
```

```
            case kDigitsDotDigitMenuItem:
                numberFormatter = CreateNumberFormatter();
                numberFormatter->SetPrecision(0.5,
                            TPositionalNumberFormatter::kRoundEven);
                numberFormatter->SetMinFractionDigits(1);
                numberFormatter->SetMaxFractionDigits(1);
                theCellNumberFormatter = numberFormatter;
                break;

            case kDigitsDotTwoDigitsMenuItem:
                numberFormatter = CreateNumberFormatter();
                numberFormatter->SetPrecision(0.005,
                            TPositionalNumberFormatter::kRoundEven);
                numberFormatter->SetMinFractionDigits(2);
                numberFormatter->SetMaxFractionDigits(2);
                theCellNumberFormatter = numberFormatter;
                break;

            case kDigitsWithCommaDotDigitMenuItem:
                numberFormatter = CreateNumberFormatter();
                numberFormatter->SetIntegerSeparator(true);
                numberFormatter->SetPrecision(0.05,
                            TPositionalNumberFormatter::kRoundEven);
                numberFormatter->SetMinFractionDigits(1);
                numberFormatter->SetMaxFractionDigits(1);
                theCellNumberFormatter = numberFormatter;
                break;

            case kDigitsWithCommaDotTwoDigitsMenuItem:
                numberFormatter = CreateNumberFormatter();
                numberFormatter->SetIntegerSeparator(true);
                numberFormatter->SetPrecision(0.005,
                            TPositionalNumberFormatter::kRoundEven);
                numberFormatter->SetMinFractionDigits(2);
                numberFormatter->SetMaxFractionDigits(2);
                theCellNumberFormatter = numberFormatter;
                break;

            case kDollarDigitsDotTwoDigitsMenuItem:
                numberFormatter = CreateCurrencyFormatter();
                theCellNumberFormatter = numberFormatter;
                break;

            case kDollarDigitsWithCommaDotTwoDigitsMenuItem:
                numberFormatter = CreateCurrencyFormatter();
                numberFormatter->SetIntegerSeparator(true);
                theCellNumberFormatter = numberFormatter;
                break;

            case kDigitsWithFractionMenuItem:
                rationalNumberFormatter = CreateRationalNumberFormatter();
                theCellNumberFormatter = rationalNumberFormatter;
                break;
        }
        fCurrentCell->AdoptNumberFormatter(theCellNumberFormatter);
    }
    return handled;
}
```

HandleViewAction

HandleViewAction is the next function of the TSpreadsheetPresenter we need to implement. This function is called whenever the user changes the focus from one cell to another. We use it to keep track of the active selection.

```
bool TSpreadsheetPresenter::HandleViewAction(TViewAction& action)
{
    bool handled = false;

    TStandardText textInField;
    TFormattableNumber formattable;
    TStandardText formatResult;
    TNumberScanResult scanResult;
    MTextControlState* textControlState;
    TNumberFormatter* theCellNumberFormatter;
    TTextControl* textControl;
    TCell* theCell;
    unsigned short row = 0;
    unsigned short col = 0;
    TSpreadsheetView*theView = (TSpreadsheetView*) action.GetSender().GetView();

    if (action.GetEventType() == TTextControlAction::kActivate)
    {
        TDeleterFor<TIteratorOver<TTextControl> > controlIterator
                                = theView->CreateControlIterator();
        TModelPointerTo<TSpreadsheetModel> model(GetModelReference());

        for (textControl = controlIterator->First();
            (row < model->GetNumberOfRows()) && (textControl != NIL);
            row++)
            for ( ; (col < model->GetNumberOfColumns()) && (textControl != NIL);
                col++, textControl = controlIterator->Next())
            {
                if (textControl->IsActive())
                {
                    double  num = 0.0;

                    if (fCurrentTextControl != 0)
                    {
                        // right now fCurrentCell is the previously selected cell.
                        textControlState = fCurrentTextControl->GetState();
                        textControlState->GetTextState(textInField);
                        TStandardText zeroText("0.0");

                        if (zeroText == textInField)
                        {
                            num = 0.0;
                            fCurrentCell->SetValue(num);
                            textControlState->SetTextState(zeroText);
                            model->CellChanged(fCurrentCell);
                        }
                        else
                        {
                            fAnchorNumberFormatter->Scan(textInField,
                                        TTextRange::GetMaximumRange(),
                                        formattable, scanResult);
```

```
                              TScanResult::EScanResult confidence =
                                  scanResult.GetConfidence();

                              if (confidence == TScanResult::kPerfect)
                              {
                                  num = formattable.GetNumber();

                                  fCurrentCell->SetValue(num);
                                  theCellNumberFormatter =
                                      fCurrentCell->GetNumberFormatter();
                                  theCellNumberFormatter->Format(formattable,
                                                              formatResult);
                                  model->CellChanged(fCurrentCell);

                                  textControlState->SetTextState(formatResult);
                              }
                              else
                              {
                                  num = 0.0;
                                  fCurrentCell->SetValue(num);
                                  textControlState->SetTextState(zeroText);
                                  model->CellChanged(fCurrentCell);
                              }
                          }

                          // now we process the newly selected current cell.
                          textControlState = textControl->GetState();
                          theCell = model->GetCellAt(row,col);
                          num  = theCell->GetValue();
                          if (num == 0.0)
                          {
                              textControlState->SetTextState(zeroText);
                          }
                          else
                          {
                              formattable.SetNumber(num);
                              fAnchorNumberFormatter->Format(formattable,
                                                          formatResult);
                              textControlState->SetTextState(formatResult);
                          }
                      }
                      fCurrentTextControl = textControl;
                      fCurrentCell = theCell;
                      model->CellChanged(theCell);
                      break;
                  }
              }
          handled = true;
      }
      return handled;
  }
```

Creating number formatters

In our formatting-menu handling code, we relied on three utility functions, CreateCurrencyFormatter, CreateNumberFormatter, and CreateRationalFormatter, to create the default number formatters for this locale. These routines retrieve formatters from the current locale and return them to the caller. The implementation of CreateNumberFormatter is as follows. The other two functions have very similar implementations and aren't shown here.

```
TFloatingPointNumberFormatter* TSpreadsheetPresenter::CreateNumberFormatter()
{
    TFloatingPointNumberFormatter *numberFormatter = NIL;

    // Get the current locale
    TLocale currentLocale = TLocale::GetCurrentLocale();

    try {
        TLocaleItem<TNumberFormatter> numberFormatterItem;

        numberFormatter = (TFloatingPointNumberFormatter*)
                            numberFormatterItem.CopyItem(TLocale::kNumberFormatID,
                                        currentLocale);
    }
    catch (const TArchiveException&) {
        // rethrow the exception.
        throw;
    }

    return numberFormatter;
}
```

IMPLEMENTING TSPREADSHEETVIEW

TSpreadsheetView is the last class we have to implement. Once again, we begin by defining the standard constructors and destructor.

```
TaligentTypeExtensionMacro(TSpreadsheetView);

TSpreadsheetView::TSpreadsheetView(TGUIBundle* bundle)
    : TDocumentComponentView(bundle)
{
}

TSpreadsheetView::TSpreadsheetView(const TSpreadsheetView& other)
    : TDocumentComponentView(other)
{
    // this method has to exist even though it is a private, and views
    // aren't supposed to be copyable.
    ::Assertion(false, "Can't copy TSpreadsheetView.");
}

TSpreadsheetView::TSpreadsheetView()
    : TDocumentComponentView()
{
}

TSpreadsheetView::~TSpreadsheetView()
{
}
```

CreateControlList

CreateControlList creates our set of TTextControl objects.

```
void TSpreadsheetView::CreateControlList(long numRows, long numCols)
{
    TViewHandle viewHandle;
    TStandardText initialText("0.0");
    TStyleSet initialStyles;

    initialStyles.Add(TTextColorStyle::GetRed());
    initialStyles.Add(TFontIdentifierStyle("TaligentSans"));
    initialStyles.Add(TFontPointSizeStyle(18));

    for (int col= 0; col < numCols; col++)
    {
        for (int row = 0; row < numRows; row++)
        {
            TTextActionControlState* state =
                    new TTextActionControlState(initialText , viewHandle);

            TTextControl* control = new TTextControl(state);

            control->SetTextBorderThickness(1);
            control->SetControlLayout(MControl::kLeftToRight);
            control->SetEnabled(TRUE);
            control->SetInitialTextStyles(initialStyles);

            control->SetAllocatedAreaInParent(TGRect(TGPoint (50 + 200 * col,
                                                              50 + 30 * row),
                                                     TGPoint(250 + 200 * col,
                                                              50 + 30 * (row + 1))));
            fControls.Add(control);
        }
    }
}
```

DrawContents

Next, we need to implement the DrawContents member function, which is called whenever the view needs to be redrawn. DrawContents draws a border around our grid of cells.

```
void TSpreadsheetView::DrawContents(TGrafPort& port) const
{
    // Just draw a border
    TGRect aRectangle (TGRect(TGPoint (50 , 50),
                       TGPoint (450, 290)));
    port.Draw(aRectangle);
}
```

SUMMING UP THE APPLICATION

This is all we needed to complete our application. It is surprising how little code is required, and how much functionality the application gets in return. As we did in Part 2, the following table lets us compare the size of the applications, in classes, member functions, and lines of code.

	Classes	Member Functions	Lines of Code
Nonframework-based Windows application	4	64	1257
Framework-based Windows application	11	516	4724
CommonPoint application	4	44	1035

Note that our CommonPoint application has even fewer member functions and lines of code than our original, nonframework-based Windows sample, while providing a great deal more functionality.

Compared with the other versions of our application, it should be clear that:

- Using existing frameworks such as those provided by the CommonPoint application system can make writing your applications a lot easier.
- Framework-based programs get more done than conventional programs with relatively little effort, once you learn how to use the framework.
- Development tools that work with frameworks can dramatically reduce the amount of boilerplate code we need to write, providing additional productivity gains over and above those already mentioned.

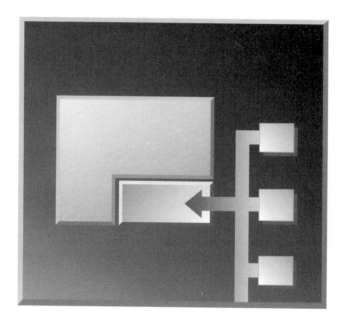

CHAPTER 14

THE POWER OF FRAMEWORKS

Let's review what we have worked on and what you have learned about frameworks. We'll take a look back at the issues that have come up in the book to see where we stand with frameworks today, and we'll look forward to see what the future of frameworks might be.

FRAMEWORKS TODAY

Over the course of this book, we've covered the state of frameworks in the software industry today. We've looked at:

- What frameworks are, and the advantages that frameworks have over "traditional" object-oriented programming: faster development cycles, increased leverage of domain expertise, improved design consistency, lower maintenance overhead, and improved extensibility.
- The principles of good framework design, which you should follow whenever you create your own frameworks. These principles can make a significant difference in the quality of your framework designs.
- The do's and don'ts of framework reuse and the ways to make the reuse process work smoothly. Reusing existing frameworks is very different from writing and using your own.
- When it makes sense to write your own framework instead of reusing an existing framework. Making the right choice can be critical to the success of your projects.
- The frameworks provided by the CommonPoint application system, showing how a complete set of well-designed, reusable frameworks can be much more than the sum of its parts.

If you've made it to this point, you should have a good understanding of what frameworks are all about and how to take advantage of their power in your own work.

THE FUTURE OF FRAMEWORKS

Even though the CommonPoint application system provides a quantum leap forward in using frameworks in the software industry, frameworks still have a long way to go before they become an everyday part of sofware engineering.

Some possible directions frameworks can grow are discussed here.

✔ NOTE   Although Taligent is working on growing its product line in many of these directions, the following information does not constitue a product announcement.

Frameworks as fundamental building blocks

Class libraries are rapidly supplanting procedural libraries as the fundamental building blocks for constructing software—a process that has been aided by visual programming environments such as Microsoft's Visual Basic. In the future, it is likely that frameworks will supplant class libraries, because frameworks provide developers with the same plug-and-play capabilities as today's class libraries, while allowing the developer to customize the framework.

Application systems gain acceptance and maturity

Application systems such as the CommonPoint application system will continue to grow and mature, adding new frameworks and adding new features to existing frameworks. Because the majority of these new features can be added to the application system while maintaining full compatibility, existing applications will be able to take advantage of these features without recompiling.

Frameworks as products

Frameworks enable (but do not require) a new business model where the speed with which new solutions are delivered to the marketplace is dramatically accelerated and where every player in the computing industry gains tremendous advantage.

In this new business model, third-party developers can and will provide frameworks that tackle specific product domains, in vertical markets and across broad product categories.

One of the key factors enabling the frameworks-as-a-business model is the inclusion of licensing mechanisms as a built-in feature of the application system, which make it possible for developers to control the distribution and use of their frameworks in a reliable way. The CommonPoint application system is the first product to include these licensing mechanisms, although other application system and OS vendors may eventually follow.

Improving design methodologies

Although the framework design techniques described in this book have been well proven, they are not the final word on good framework design. As framework technology matures in the marketplace, improved methodologies will undoubtedly become available.

Improving design and development tools

Developing object-oriented software, and in particular framework-based software, poses special challenges to the developer. Managing an extensive library of frameworks requires special tools that let developers find and use frameworks more efficiently than they can with today's development tools.

The Taligent *cp*Professional development environment provides a powerful object-oriented development environment designed to expedite framework-based application development. Future versions of *cp*Professional, along with other advanced development tools from Taligent and other companies, will make it possible to develop applications with even less programming and facilitate the development and reuse of frameworks throughout a development organization.

Patterns and framework design

Patterns can be very helpful in the correct design of frameworks. The book *Design Patterns: Elements of Reusable Object-oriented Software* (Gamma et al. 1995) provides a basic set of patterns that covers many of the patterns used in today's frameworks. As the knowledge of patterns throughout the software development world grows, the library of patterns will undoubtedly improve, making it easier for developers to design their frameworks right the first time.

In the future, development tools may provide more direct support for pattern-based programming. Imagine a tool that allowed you to design your framework by plugging prebuilt, pretested design patterns into your framework. Such a tool would greatly speed the creation of domain-specific frameworks.

Frameworks and component software

Component software is another emerging trend in the software development arena. Component software allows applications to be created with little or no programming by combining already-created software components. The CommonPoint application system provides support for components, and OpenDoc and OLE provide support for a more limited component model. Future versions of CommonPoint will provide additional components for use by custom software development, and Taligent and others will provide sophisticated component-based programming tools.

THE PROMISE OF FRAMEWORKS

Clearly, the future of framework-based programming holds a lot of promise. Whether that promise can become reality depends on the efforts of software developers such as yourself. Taligent is doing everything it can to help software developers succeed with frameworks. We hope that you will consider using a framework to solve your next big programming problem and that you will look into using the CommonPoint application system as the base for your future application development.

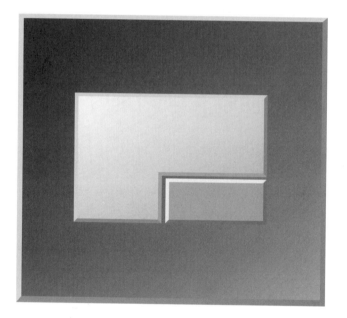

Appendix A

Reading notation diagrams

The notation diagrams used throughout this book are designed to show the static relationships between classes. These diagrams are selective about which classes and relationships appear and do not always include all classes in a subsystem or framework.

Notation diagrams use the following conventions to depict classes and relationships.

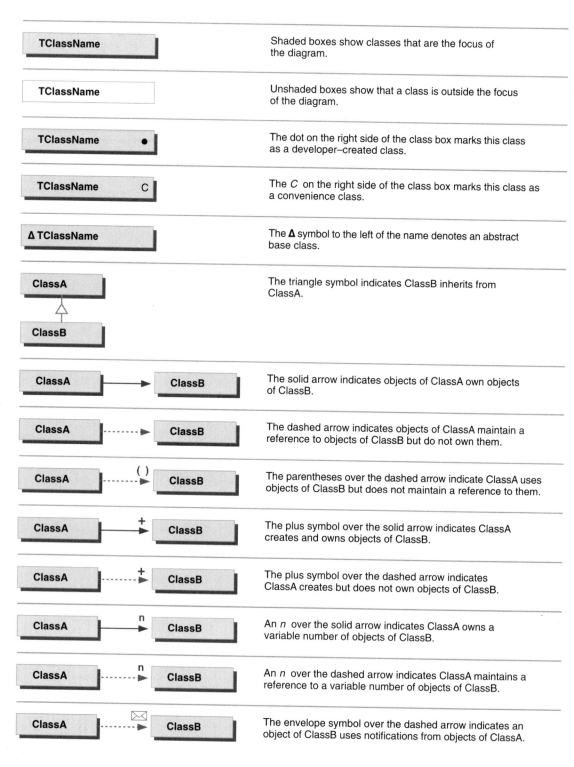

Shaded boxes show classes that are the focus of the diagram.

Unshaded boxes show that a class is outside the focus of the diagram.

The dot on the right side of the class box marks this class as a developer–created class.

The *C* on the right side of the class box marks this class as a convenience class.

The **Δ** symbol to the left of the name denotes an abstract base class.

The triangle symbol indicates ClassB inherits from ClassA.

The solid arrow indicates objects of ClassA own objects of ClassB.

The dashed arrow indicates objects of ClassA maintain a reference to objects of ClassB but do not own them.

The parentheses over the dashed arrow indicate ClassA uses objects of ClassB but does not maintain a reference to them.

The plus symbol over the solid arrow indicates ClassA creates and owns objects of ClassB.

The plus symbol over the dashed arrow indicates ClassA creates but does not own objects of ClassB.

An *n* over the solid arrow indicates ClassA owns a variable number of objects of ClassB.

An *n* over the dashed arrow indicates ClassA maintains a reference to a variable number of objects of ClassB.

The envelope symbol over the dashed arrow indicates an object of ClassB uses notifications from objects of ClassA.

Notation diagrams show the member functions associated with a class.

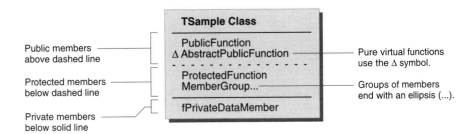

The simple class diagram below shows an example of the notation.

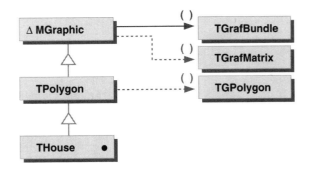

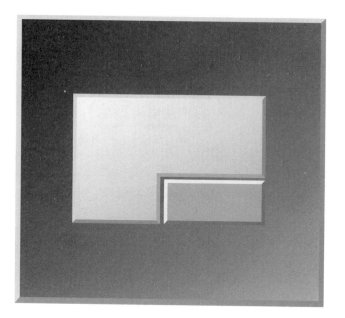

APPENDIX B

USING THE CD-ROM

The CD-ROM that accompanies this book contains an interactive demonstration of framework development, along with the binary executable and source code for every version of the application discussed in this book.

USING THE INTERACTIVE PRESENTATION

The interactive presentation covers the development of a framework-based spreadsheet application developed for the Microsoft Windows platform.

The steps you need to follow to view the interactive presentation vary depending upon the operating system your personal computer is running. Refer to the section that corresponds to your system.

Starting the presentation using Microsoft Windows

To view the interactive presentation on Microsoft Windows, follow these steps:

1 Insert the CD-ROM into your CD drive.

We'll assume that your CD drive is drive D:. If your CD drive has a different letter, substitute the correct drive letter.

2 Open the File Manager, and select the icon for drive D: from the icon strip at the top of the File Manager window.

3 Double-click the file PWRFW.EXE from the pane on the right side of the File Manager window.

This runs the interactive presentation.

Starting the presentation using IBM OS/2

To view the interactive presentation on IBM OS/2, follow these steps:

1 Insert the CD-ROM into your CD drive.

We'll assume that your CD drive is drive D:. If your CD drive has a different letter, substitute the correct drive letter.

2 Click to open the OS/2 System icon, click the Drives icon, and then click the Drive D icon.

The contents of the CD-ROM are displayed.

3 Double-click the PWRFW icon in the Drive D window.

This runs the interactive presentation.

Using the presentation (Windows or OS/2)

When the presentation starts, you see a title screen with two buttons on it.

TITLE SCREEN OF THE INTERACTIVE PRESENTATION

When you click the About This CD button, a series of screens appears explaining how the interactive presentation is put together. It also shows you the legal notices.

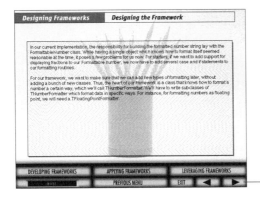

Click the right arrow to move through the presentation.

A TYPICAL INFORMATION SCREEN

You progress through the screens by clicking the right arrow at the bottom of the screen. Once you've finished reading the information in this section, you return to the title screen.

✔ NOTE   Don't be concerned if your screen does not match the one shown here exactly: the content of the interactive presentation may have changed slightly since these screen shots were captured.

Now you're ready to look at the rest of the presentation. Click the Exploring Frameworks button on the right of the title screen. A menu screen similar to the one shown below appears. You can click one of the buttons in the middle of the screen to go to a specific section of the presentation directly, or you can click the right arrow to move through the presentation one slide at a time.

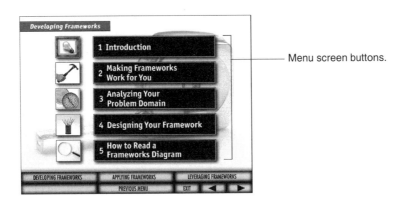

Menu screen buttons.

A TYPICAL MENU SCREEN

You can also click the PREVIOUS MENU button to return to the menu that contains the section of the presentation that you're currently viewing. If you click this button repeatedly, you'll eventually arrive at the top level menu screen.

The EXIT button exits the presentation.

At the bottom left, a status display labeled ...MORE... appears when you are viewing one of a series of related screens. If you are viewing a single screen, or if you are viewing the last slide in a series, the status area is blank.

Notice the buttons labeled DEVELOPING FRAMEWORKS, APPLYING FRAMEWORKS, and LEVERAGING FRAMEWORKS. Clicking one of these buttons takes you directly to the main menu of the corresponding section of the presentation.

These are all the instructions you need to use the interactive presentation.

RUNNING THE SAMPLE APPLICATIONS

Binary executables are provided for each version of the spreadsheet application, for both Windows and OS/2.

Microsoft Windows

The executables for the Microsoft Windows versions of the applications is found on the CD-ROM in the following directories:

\POFSRC\WIN31

\POFSAMP1\	Contains the first, nonframework-based spreadsheet.
\POFSAMP2\	Contains the framework-based spreadsheet.
\POFSAMP3\	Contains the extended framework-based spreadsheet, with support for rational numbers.

To run one of these spreadsheet applications on Microsoft Windows, follow
these steps:

1 Insert the CD-ROM into your CD drive.

We'll assume that your CD drive is drive D:. If your CD drive has a different
letter, substitute the correct drive letter.

2 Open the File Manager, and select the icon for drive D: from the icon strip at
the top of the File Manager window.

In the left pane of the File Manager window, select the folder that
corresponds to the application that you want to run, as listed in the table
above.

3 Double-click the file SAMPLE1.EXE, SAMPLE2.EXE, or SAMPLE3.EXE,
depending on which sample you want to run, from the pane on the right side
of the File Manager window.

This runs the interactive presentation.

IBM OS/2

The executables for the OS/2 versions of the applications is found on the
CD-ROM in the following directories:

\POFSRC\OS2

\POFSAMP1\	Contains the first, nonframework-based spreadsheet.
\POFSAMP2\	Contains the framework-based spreadsheet.
\POFSAMP3\	Contains the extended framework-based spreadsheet, with support for rational numbers.

To run one of these spreadsheet applications on OS/2, follow these steps:

1 Insert the CD-ROM into your CD drive.

We'll assume that your CD drive is drive D:. If your CD drive has a different
letter, substitute the correct drive letter.

2 Click to open the OS/2 System icon, click the Drives icon, and then click the
Drive D icon.

The contents of the CD-ROM are displayed.

3 Double-click the icon labeled SAMPLE1, SAMPLE2, or SAMPLE3,
depending on which sample you want to run.

USING THE SPREADSHEET SOURCE CODE

You can browse the source code for the various versions of the spreadsheet application.

Microsoft Windows

The source code to the Microsoft Windows versions of the application is found on the CD-ROM in the following directories:

\POFSRC\WIN31

\POFSAMP1\	Contains the first, nonframework-based spreadsheet.
\POFSAMP2\	Contains the framework-based spreadsheet.
\POFSAMP3\	Contains the extended framework-based spreadsheet, with support for rational numbers.

You can view the source code files using any text editor or development environment, although the files are intended to be used with the Borland C++ 4.5 development environment.

To compile the spreadsheet application on Microsoft Windows, follow these steps:

1 Copy the source code directory (or directories) you want to compile to your hard drive (usually Drive C).

2 If you have not already done so, start the Borland C++ development environment.

3 From Borland C++, choose Open Project... from the Project menu.

In the dialog box, navigate to the directory to which you copied the source code files, and open the file that has an .IDE suffix.

4 Choose Project... from the Options menu.

Modify all the include, library, and binary directory paths to point to your copy of the source code directory.

5 Click the Make and Run icon on the toolbar (the lightning bolt), or choose Make all from the Project menu, and then choose Run from the Debug menu.

The application is compiled, linked, and run.

IBM OS/2

The source code to the IBM OS/2 versions of the application is found on the CD-ROM in the following directories:

\POFSRC\OS2

\POFSAMP1\	Contains the first, nonframework-based spreadsheet.
\POFSAMP2\	Contains the framework-based spreadsheet.
\POFSAMP3\	Contains the extended framework-based spreadsheet, with support for rational numbers.

You can view the source files using any text editor or development environment, although the files are intended to be used with the IBM C Set ++ 2.1 development environment.

To compile the spreadsheet application on OS/2, follow these steps:

1 Copy the source code directory (or directories) you want to compile from the CD-ROM to your hard drive (usually Drive C).

2 Open an IBM C/C++ Tools 2.01 Window.

3 Change directories to the directory on your hard disk that contains the example that you want to compile.

4 Edit the batch file, called S1.CMD, S2.CMD, or S3.CMD, depending on which version of the spreadsheet you are working.

5 Edit the directory paths to point to your source code directories.

6 To build the application, run the batch file by typing S1, S2, or S3, as appropriate.

7 Once the application has been compiled and linked, you can execute it by typing SAMPLE1, SAMPLE2, or SAMPLE3, as appropriate.

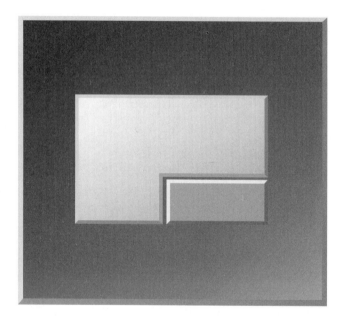

REFERENCES

- Andert, Glenn. 1994. "Object Frameworks in the Taligent OS." *Proceedings of the IEEE COMPCON* Spring 94.

- Birrer, Andreas and Thomas Eggenschwiler. 1993. "Frameworks in the Financial Engineering Domain: An Experience Report." *European Conference on Object-Oriented Programming (1993).*

- Booch, Grady. 1994. "Designing an Application Framework." *Dr. Dobb's Journal* 19, no. 2 (February).

- Coplien, James. 1992. *Advanced C++ Programming Styles and Idioms.* Reading, MA: Addison-Wesley.

- Cotter, Sean with Mike Potel. 1995. *Inside Taligent Technology.* Reading, MA: Addison-Wesley.

- Freytag, Asmus. 1994. "Build a Multilingual User Interface for Your Application with Win32®." *Microsoft Systems Journal* 9 no. 6 (June).

- Gamma, Erich, Richard Helm, Ralph Johnson, and John Vlissades. 1993. "Design Patterns: Elements of Reusable Object-oriented Software." *European Conference on Object-Oriented Programming (1993).*

- Gamma, Erich, Richard Helm, Ralph Johnson, and John Vlissades. 1995. *Design Patterns: Elements of Reusable Object-oriented Software.* Reading, MA: Addison-Wesley.

- Hall, William S. 1994. "Internationalization in Windows NT, Part I: Programming with Unicode." *Microsoft Systems Journal* 9 no. 6 (June).

    ———. 1994. "Internationalization in Windows NT, Part II: Programming with Unicode." *Microsoft Systems Journal* 9 no. 7 (July).

- Johnson, Ralph E. 1993. "How to Design Frameworks." OOPSLA '93 Tutorial Notes.

- Johnson, Ralph E. and Brian Foote. 1988. "Designing Reusable Classes." *The Journal of Object-Oriented Programming*, Vol. 1, no. 2.

- Meyer, Bertrand. 1988. *Object-Oriented Software Construction*. Englewood-Cliffs, NJ: Prentice Hall.

- Nelson, Carl. 1994. "A Forum for Fitting the Task." *IEEE Computer* 27, no. 3 (March).

- Taligent, Inc. 1994. *Taligent's Guide to Designing Programs*. Reading, MA: Addison-Wesley.

- Taligent, Inc. 1995. *Text, Native Language Support, and Time Media*. CommonPoint application system Version B For AIX® developer documentation.

- Wilson, Dave. 1994. "Designing Object Oriented Frameworks" (seminar). Personal Concepts, Palo Alto, CA.

- Wirfs-Brock, Rebecca, Brian Wilkerson, and Lauren Wiener. 1990. *Designing Object-Oriented Software*. Englewood Cliffs, NJ: Prentice Hall.

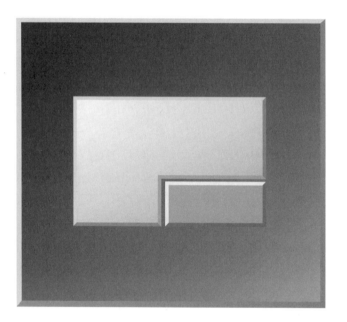

RECOMMENDED MATERIALS FOR FURTHER READING

The experiences of other developers are a great source of information and inspiration—you should read about what other groups are doing, as well as publish articles about your own endeavors.

This section includes standard object-oriented design references and new publications and articles about frameworks from a variety of sources. Many of the examples included in this book are based on information obtained from the articles listed here.

For more information about reading resources, see the Taligent home page on the World Wide Web (`http://www.taligent.com`). Taligent provides a list of recommended resources in the document, "Object Technology Resources," available from the home page or directly from Taligent.

INTRODUCTION TO OBJECT TECHNOLOGY

- Taylor, David A. *Object-Oriented Technology: A Manager's Guide.* Reading, MA: Addison-Wesley, 1990.
- Tkach, Daniel, and Richard Peptic. *Object Technology in Application Development.* Redwood City, CA: Benjamin/Cummings, 1994.

OBJECT-ORIENTED DESIGN AND ANALYSIS

- Booch, Grady. *Object-Oriented Analysis and Design with Applications,* 2nd ed. Redwood City, CA: Benjamin/Cummings, 1994.
- Coad, Peter. "Object-Oriented Patterns." *Communications of the ACM* 35, no. 9 (September 1992).
- Coleman, Derek, and Patrick Arnold, and Stephanie Bodoff, Chris Dollin, Helena Gilchrist, Fiona Hayes, and Paul Jeremaes. *Object-Oriented Development: The Fusion Method.* Englewood-Cliffs, NJ: Prentice Hall, 1994.
- Eggenschwiler, Thomas, and Erich Gamma. "ET++ SwapsManager: Using Object Technology in the Financial Engineering Domain." *OOPSLA '92 Conference Proceedings, ACM SIG Notices* 27, no. 10 (1992).
- Gamma, Erich, and Richard Helm, Ralph Johnson, and John Vlissades. *Design Patterns: Elements of Reusable Object-Oriented Software.* Reading, MA: Addison-Wesley, 1993.
- Goldstein, Neal, and Jeff Alger. *Developing Object-Oriented Software for the Macintosh.* Reading, MA: Addison-Wesley, 1992.
- Jacobson, Ivar, and Magnus Christerson, Partik Jonsson, and Gunnar Overgaard. *Object-Oriented Software Engineering* (Revised 4th printing). Reading, MA: Addison-Wesley, 1993.
- Johnson, Ralph E. "How to Design Frameworks." OOPSLA '93 Tutorial Notes.
- Meyer, Bertrand. *Object-Oriented Software Construction.* Englewood-Cliffs, NJ: Prentice Hall, 1988.
- Wirfs-Brock, Rebecca, Brian Wilkerson, and Lauren Wiener. *Designing Object-Oriented Software.* Englewood Cliffs, NJ: Prentice Hall, 1990.
- Wong, William. *Plug & Play Programming, An Object-Oriented Construction Kit.* New York, NY: M&T Books, 1993.

LEARNING C++

- Cargill, Tom. *C++ Programming Style*. Reading, MA: Addison-Wesley, 1992.
- Coplien, James. *Advanced C++ Programming Styles and Idioms*. Reading, MA: Addison-Wesley, 1992.
- Stroustrup, Bjarne. *The C++ Programming Language,* 2nd ed. Reading, MA: Addison-Wesley, 1991.

LEARNING MORE ABOUT TALIGENT

- Cotter, Sean with Mike Potel. *Inside Taligent Technology*. Reading, MA: Addison-Wesley, 1995.
- Taligent, Inc. *Building Object-Oriented Frameworks* (white paper). 1994.
- Taligent, Inc. *Leveraging Object-Oriented Frameworks* (white paper). 1993.
- Taligent, Inc. *Taligent's Guide to Designing Programs: Well-Mannered Object-Oriented Design in C++*. Reading, MA: Addison-Wesley, 1994.

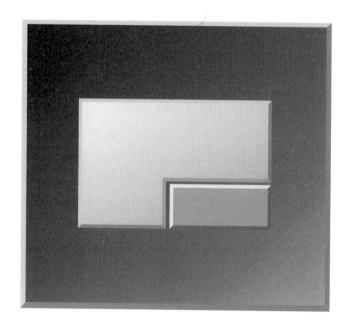

GLOSSARY

abstraction	The process of extracting the essential characteristics of a problem and its solutions to develop a framework composed of interrelated objects. Each object should represent a single variation of an abstraction and have a small, focused set of responsibilities.
black-box framework	A metaphor for a framework whose inner workings are concealed from the framework client. Such frameworks are designed to be used as-is and do not expose an API for extending the framework. COMPARE *white-box framework* SEE ALSO *composition, inheritance*
callback	A function or procedure that the framework executes at some point in the flow of control. Callbacks are passed to a framework to customize the behavior of the framework. SEE ALSO *functor*
class	A data structure that serves as a pattern for the creation of objects. A class can be thought of as a programmer-defined type, in which you specify the data members and the member functions of objects belonging to the class.
class library	A collection of one or more classes that implement an area of functionality. Programmers use a class library by instantiating its classes and invoking their methods. COMPARE *framework*
client API	The part of a framework's interface that allows a client to access the default behavior of the framework and use the framework without changing its fundamental internal operations. COMPARE *customization API*

command

In user interfaces, an instruction to a program from the end user that causes an action to take place. The user can choose the command from a menu, type it from the keyboard, or execute it from a button.

component

A discrete software entity that can be interactively combined with or connected to other elements to create a custom software solution. In the CommonPoint system, the key programming abstraction for data-centered applications is the embeddable component—a special type of ensemble that can be integrated with any compound document.

SEE ALSO   *ensemble, module*

composition

A technique for using frameworks in which the developer instantiates and combines existing classes to change the framework's behavior.

COMPARE   *inheritance*

convenience class

A specialized class that provides domain-specific functionality. Convenience classes are often simple, concrete implementations of abstract base classes and are normally designed to be used directly. Frameworks often provide convenience classes as shortcuts for framework clients.

coupling

The interdependencies among frameworks and between frameworks and ensemble code. When these interdependencies are isolated in intermediary classes, frameworks are described as loosely-coupled. Because dependencies can create bottlenecks and result in fragile code, frameworks should be loosely-coupled wherever possible.

customization API

The part of a framework's interface that allows a client to alter the behavior of the framework by replacing parts of the framework implementation.

COMPARE   *client API*

data abstraction

The process of representing information in terms of its interface with the user and defining new data types for these representations. Abstraction separates the external behavior of an object from its internal implementation. In C++, classes support data abstraction.

decomposition

SEE   *factoring*

design pattern

A microarchitecture for a recurring element in an object-oriented design.

encapsulation	The protection of the attributes and behaviors of an object from direct access by other objects. Typically, an object's structure and its member function implementations are not exposed. Through encapsulation, a program's data and functionality are confined within individual objects instead of being scattered throughout the code. Also known as *information hiding* or *data hiding*.
ensemble	The developer code that captures the specifics of a particular software solution based on one or more frameworks. The domain knowledge, expertise, rules, and policies provided by the developer form the ensemble. Together, the ensemble and the frameworks form the application (or part of a larger application) that solves the specific domain problem. COMPARE *framework*
factoring	The process of breaking down a problem into a set of discrete subproblems and determining which of those problems can be solved by creating new frameworks. Also known as *decomposition*.
framework	A group of interrelated classes that provide a structure for solving a set of related problems. A framework abstracts the essential entities, state, and behavior in its problem domain. It provides key mechanisms, defines the interaction protocols for key scenarios, and encapsulates and enforces fundamental invariants. Programmers can use, extend, or customize frameworks for specific computing solutions. COMPARE *class library*
functor	An object with one significant function that is executed by the framework at some point in the flow of control. Functors are passed to a framework to customize the behavior of the framework. SEE ALSO *callback*
helper class	A class that provides a behavior used by one or more other classes.
information hiding	SEE *encapsulation*
inheritance	A technique for using frameworks in which the developer derives new classes to change the framework's behavior. Inheritance-focused frameworks typically manage the flow of control by calling specific functions overridden by developers. COMPARE *composition*

instance	An occurrence of an object. SEE *object*
invariant	Part of a solution in a particular problem domain that remains constant from one problem to another. Such invariants can be captured in a framework, providing a shared protocol for solutions in that domain. SEE ALSO *framework*
locale	A collection of all the preferred objects for a particular geographic region. These include number, date, and time formatters, keyboard layout, and language-specific text processing objects.
localization	The process of preparing a product for release in a particular geographic region by tailoring it to conform to the local language, customs, and conventions.
modularity	The property of a system in which abstractions have been packaged into discrete units to facilitate the independent design and revision of different parts of the system.
module	A discrete unit that represents part of a system or application. SEE ALSO *modularity, component*
multiple inheritance	The ability to derive a class from more than one base class. Multiple inheritance allows you to combine independent concepts, represented as classes, into a composite concept represented as a derived class.
object	A representation of an entity in terms of its attributes (the data it can contain) and its behaviors (the operations it can perform on that data). An object can represent a programming entity such as a pushdown stack or a window, or it can represent an abstraction of a real-world entity such as a chess piece or a rectangle. An object is an instance of a class.
override	Replacing a member function inherited from a base class with a member function of the same name in a derived class, typically to change or add to the behavior.
parameterized type	SEE *template*
polymorphism	The mechanism by which objects of different classes related through inheritance respond uniquely to the same member function call.

selection	A specification of a set of data elements that can be acted upon by a command.
template	In C++, a class defined to have a parameter of unknown type. The types of the parameters are supplied when an object of the class is instantiated. Also known as *generic* or *parameterized type*.
white-box framework	A metaphor for a framework whose inner workings are exposed through an API that allows framework clients to extend the framework and modify its behavior. COMPARE *black-box framework* SEE ALSO *composition, inheritance*
wrapper	An encapsulator for another object; the wrapper makes the object accessible to, or usable by, other objects.

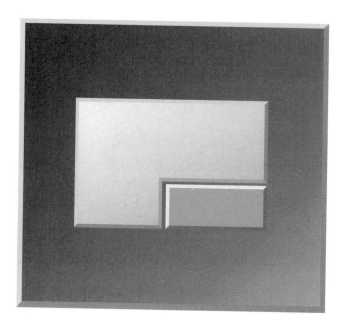

SUBJECT INDEX

S

CODE INDEX

IMPORTANT— READ CAREFULLY BEFORE OPENING.

By opening this sealed disk package, you indicate your acceptance of the following Taligent License Agreement.

This is a legal agreement between you, the end user, and Taligent, Inc. BY OPENING THIS SEALED DISK PACKAGE, YOU ARE AGREEING TO BE BOUND BY THE TERMS OF THIS AGREEMENT. IF YOU DO NOT AGREE TO THE TERMS OF THIS AGREEMENT, PROMPTLY RETURN THE UNOPENED DISK PACKAGE AND THE ACCOMPANYING ITEMS (including written materials and binders or other containers) TO THE PLACE YOU OBTAINED THEM FOR A FULL REFUND.

TALIGENT LICENSE TERMS

1. License. Taligent grants to you the right to use one copy of the enclosed Taligent software program (the "SOFTWARE") on a single terminal connected to a single computer (i.e. with a single CPU). You may not network the SOFTWARE or otherwise use it on more than one computer or computer terminal at the same time. The SOFTWARE is provided for instructional purposes and is not intended for productive use.

2. COPYRIGHT. The SOFTWARE is owned by Taligent or its suppliers and is protected by United States copyright laws and international treaty provisions. Therefore, you must treat the SOFTWARE like any other copyrighted material (e.g. a book or musical recording) except that you may either (a) make one copy of the SOFTWARE solely for backup or archival purposes, or (b) transfer the SOFTWARE to a single hard disk provided you keep the original solely for backup or archival purposes. You may not make derivative works of the SOFTWARE or copy the written materials accompanying the software.

3. RIGHTS RESERVED. All right, title and interest to all intellectual property with respect to the SOFTWARE including any patent, copyright, trademark or trade name rights shall remain exclusively with Taligent or its suppliers.

3. OTHER RESTRICTIONS. You may not rent or lease the SOFTWARE, but you may transfer the SOFTWARE and accompanying written materials on a permanent basis provided you retain no copies and the recipient agrees to be bound by the terms of this Agreement.

4. SOURCE CODE. The source code of the SOFTWARE licensed hereunder represents and embodies trade secrets of Taligent and/or its licensors. The source code and embodied trade secrets are not licensed to you and any modifications, additions or deletions to the source code are strictly prohibited. You agree not to disassemble, decompile, or otherwise reverse engineer the SOFTWARE in order to discover the source code and/or the trade secrets contained in the source code.

5. CUSTOMER REMEDIES. Taligent's entire liability and your exclusive remedy shall be, at Taligent's option, either (a) return of the price paid or (b) repair or replacement of any SOFTWARE which is found to be defective within 90 days of licensing and which is returned to Taligent with a copy of your receipt. This Limited Warranty is void if failure of the SOFTWARE has resulted from accident, abuse, or misapplication. Any replacement SOFTWARE will be warranted for the remainder of the original warranty period or 30 days, whichever is longer.

6. NO OTHER WARRANTIES. TALIGENT DISCLAIMS ALL OTHER WARRANTIES, EITHER EXPRESS OR IMPLIED, INCLUDING BUT NOT LIMITED TO IMPLIED WARRANTIES OF MERCHANTABILITY AND FITNESS FOR A PARTICULAR PURPOSE, WITH RESPECT TO THE SOFTWARE AND THE ACCOMPANYING WRITTEN MATERIALS. THIS LIMITED WARRANTY GIVES YOU SPECIFIC LEGAL RIGHTS. YOU MAY HAVE OTHERS, WHICH VARY FROM STATE TO STATE.

7. NO LIABILITY FOR CONSEQUENTIAL DAMAGES. IN NO EVENT SHALL TALIGENT OR ITS SUPPLIERS BE LIABLE FOR ANY DAMAGES WHATSOEVER (INCLUDING, WITHOUT LIMITATION, DAMAGES FOR LOSS OF BUSINESS PROFITS, BUSINESS INTERRUPTION, LOSS OF BUSINESS INFORMATION, OR OTHER PECUNIARY LOSS) ARISING OUT OF THE USE OF OR INABILITY TO USE THIS TALIGENT PRODUCT, EVEN IF TALIGENT HAS BEEN ADVISED OF THE POSSIBILITY OF SUCH DAMAGES. BECAUSE SOME STATES DO NOT ALLOW THE EXCLUSION OR LIMITATION OF LIABILITY FOR CONSEQUENTIAL OR INCIDENTAL DAMAGES, THE ABOVE LIMITATION MAY NOT APPLY TO YOU.

8. U.S. GOVERNMENT RESTRICTED RIGHTS. The SOFTWARE and documentation are provided with RESTRICTED RIGHTS. Use, duplication, or disclosure by the Government is subject to restrictions as set forth in subdivision (b)(3)(ii) of "The Rights in Technical Data and Computer Software" clause at 252.227-7013. Contractor/manufacturer is Taligent, Inc. 10201 North De Anza Blvd., Cupertino, CA 95014-2233.

9. GOVERNING LAW. This Agreement is governed by the laws of the State of California.

ADDISON-WESLEY WARRANTY TERMS

Addison-Wesley warrants the enclosed disk to be free of defects in materials and faulty workmanship under normal use for a period of ninety days after purchase. If a defect is discovered in the disk during this warranty period, a replacement disk can be obtained at no charge by sending the defective disk, postage prepaid, with proof of purchase to:
Addison-Wesley Publishing Company
Editorial Department
Trade Computer Books Division
One Jacob Way
Reading, MA 01867

After the ninety-day period, a replacement will be sent upon receipt of the defective disk and a check or money order for $10.00, payable to Addison-Wesley Publishing Company.

Addison-Wesley makes no warranty or representation, either express or implied, with respect to this software, its quality, performance, merchantability, or fitness for a particular purpose. In no event will Addison-Wesley, its distributors, or dealers be liable for direct, indirect, special, incidental, or consequential damages arising out of the use or inability to use the software. The exclusion of implied warranties is not permitted in some states. Therefore, the above exclusion may not apply to you. This warranty provides you with specific legal rights. There may be other rights that you may have that vary from state to state.